IN
PRAISE
OF
HARD
INDUSTRIES

Books by Eamonn Fingleton

Blindside: Why Japan Is Still on Track to
Overtake the U.S. by the Year 2000

In Praise of Hard Industries:
Why Manufacturing, Not the Information
Economy, Is the Key to Future Prosperity

The Penguin Money Book
(WITH TOM TICKELL)

IN
PRAISE
OF
HARD
INDUSTRIES

Why manufacturing,
not the information economy,
is the key to
future prosperity

EAMONN
FINGLETON

HOUGHTON MIFFLIN COMPANY

BOSTON · NEW YORK   1999

For information about permission to reproduce selections
from this book, write to Permissions, Houghton Mifflin Company,
215 Park Avenue South, New York, New York 10003.

Library of Congress Cataloging-in-Publication Data
Fingleton, Eamonn.
In praise of hard industries : why manufacturing, not the informa-
tion economy, is the key to future prosperity / Eamonn Fingleton.
    p.   cm.
Includes bibliographical references and index.
ISBN 0-395-89968-0
1. Manufacturing industries — United States — Forecasting.
2. Manufacturing industries — OECD countries — Forecasting.
3. Industries — United States — Forecasting. 4. Industries —
OECD countries — Forecasting. I. Title.
HD9725.F56 1999
338.4'767 — dc21   99-26208 CIP

Printed in the United States of America

Book design by Robert Overholtzer

QUM 10 9 8 7 6 5 4 3 2 1

In gratitude to my wife, Yasuko,
for encouragement and support
over many years

Contents

I. Postindustrialism Versus Manufacturing

1. Three Strikes Against the New Economy   3

II. Postindustrialism's Drawbacks

2. A Hard Look at Computer Software   37
3. Finance: A Cuckoo in the Economy's Nest   68
4. From Cyberspace to Tinseltown   87

III. Manufacturing's Advantages

5. A Showcase of Manufacturing Strengths   115
6. Golden Oldies: Ships, Textiles, Steel   143
7. The Future: An Expanding Universe   165

IV. Toward a Manufacturing Renaissance

8. Time to Take the Blinders Off   199
9. An Action Plan   227

Notes   239
Bibliography   249
Acknowledgments   253
Index   255

I

Postindustrialism
Versus Manufacturing

1

Three Strikes Against
the New Economy

You can hardly pick up a newspaper these days without reading yet
another glowing account of the golden prospects supposedly in store
for the United States in the so-called postindustrial era. If media comment is any guide, almost everyone these days is convinced that new
information-based businesses and other postindustrial activities have
superseded manufacturing as the font of prosperity.

There is, it seems, a natural progression here. Just as in the early
nineteenth century the United Kingdom exploited the bountiful possibilities of the manufacturing age to become the world's leading economy, a far-sighted United States is now poised to lead the world in a
leap to a still more sophisticated level of economic endeavor in the
postindustrial age.

This euphoric cast on America's so-called New Economy has been
subjected to remarkably little reality checking. But the truth is that
America's steady retreat from manufacturing cries out for close scru-
tiny. For there are major holes in the case for postindustrialism. Not
only do those who advocate postindustrialism overestimate the prospects for postindustrial services, but they greatly underestimate the
prospects for manufacturing. A major problem with the argument of
postindustrialists is that they do not understand how sophisticated
modern manufacturing truly is.

Before looking at the reality of modern manufacturing, however, let's first be clear about postindustrialism. The term covers a bewildering variety of businesses whose only obvious shared characteristic is what they are *not:* they are not manufacturing. Broadly defined, virtually all service industries might be considered part of the postindustrial economy. For the purposes of this book, however, we bend over backward to be fair to the postindustrialists and to judge their case on those advanced or sophisticated areas of the service economy whose prospects they regard as particularly promising. We therefore focus mainly on the information industry, which, as defined for statistical purposes recently by the U.S. government, consists of publishing, movies, broadcasting, telecommunications, and computer software. We also include within our definition of postindustrial services such other advanced areas of the service economy as financial services, database management, the Internet, consulting, accounting, advertising, and the law.

One confusing point that ought to be cleared up right away is that some statisticians have recently started classifying computer software as a manufacturing industry. This is obviously a perverse use of words, and one that is explicable only as an effort by embarrassed government officials to cover up the extent to which *real* manufacturing has declined in certain key Western nations. Throughout this book, we treat software for what it obviously is — a postindustrial service.

Our task is to weigh the economic merits of postindustrial activities against those of what might be called hard industries. This term is intended to denote capital-intensive, technically sophisticated forms of manufacturing. Thus, it excludes most types of final assembly of consumer products, which is generally a labor-intensive and unsophisticated activity. This distinction needs to be emphasized because postindustrialists implicitly define manufacturing as merely labor-intensive work of the assembly type. In so doing, they set up a straw man, for there is no question that, in an increasingly integrated world economy, many kinds of consumer products can no longer be assembled economically in high-wage nations. What the postindustrialists overlook, however, is that assembly is only the final, and generally by far the least sophisticated, step in the making of modern consumer goods. Earlier steps such as the making of components and materials are typically highly sophisticated. And the making of components and materials is preceded by a still more sophisticated step — the manufacture of the *production machines* that make the world's components and materials.

These higher levels of manufacturing used to be the backbone of American prosperity in the days of undisputed U.S. leadership of the world economy in the 1950s. Unfortunately for the United States, they have now migrated elsewhere — and in particular to nations that have adopted carefully honed national strategies to boost their manufacturing prowess.

One nation that has been outstandingly successful in expanding its share of advanced manufacturing in recent decades is Japan. The history of the Japanese electronics industry in particular is an object lesson in how a nation can climb the ladder of manufacturing sophistication. Having started out in the 1950s as a lowly assembler of imported components, the Japanese electronics industry long ago phased out most of its assembly operations to make way for more sophisticated activities — albeit activities that are almost entirely overlooked by consumers and even by business reporters and economic commentators. Among the most notable of such activities is the manufacture of high-tech electronic components. The Japanese electronics industry has also moved heavily into making the advanced materials and production machinery used throughout the world electronics industry. Among the other nations that have been similarly successful in advancing to ever more sophisticated levels of manufacturing are Germany, Switzerland, and Singapore. As we will see, these nations, like Japan, have generally outpaced the United States economically over the long run.

That said, we should make it clear that this book does not seek to disparage *all* postindustrial activities, let alone all service industries. Nor does it hold up all manufacturing activities as inherently superior. In fact, advanced nations clearly need a judicious balance of manufacturing and services, not least postindustrial services. Apart from anything else, many postindustrial services are necessary to support and enhance a nation's manufacturing base. The point, however, is that postindustrialism should not be embraced blindly just because it is fashionable. Nor should nations lightly allow their manufacturing prowess to drain away.

For as we will see, postindustrialism entails many hidden drawbacks. Of these the most important are

- An unbalanced mix of jobs
- Slow income growth
- Poor export prospects

These drawbacks constitute — in baseball terms — three strikes against the New Economy.

Strike one against the New Economy: a bad job mix

The most obvious problem with the New Economy is that it creates an unbalanced mix of jobs. Whether we are talking about financial engineering, legal services, computer software, Web site building, health care, broadcasting, database management, consulting, scientific research, or telecommunications, most postindustrial jobs are for people of considerably higher than average intelligence — typically people whose IQs rank in the top 20 percent on IQ tests, if not in the top 5 percent or even 1 percent. In this regard, postindustrialism contrasts sharply with manufacturing, which, of course, generally creates a well-balanced range of jobs.

Thus, for workers who lack the rarefied talents needed to succeed in postindustrial services, America's shift to the New Economy is little short of a disaster. In fact, the job prospects for such workers are so discouraging that even the postindustrialists don't bother to sugarcoat the pill. As estimated by the postindustrial economic commentator Michael Rothschild, up to 20 percent of the American workforce will be marginalized by the move to an information-based economy. That amounts to a shocking 25 million people — or roughly four times the total number of jobless workers in the United States as of 1998!

Yet Rothschild and his cohorts see the sacrifice of so large a share of the workforce as not only inevitable but even acceptable — because the collateral advantages of postindustrialism for the rest of the economy are supposedly so large. The postindustrialists imagine in particular that postindustrialism is a formula for generally fast growth in incomes. Would that it were so. For subpar income growth is the second strike against the New Economy.

Strike two against the New Economy: slow income growth

That the drift in the United States into postindustrialism results in weak income growth is one of the most serious, albeit one of the least recognized, drawbacks of the New Economy.

Yet the evidence is undeniable. Nearly two decades after the United States began its fateful drift into full-scale postindustrialism, international economic comparisons consistently show that Americans have lagged in income growth in the interim. The ultimate authority on this is *OECD in Figures,* a yearbook published by the Paris-based Organization for Economic Cooperation and Development. For those who believe in the superiority of the U.S. postindustrial strategy, the 1998 edition of this yearbook makes distinctly chastening reading. It shows that, with a per capita income at last count of just $27,821 a year, the United States trailed no fewer than eight other nations. These include Japan, Denmark, Sweden, Germany, and Austria, all of which devote a larger share of their labor force to manufacturing than the United States. Most telling of all is the performance of Switzerland, a manufacturing-oriented economy whose per capita income of $41,411 is the highest of any OECD nation. Although in the popular mind Swiss manufacturing is more or less synonymous with cuckoo clocks, Switzerland's real strength lies elsewhere. A world leader in machine tools and in sophisticated equipment for the textile, chemical, and electricity-generating industries, Switzerland is the very model of an advanced manufacturing economy.

That said, not all the world's high-income nations are noted for their large manufacturing sectors. In fact, the same OECD yearbook shows that the United States is surpassed in income by two countries with quite small manufacturing sectors, Norway and Luxembourg. But even in these cases, there is little to encourage the postindustrialists. Take Luxembourg. With 17.0 percent of its labor force in manufacturing compared with 17.3 percent in the United States, it is hardly more deindustrialized than the United States. Moreover, it owes its income edge to a unique factor that the United States clearly cannot hope to emulate: it is a major international tax haven whose receipts of foreign financial flows — many from questionable sources — are vast in relation to its tiny population of 418,000. Norway's nonmanufacturing prosperity is an equally special case. Why? Because with a population of just 4.4 million, Norway ranks as the world's second-largest oil exporter after Saudi Arabia!

In any case, the absolute levels of incomes we have been discussing so far are less important than the pace of income growth. And here the facts are even more clearly against the postindustrialists.

A particularly appropriate starting point for any analysis of income growth is 1980. This was the year when the merits of postindustrialism were first widely debated in the United States. The debate began after the social philosopher Amitai Etzioni published a gloomy analysis of U.S. deindustrialization. His concern about America's incipient drift out of manufacturing was widely challenged by many feel-good commentators, who proceeded to enunciate the now widely accepted doctrine that a shift to postindustrialism would boost U.S. income growth.

Yet with almost no exceptions, manufacturing-oriented economies have outpaced the United States in income growth in the interim. Take the sixteen-year period to 1996, the last year for which full OECD figures are available as this book goes to press. In that time, the United States boosted its per capita income at current prices — that is, before adjustment for inflation — by a total of 134 percent. Although at first sight this growth seems impressive, it was bested by no less than twelve other OECD nations. In order of income growth, these were South Korea, Japan, Portugal, Ireland, Luxembourg, Austria, Italy, Spain, Denmark, New Zealand, Germany, and Switzerland. And with the single exception of Luxembourg, all these nations boasted a greater commitment to manufacturing employment than the United States. In fact, many of them are renowned for their outsized manufacturing sectors — most notably Germany, Japan, and South Korea. Less well known, but perhaps even more significant, is that Spain and Ireland have determinedly pursued national policies to build their manufacturing sectors in the last three decades, and they too have been rewarded with notably superior income growth.

If these manufacturing-oriented nations had outperformed only the United States, the evidence would be convincing enough. But in fact, they have also outperformed several other nations that have embraced postindustrialism almost as enthusiastically as the United States. Perhaps the most notable case in point is the United Kingdom, whose cumulative income growth, as measured in current dollars, in the sixteen-year period came to just 106 percent. This put it twenty-first in a field of twenty-six OECD nations. Canada, another rapidly deindustrializing nation, came in second to last (ahead only of perennially ill-starred Mexico), having mustered income growth of just 81 percent.

Given the strength of the statistical evidence to the contrary, why did the postindustrialists ever consider the information economy a superior formula for income growth in the first place? They have been blindsided by a subtle fallacy in economic reasoning. This fallacy is clearly apparent in the views of, for instance, John Naisbitt, the author of *Megatrends* and one of the earliest cheerleaders for postindustrialism. Noting correctly that the wages of America's postindustrial workers are generally much higher than the American average, Naisbitt jumps to the completely fallacious conclusion that a general shift by the United States into postindustrialism will result in a general boost to wages. The fallacy here is Naisbitt's assumption that postindustrial wages are high by dint of the innately superior economic virtues of postindustrial services. In reality, of course, the high wages paid in typical postindustrial businesses, such as software, merely reflect the fact that such businesses generally recruit exceptionally intelligent and capable workers, in essence workers who could expect to earn superior wages in almost any field they chose to enter. In particular, such workers could earn at least equally high wages in a manufacturing-based economy. Naisbitt utterly overlooks the plight of the rest of the workforce, especially the millions of ordinary workers left out in the cold by the shift to the New Economy. It is their plight, of course, that is behind the persistent underperformance of the United States in international comparisons of income growth.

Nevertheless, many postindustrialists cling doggedly to their faith in the New Economy's superior income performance. How do they explain away the contrary evidence? By raising various objections to the methodology underlying the OECD comparisons. They seize, for instance, on the fact that the period under consideration does not include 1997 and 1998, years in which such manufacturing-oriented economies as South Korea and Japan suffered well-publicized economic problems. But including these two years would make little difference to the outcome. And even if we eliminate South Korea and Japan from the discussion, we are left with many other manufacturing-oriented economies that have clearly been beating the United States in income growth and/or absolute income levels.

In any case, two bad years are not remotely enough to eliminate

South Korea and Japan from the reckoning. Take South Korea. In the sixteen years to 1996, its cumulative income growth was a stunning 546 percent. By comparison with this performance, the subsequent strains suffered by that nation have been no more than speed bumps. In fact, it is likely that when all the figures are available, we will find that South Korea remains far and away the league leader in income growth for the entire period from 1980 to 1998.

Equally in the case of Japan, the strains suffered in 1997 and 1998 were nowhere near so serious as to wipe out the superiority of its record in the previous sixteen years. We have more to say about Japan later, but for now let's be clear about one thing: the impression that the Japanese economy "collapsed" in the 1990s is a myth. Of course, not everything in the Japanese economy has been going well. In particular, as the media have continually emphasized, Japan's stock market has been in the doldrums for years after crashing in the first years of the decade, and the Japanese banking system has been laid low by major troubles in the Tokyo real estate industry. But given that this present writer was one of the few Tokyo-based financial observers who in the late 1980s issued prescient and outspoken warnings of the coming crashes in banking and stocks, he can claim to have some insight into the true nature of the problems in Japanese finance. On his analysis, the significance of Japan's financial problems for the wider Japanese economy has been greatly exaggerated. And the result has been that American policymakers have been encouraged to overlook Japan's many hidden strengths in the 1990s.

A second objection the postindustrialists raise to the OECD comparisons concerns the exchange rates used for converting foreign nations' incomes into dollars. Although the OECD's figures are converted at market exchange rates (and it is hard to think of a more objective methodology than that), the postindustrialists believe this method is unfair to the United States. They maintain that the purchasing power of the dollar within the United States is greater than what one dollar can buy abroad if converted into local currency at market exchange rates. They therefore embrace a system of comparison in which "purchasing power parity" exchange rates are used to assign a lower-than-market valuation to wages earned by workers in Japan, Germany, Switzerland, Singapore, and other advanced foreign nations.

At first sight, this methodology seems to make sense. After all, an

American family posted to, say, Singapore, will soon discover that replicating an American lifestyle there is much more expensive than in Peoria. To the postindustrialists, therefore, the fact that wage levels in Singapore are somewhat higher than those in the United States hardly proves that Singaporeans are better off than Americans. But the postindustrialists forget that, by the same token, citizens of Singapore who try to replicate their home-country standard of living in Peoria also face sticker shock. They may, for instance, need to maintain two or three cars just to get through the day, whereas, by contrast, in Singapore the supermodern public transport system is so comfortable and safe that even many well-off citizens see little need to own a car. The Singaporeans will also face sticker shock when it comes to educating their children. How much will they have to pay for private education to make sure their children get as good a start in life as they would in an ordinary Singaporean state school? And for that matter, is there any private school in Peoria, however expensive, as safe from the drug culture as an ordinary Singaporean school?

The postindustrialists' purchasing power parity method tends to throw up particularly anomalous results in the case of the principal U.S. economic competitor, Japan. On a purchasing power parity basis, the Japanese come out looking distinctly less affluent than Americans. This impression seems to be confirmed by the high prices the Japanese must pay for items such as housing, beef, and entertainment. But are the Japanese really so poor? Hardly. In fact, on many of the most important measures, the Japanese are clearly richer than Americans. Take the most important measure of them all, life expectancy. If the past is any guide, this highly objective measure is closely correlated with living standards. Remember that in the early years after World War II the world's highest life expectancies were found in Sweden and Norway, nations that by common consent at that time led the world in affluence. These days, however, the Japanese are the world's longest-lived people. In the space of just sixty years, their life expectancy has gone from about fifteen years shorter than that of Americans to nearly four years longer. The key factor driving this trend has clearly been rising living standards. It is obvious, therefore, that there is something wrong with a purchasing power parity methodology that portrays the Japanese today as significantly less affluent than Americans.

There are many hidden flaws in the purchasing power parity

method. Although it may accurately capture the variation in the price of a McDonald's hamburger around the world, it is far from reliable in assessing less easily measured items such as infant care and preventive medicine, areas in which superior Japanese standards do much to explain Japan's world-beating longevity rates.

Much more could be said about the major blindspots in the purchasing power parity method. But all we need to note here is that purchasing power parity is an ethnocentric yardstick that should have no place in a scientific debate. What matters is the undeniable fact that, measured at market exchange rates, employers in many foreign countries pay wages that are considerably higher than American employers pay. Thus, it is a myth that manufacturing-oriented economies are ipso facto low-wage economies. And, of course, the postindustrialists' suggestion that manufacturing economies are destined to suffer slower income growth than postindustrial ones is clearly even more misguided.

The end result of postindustrialism is not only poorer income prospects for individual American workers but a general decline in U.S. economic strength. This decline is greatly compounded by the New Economy's tendency to weaken the nation's trade position. To that subject we now turn.

Strike three against the New Economy: a dearth of exports

The third big drawback of postindustrialism is that it weakens a nation's prowess in overseas trade. It is a problem that has received remarkably little attention from the postindustrialists. In fact, such leading advocates of postindustrialism as Daniel Bell, John Naisbitt, and Kevin Kelly make virtually no reference to exports in their writings. But there is no getting away from the fact that the export problem is not only obvious but extremely serious.

Virtually all postindustrial activities are handicapped in export markets by fundamental cultural differences. Take the much-hyped new American information businesses that have mushroomed with the rise of the Internet. Almost all their revenues come from within the United States because in overseas markets their sales are hindered by several cultural and regulatory factors, of which the most obvious is language.

English may be a universal language, but most non-native speakers are hardly more likely to be comfortable reading English-language websites than, say, English-language magazines. Differing national tastes also limit the export potential for Internet-based information businesses: an American database of baseball scores, for instance, has little appeal in Britain, let alone in Germany or France.

Many kinds of information are inherently local in appeal and therefore generate minimal exports. Information on traffic conditions in Vermont, for instance, is likely to be of little value in Virginia, let alone in Vietnam. Similarly, a database on Nebraskan car insurance rates has limited value in North Carolina, let alone in the Netherlands or Nepal. The problems in exporting information are in fact endless. It is not surprising that, as noted by the Internet consultant Alfred Glossbrenner, American information providers' export sales are "negligible."

As we will see in chapter 2, similar cultural problems are also much in evidence in curtailing the American computer software industry's export prospects. These problems are perhaps most obvious in the case of personal computer programs, which must, of course, be comprehensively altered for other nations' writing systems and customs. The costs involved cut deeply into U.S. export revenues. In particular, the user interface — the array of commands and menus by which the user operates the computer — must be tailored to the user's culture. Much more is involved than merely writing the commands and menus in the user's national language. The interface for many application programs, such as accounting and factory-management systems, may require a total makeover to fit the customs and procedures of other nations. Sometimes the user interface may even have to be tailor-made to suit the needs of individual companies within a single country. Thus, for all the hype about the world-beating lead in software enjoyed by the United States, most American software businesses generate little if any revenue abroad and therefore do remarkably little for the chronically troubled U.S. balance of payments.

Culture is also a barrier to exports in many other highly paid information-based professions. The United Kingdom's famously strong advertising agencies provide a good example. Among the largest and most globalized agencies in the world, they shape the worldwide advertising activities of such globally active corporations as Ford, IBM, Philip Morris, Procter & Gamble, and Toyota. Nonetheless, their contribution to Britain's balance of payments is quite puny. The reason is obvious: few of the jobs involved in serving their global clients are British jobs. To create advertising for the American market, for instance, British advertising agencies rely heavily on thousands of American advertising professionals in New York and elsewhere in the United States. And of course, *a fortiori* in non-English-speaking markets, such as Japan or Germany, British advertising firms must rely almost entirely on locally recruited professionals to serve clients in those countries. Thus, most of their foreign revenues are eaten up by costs incurred abroad. At the end of the day, all the British economy receives is a trickle of dividends on the capital invested overseas.

The story is much the same in other information-based businesses. Take the American legal profession. It accounts for fully 2 percent of the U.S. gross domestic product, yet it contributes virtually nothing to the U.S. balance of payments. In truth, with the exception of some special clients such as foreign corporations operating within U.S. borders, foreigners have no need for American legal advice.

So much for cultural barriers to postindustrial exports. But these are far from the only impediments limiting overseas sales of U.S. postindustrial services. Another key impediment to trade in postindustrial services is regulation in foreign markets, which is generally a much bigger problem for exporters of services than for exporters of manufactured goods.

Regulation is a particularly serious problem in financial services, an industry that ranks second only to computer software in the hopes pinned on it by the postindustrialists. If we believe the postindustrialists, nations like the United States and the United Kingdom can look forward to rich pickings as other nations open their financial markets to overseas competition in the years ahead. Unfortunately, this prospect is largely fantasy. It ignores the fact that regulators in many overseas financial markets are not as "global" in their outlook as those in the United States, let alone those in that ultimate postindustrial pioneer, the United Kingdom. As we will see in chapter 3, regulators in many key nations believe it is crucial to maintain their grip on their nations' financial systems, even if they rarely acknowledge this publicly.

Another major problem for many would-be postindustrial exporters is inadequate protection of their intellectual property rights. In particular, piracy in foreign markets severely depletes the flow of foreign revenues to many important postindustrial businesses, most notably computer software, movies, and music. Perhaps the most worrying aspect of the problem is that illegal copying of copyrighted work is getting ever easier thanks to technological advances. Pirating is rife in the CD industry, for instance, in part because the investment needed to set up a CD replication operation is, in real terms, only a fraction of the cost of a record-pressing plant in the era of gramophone records. Now, of course, the rise of the Internet has made it even easier to profit from other people's work.

It is important to remember that piracy is a double whammy for American postindustrial exporters. First, of course, it deprives them of sales volume. The second effect, while less obvious, is perhaps even more serious: it puts them into head-to-head competition with cut-price versions of their own products — with devastating implications for their pricing strategy.

As if America's poor prospects for exports were not bad enough, there is another problem with the trade side of postindustrialism — rising imports. At first sight, the idea of the United States importing postindustrial services on a large scale is hard to reconcile with our observation that cross-border trade in postindustrial services is heavily curtailed by cultural and other barriers. But in fact, there is no contradiction here, because the barriers to trade in postindustrial services are often not totally insurmountable. Rather, they are expensive to surmount. Typically, the only real problem in exporting postindustrial services is that postindustrial products have to be adapted considerably for foreign markets. Although this adds to costs and thus is a major drawback for high-wage countries, it is hardly fatal for low-wage countries.

The full seriousness of the import threat becomes apparent only when one realizes that postindustrial services are highly labor-intensive — typically more so even than such labor-intensive manufacturing activities as the final assembly of televisions and radios. By definition in a labor-intensive industry, the cost of labor is a decisive factor in export competitiveness. Thus, as global competition intensifies, the First World's postindustrial businesses can be expected to outsource more and more of their services from low-wage nations in the Second and Third Worlds.

Even such a sophisticated business as the American computer software industry is far from invulnerable to the threat of Third World competition. At first sight, this seems hard to credit. After all, computer software is generally regarded as the ultimate "knowledge industry," an industry that requires not only a great deal of sophisticated know-how but a special streak of creativity that only a few countries are supposed to have. How can Third World countries possibly aspire to go toe to toe with the United States in such an industry? Actually, very easily.

Let's address the creativity argument first. All conventional wisdom to the contrary, there is little evidence that simply by dint of their nationality Americans are more creative than other people — and certainly there is no reason to hope, as the postindustrialists do, that a purported edge in creativity will render the United States invulnerable to foreign competition in the postindustrial era. In fact, the evidence the postindustrialists adduce for their belief in superior American creativity is remarkably flimsy. They make much, for instance, of the fact that Americans are disproportionately successful in winning Nobel Prizes for science and technology. But is this a reliable measure of creativity? Actually no. Why? Because Nobel Prizes for science are awarded mainly for breakthroughs in only one narrow field, *fundamental* science. And the success of a nation's scientists in fundamental science is a function far less of their inherent creativity than of how much government money is available for such science. Since the U.S. government is by far the world's biggest spender on fundamental science, American scientists not surprisingly win more than their share of the prizes. We have more to say about the creativity question later. But for now let's agree that creativity is a human attribute that is manifested in different forms in different cultures and is not notably absent among appropriately trained workers in even the poorest nations.

In any case, as we will see in chapter 2, the role that creativity plays in the software industry has been greatly exaggerated. Certainly the incontrovertible facts of the industry give the lie to the idea that Americans have a special lock on software-writing skills. Many other nations, including some of the world's poorest, have demonstrated that they have what it takes to compete in the industry. Moreover, the know-how to enter the software business is amazingly easy for the developing world to acquire. That opens up the possibility that American software workers will increasingly be undercut by low-wage workers abroad. In fact, as William Wolman and Anne Colamosca have pointed out in their book *The Judas Economy,* the threat of Third World imports is potentially far greater in software than in hardware.

Thanks to breakthroughs in satellite communications, Third World software companies can now deliver their products instantaneously and cheaply to customers anywhere in the world. By contrast, the Third World is heavily handicapped in trying to export manufactured goods to the West because of abysmal local transportation systems, not to mention the high cost of shipping bulky goods to far-off overseas markets.

The conclusion, therefore, is that, from the point of view of the American balance of payments, the shift to postindustrialism is double trouble. First, it weakens the nation's export strength. Second, it exposes the United States to the prospect of rapidly increasing imports. That said, many Americans find it easy to overlook the fact that postindustrial businesses do not do much for the balance of payments. After all, the huge U.S. current account deficits do not directly affect the quality of life within the nation — at least not in the short run. But in the long run, trade matters — and matters fundamentally. A nation that allows its trade position to deteriorate too far for too long cannot expect to remain the world's leading economy indefinitely.

In truth, almost anywhere the postindustrialists' case is tested, it turns out to be more sizzle than steak. Having understood the New Economy's weaknesses, let's now consider the crucial and much-overlooked strengths of manufacturing.

In praise of hard industries

As we have already noted, the most obvious advantage of manufacturing is that it creates jobs for a wide range of people. In fact, even in the most sophisticated areas of manufacturing, jobs abound for the sort of blue-collar workers who are being increasingly marginalized in postindustrial economies. Take the most advanced areas of the steel industry. Many steel industry jobs have become simpler and easier to carry out as steelmakers have moved to ever higher levels of automation over the years. In many manufacturing industries these days so much knowledge can be built into the production machines that even a worker of less than average intelligence can operate them effectively.

As Bennett Harrison of New York's New School has pointed out, all conventional wisdom to the contrary, unskilled workers "barely off the farm" can be readily trained to operate computer-controlled presses and similarly sophisticated production machinery. In Harrison's terms, today's high-tech production machinery is not "skill-demanding" but "skill-enabling." Quoting a study by the economist David Howell, Harrison rebuts the widespread belief that a move to more advanced production techniques necessarily results in the marginalization of workers of average intelligence. Referring to the trend for low-paid workers to suffer declining real wages in the United States in recent years, he comments: "If wages of poorly educated workers are falling, we need to look for explanations other than technology. After all, the same technologies have penetrated factories and offices in Europe and Asia, yet nowhere outside of the United States have low-end wages fallen so far and so fast."

Of course, high-tech manufacturing is necessarily very capital-intensive. To the postindustrialists, this seems like a major disadvantage. But this view could hardly be more wrong. Remember that in general the more capital is invested in a factory, the higher its labor productivity is likely to be. And superior productivity is, of course, the royal road to high wages. Moreover, the fact that an industry is capital-intensive almost automatically elevates it beyond the reach of competitors in low-wage nations. The truth is that many manufacturing industries are becoming ever more capital-intensive all the time, thereby raising ever higher the barriers to entry for poorer nations.

Even quite mature manufacturing industries can be notably capital-intensive — and particularly the more advanced sectors of such industries. Take the textile industry. Although the production of textiles is generally regarded as labor-intensive, many of the textile industry's subsectors are highly capital-intensive and therefore tend to be dominated by rich nations. Spinning is a good example. As recounted in the *Wall Street Journal,* the capital required in a state-of-the-art spinning mill these days can amount to as much as $300,000 per job. It is hardly surprising, therefore, that the world's most productive spinning mills are located in affluent northern Italy, not in dirt-poor India or Pakistan.

Perhaps the ultimate example of high capital intensity is the components side of the electronics industry. As we will see, the investment per job in some Japanese component factories can reach well over $1 million — or more than one hundred times the rate of capital intensity in some parts of the world software industry.

It goes without saying that in capital-intensive businesses factory wages are likely to represent only a small proportion of total costs. They are dwarfed by depreciation, financing charges, royalties for intellectual property, research and development expenses, and other high overheads. Just how small the wage component of costs can be was startlingly illustrated in the case of a cellular phone factory built by Motorola a few years ago. After looking at many alternative sites around the world, Motorola decided to locate the factory in ultra-high-wage Germany. Germany's high wage costs mattered little because wages accounted for only 3 percent of the company's total expected costs. In truth, from the point of view of an advanced manufacturing company, the need to offer superhigh wages is a small price to pay for the many advantages of a German location. Whereas higher German wages add only slightly to total costs, Germany offers a world-beating manufacturing infrastructure complete with superb utilities, reliable delivery services, honest regulators, and a pleasant residential environment for expatriate executives. And of course, there is also the advantage of Germany's well-educated and disciplined workforce. As Norbert Quinkert, chairman of Motorola's German operations, points out, the advantage to the company of choosing a lower-wage location such as Britain was actually negligible in the larger scheme of things.

If capital intensity were the only advantage that manufacturing had over postindustrial services, the case for manufacturing would be strong enough. But manufacturing boasts another key advantage: it enables incumbents in an industry to build up a huge endowment of proprietary know-how that gives them a wide productivity edge over new entrants to the industry.

Some of this know-how is explicitly protected by patents, but often the most valuable know-how is unpatented proprietary production technology. Typically such know-how can be acquired only by dint of many years of learning by doing.

Just how formidable an advantage superior manufacturing know-how can be is best seen from the point of view of a new entrant to an industry. Lacking the benefit of the incumbents' know-how, a new entrant is condemned to achieve notably poor labor productivity rates. Thus, even if a new entrant operates from a developing nation and therefore enjoys a large advantage in lower wages, its unit costs will start out considerably higher than those of the incumbents, and it will probably have to continue to absorb losses for many years as it struggles to catch up in know-how. In practice, the struggle is an unequal one — and unless the new entrant enjoys the full support of an extremely far-sighted, nationally organized effort, such as that mounted by the Japanese government over the last one hundred years, it will undoubtedly think twice about entering the field in the first place.

It is difficult to exaggerate what a great advantage incumbents typically enjoy in many areas of advanced manufacturing these days. Take a product like liquid-crystal displays. Most familiar as the flat screens used in notebook personal computers, these seem at first sight to pose no great manufacturing challenge. In one sense this is correct. Basically an adaptation of semiconductor technology, they are made using similar manufacturing equipment. In theory at least, many companies around the world could enter this extremely fast-growing business. But in practice, few have done so, with the result that the world market is utterly dominated by a handful of Japanese manufacturers. In fact, Osaka-based Sharp Corporation alone enjoys a world market share of close to 50 percent.

Why such market concentration? The key to the mystery is something called "yield" — the percentage of flaw-free products in a given production batch. A liquid-crystal display is flaw-free only if all of the countless "dots" that constitute its screen are fully functional. The misbehavior of even a single dot is not only noticeable to the human eye but intolerably distracting. Since each dot is controlled by a separate tiny transistor, every single one of hundreds of thousands of transistors must function as advertised. Given that, among other things, the tiniest contamination, such as a microscopic speck of dust, can render such transistors dysfunctional, the quality-control challenge in producing these devices is enormous. A new entrant to the industry would be lucky to get a yield of good screens of as much as 10 percent. By contrast, the leading incumbents in the industry are believed routinely to achieve yields of 90 percent or more. Thus, differences in yield alone can give incumbents in this industry a nine-to-one productivity advantage over new entrants.

One obvious step a company can take to improve yield is to filter the factory air with extreme care. But this is easier said than done, and even when a liquid-crystal display company takes all obvious precautions, it can still end up with a notably poor yield.

Admittedly, not all manufacturing involves entry barriers as formidable as this. But even the manufacture of relatively simple materials often requires a great deal of valuable proprietary know-how that is difficult for would-be entrants to an industry to acquire. Take something as simple as adhesives. As an expert at the Shell/Royal Dutch oil group has pointed out, the exact chemical structure of an adhesive is often almost impossible for competitors to determine. A manufacturing company may literally need to have unrestricted access to its competitors' factories if it is to understand their production processes. In the nature of things, such access is generally denied; thus, in seeking to close the technology gap with more advanced competitors, manufacturing companies often resort to amazing — and often highly controversial — tactics. Take, for instance, some Japanese aerospace executives who wanted to acquire American aerospace know-how. As recounted by Larry Kahaner in *Competitive Intelligence,* these executives wore shoes with especially soft soles when touring American aerospace factories. Their objective was to pick up from the factory floor microscopic metal shavings, which were later analyzed for clues to the Americans' manufacturing secrets.

Of course, with reasonable luck, a security-conscious manufacturing company can keep most of its production know-how secret for years, if not decades. Even in mature manufacturing industries, proprietary know-how often provides incumbents with enduring protection against new competition. The photographic film industry provides a striking example. Because its product is based on nineteenth-century breakthroughs in silver chemistry, this industry might seem like an easy target for, say, the East Asian tiger economies. But in reality, it has remained all but impregnable to them. Even the Koreans are no more than a negligible force in the industry: although they make some film at home, they do little exporting and are highly dependent on inputs imported from Japan and the United States. A key problem for the Koreans, as for other would-be entrants, is that they cannot match the enormous endowment of know-how that the incumbents have built up over several decades of learning by doing.

The most recent major entrants to the business, Fuji Photo Film of Japan and Polaroid of the United States, got their start as long ago as the mid-1930s — and their stories only serve to underline how high the entry barriers truly are. Fuji Photo would probably never have gotten off the ground but for the fact that Japan's then-military government deemed photographic film an essential war matériel; thus, Japan spared no expense in establishing an indigenous source of supply ahead of Pearl Harbor. Polaroid's rise was propelled by a similarly unique force: the enormous creativity of Edwin Land, one of the most brilliant inventors of the twentieth century. Yet even with the benefit of Land's technological innovations, Polaroid has remained no more than a niche player that continues to depend on competitors for certain key inputs.

The fact remains that, at the end of the twentieth century, the global photographic film market is still dominated by just three companies, Eastman Kodak, Fuji Photo Film, and Agfa-Gevaert. Based, respectively, in the United States, Japan, and the European Union (EU), these are all quintessential First World manufacturing employers. Admittedly, Eastman Kodak has been losing market share in recent years, but it is important to note that it is being challenged not by a low-wage competitor but by Fuji Photo, a Tokyo-based company whose wage rates are considerably higher than American levels.

The same pattern of large entry barriers is apparent right across the board in advanced manufacturing. It is obvious, therefore, that nations with a heavy orientation toward advanced manufacturing enjoy a fundamental edge in world economic competition — hence, for instance, the pattern we have already noted whereby manufacturing-oriented economies have shown remarkably strong income growth in recent years. And the result is that both Japan and Germany have now decisively passed the United States in wage rates. As recorded in the 1998 edition of *Japan: An International Comparison,* a publication of the Japan Institute for Social and Economic Affairs, the average hourly wage was $21.01 in Japan, $14.79 in Germany, and just $12.37 in the United States.

Moreover, Japan, in common with such other advanced manufacturing economies as Austria, Switzerland, and Singapore, has generally enjoyed lower unemployment than the United States in the 1990s. Admittedly, one notable manufacturing-oriented economy has been doing less well in this regard. That country is Germany, whose unemployment rate was running at 11 percent as of 1998. Germany's problems, however, stem not from its manufacturing orientation per se, but rather from the fact that its economy has been suffering continuing dislocation following German reunification. (In 1998, nearly a decade after reunification, unemployment in the territories of the former East Germany was still running more than double that of the rest of the country.) An additional problem has been the increasing burden that Germany's leadership role in the European Union places on the German economy; in particular, Germany suffers disproportionately from the fact that EU nations have been exporting unemployment to one another for decades. Germany apart, unemployment rates in most other high-wage manufacturing economies have remained notably low in the 1990s. Take Japan. Although Japanese unemployment in 1999 slightly exceeded that of the United States, it has averaged less than 4 percent for the decade as a whole. American press commentators sometimes suggest that Japanese unemployment figures are understated, but as research by both the U.S. Department of Labor and the OECD has shown, this is a dogma-driven assertion unsupported by the facts. That there is no large hidden army of unemployed people in Japan is also confirmed by the experience of foreign employers, who consistently complain of shortages of many types of labor.

If manufacturing merely delivered high wages and low unemployment, its contribution would be impressive enough. But it also delivers another crucial economic blessing: a powerful trade performance. This reflects the fact that manufactured goods are generally much more universal in appeal than services — a fact that is abundantly apparent in the consistently large current account surpluses that most of the successful manufacturing-based economies have achieved in recent years. It is a notable fact, for instance, that of the eleven manufacturing-oriented member nations of the OECD that have surpassed the United States in income growth in recent years, all but three were running current account surpluses at last count. Meanwhile, the two great postindustrial economies, the United States and the United Kingdom, have consistently been running large current account deficits for many years.

To sum up, whether judged by jobs, wages, or trade, manufacturing scores over postindustrial services.

The future of manufacturing: a historic challenge

We have seen that manufacturing industries are highly effective in boosting the prosperity of many major economies today. But can manufacturing continue to deliver a superior economic performance in the decades ahead? The postindustrialists, of course, think not. Insisting that the world economy is already suffering from an acute excess of manufacturing capacity, they predict that this excess will only worsen in the decades ahead. It is a frightening picture — but one based on a wholly mistaken reading of how the world economy works.

In reality, the long-term outlook for manufacturing is for expansion almost right across the industrial waterfront. Perhaps the easiest way to understand the truly bright future of manufacturing is to remember that about 90 percent of the world's population is poor. As the world's developing nations bootstrap themselves out of poverty, how will they spend their money? Do they ache to acquire such postindustrial products as Wall Street's latest portfolio hedging services, personal homepage software, or databases of American newspaper clippings? Probably not. More than anything, what developing economies want is, of course, material goods. They are not alone in this preference. Even in the most developed parts of the world, there are plenty of material wants waiting to be satisfied. In fact, almost no one anywhere feels as affluent as he or she would like to be, and asked to compile a wish list of wants they would like to satisfy, most people would place more emphasis on material goods than on postindustrial services.

Thus, manufacturers face an enormous and highly exciting challenge. As in the past, they must aim to create ever more goods, but now they must strive, in the process, to use fewer of the earth's scarce resources. They must create ever greater abundance by developing more inexpensive materials and more efficient production technologies. The extent of the challenge can be summed up in one sentence: if the rest of the world is ever to enjoy an American-style standard of living, the world's output of material goods will have to increase at least fivefold. This formidable challenge will be made even more so by the fact that manufacturing will have to become much more environmentally friendly in the future than it has been in the past.

Of course, to many the idea that poor nations can ever hope to enjoy an American-style standard of living seems utopian at best. But is it? Certainly there is no question that even with the best luck in the world, many nations will remain poor as far ahead as anyone can see. On the optimistic side, however, there is nothing utopian about assuming manufacturers will continue to improve the efficiency of their production processes and thereby spread prosperity ever farther around the world. This is exactly what manufacturers have been doing since the beginning of the Industrial Revolution, and they are clearly continuing apace in our own time.

One notable way in which manufacturers have been improving their efficiency — and boosting their output — in recent years has been in cutting down their use of expensive, rare materials and instead making greater use of inexpensive, abundant ones. Whereas in former times many manufacturing industries consumed large amounts of scarce materials such as copper, zinc, and tin, they now use mainly abundant materials such as silicon and carbon. Take the telecommunications industry. In the old days it needed vast amounts of scarce copper to make telephone cables. These days, by contrast, it achieves far better results with an almost laughably commonplace material — glass. Just seventy pounds of glass in the form of optical fibers can transmit as much telephone traffic as one ton of copper. Moreover, optical fibers require only one-twentieth as much energy as copper to produce. This is a classic example of how leading manufacturers are making more with less. The result is that the price of material products keeps falling in real terms, and Western-style affluence is spreading ever farther into the developing world.

Another conspicuous example of how new technologies can spread prosperity is the development of the compact disk. Standard five-inch CDs are only about one-eighth the weight of the old ten-inch gramophone records they replaced. Thus, since both the vinyl in gramophone records and the polycarbonate in compact disks are derived from petroleum, there has been a reduction of roughly 90 percent in the drain on the earth's resources. In other words, the CD revolution has enabled the world's music lovers to get ten times more music out of a barrel of oil.

The low manufacturing cost of CDs — they can be stamped out for as little as thirty cents each — has helped spread abundance in formerly poor parts of the world. According to Peter Newcomb of *Forbes,* more than 11 billion CD disks had been sold as of 1998 — equal to about ten disks for every household on the planet.

Not surprisingly, therefore, CDs are a ubiquitous consumer item in many nations where twenty years ago gramophone records were a luxury beyond the reach of all but the richest citizens. Notable examples of such nations include South Korea, Malaysia, Thailand, Indonesia, and China.

At the same time, there has been a parallel miniaturization of CD players, many of which are less than one-thirtieth the weight of the trunk-sized record-players of the 1950s. This has yielded major savings not only in scarce materials such as copper and wood but in the machines' power consumption. Again the message is clear: manufacturers are making more with less, and in so doing they are helping spread prosperity ever farther into formerly poor parts of the world. For our purposes here, the key point is that the CD revolution has created a host of opportunities for some of the world's top manufacturers — most notably Sony Corporation, which, as we will see, dominates the world market in the key laser manufacturing technology that has made the CD possible.

For as long as scientists and engineers continue to make new technological discoveries, the process of creating more with less is clearly set to continue and can be counted on to create similarly exciting opportunities for a host of other advanced manufacturers as the developing world increases its share of consumption of countless products that the First World has long taken for granted — most notably consumer durables such as motorcycles, cars, refrigerators, air conditioners, washing machines, television sets, heaters, telephones, and personal computers. Of course, many of the final assembly plants producing these goods will be located in the developing world, but they will typically be owned by First World manufacturers, and the source of most of their key materials and components will certainly be the First World's most advanced manufacturing nations.

More generally, as technological progress projects prosperity farther and farther into the developing world, First World manufacturers will enjoy major new markets for pollution control equipment, power-generation plant, telephone-switching gear, communications satellites, railroad locomotives, airplanes, medical equipment, scientific instruments, oil rigs, pipelines, bulldozers, excavators, and many other kinds of sophisticated capital equipment.

The expansion of world manufacturing opportunities will be accelerated by the high savings rates that characterize many parts of the developing world. A high savings rate enables a nation to invest heavily not only in private industry but also in public infrastructure. Either kind of investment provides a boost to total output, particularly to exports. All this in turn enables such a nation to increase its imports of foreign products. High savings rates look likely to prove particularly enduring in East Asia, where one nation after another has launched notably effective policies in the last fifty years to buttress its citizens' savings habit. In Singapore, for instance, workers and employers have for many years been required by law to invest an effective 34 percent of wages in the government's Central Provident Fund. Other East Asian governments have similar if less direct ways of promoting savings (typically with measures that directly suppress consumption).

Given high savings rates and various other positive factors at work in the global economy today, the proportion of the world's population that enjoys a full First World–style standard of living is likely to jump from about one-tenth today to nearly one-third by the mid-twenty-first century. At the end of the day, the success of the First World's most advanced nations in performing more-for-less alchemy in manufacturing industries will be the single most important force driving the world's increasing prosperity.

Thus, beyond the economic case for manufacturing, there is a crucial political one that has been overlooked by the postindustrialists: leading manufacturing nations enjoy enormous scope to project economic power beyond their borders. This power derives from control of production know-how, which, when transferred abroad, can greatly improve other nations' productivity and by extension their income levels. Such know-how is so coveted that a great manufacturing nation can pick and choose which nations to bestow it on and can insist on extensive favors from them in return.

Just how significant this sort of power can be was already apparent several decades ago when, in the aftermath of World War II, the leading nations of both Western Europe and East Asia assiduously courted the United States for transfers of American production know-how. In return, they were prepared to sign off on most of the U.S. foreign policy agenda — including even such controversial geopolitical gambits as the Vietnam War.

Of course, these days the ability of the United States to project economic power abroad has greatly diminished as it has withdrawn from one advanced field of manufacturing after another. Thus, although the United States is still courted for transfers of production know-how, increasingly nations like Japan and Germany are the focus of even more ardent wooing. The reason is clear: these nations now possess a huge fund of valuable manufacturing technologies that can be shared with other nations to considerable mutual advantage. Such sharing has clearly bolstered Japan's sway around the world, particularly in East Asia. Germany's sway in both Western and now Eastern Europe has been similarly bolstered as other nations vie with one another for direct investment by German manufacturing companies.

In the long run, therefore, the huge economic patronage enjoyed by the great manufacturing nations of the future will serve as a powerful counterweight to the vaunted position of the United States as the world's sole remaining military superpower.

Trusting the market: the tyranny of a treacherous ideology

We have seen that the postindustrialists' case for the New Economy is a tangle of misinformation and choplogic. Why do so many otherwise intelligent and well-informed people fail to recognize the obvious holes in their theories? As we will see in chapter 8, the postindustrialists suffer major blindspots concerning everything from the true state of American deindustrialization to the extent of the Japanese economic challenge. But more than anything, their problem is that they place a childlike faith in the efficacy of free markets. They assume that since postindustrialism has emerged first in the avowedly free-market economy of the United States, it is a self-evidently good thing. They have been led astray by advocates of extreme laissez-faire, who believe, echoing Alexander Pope's admiration for the work of the Creator, that in a free-market economy "whatever is, is right."

Admittedly, at first sight the idea that the rise of postindustrialism in the United States reflects the superior efficacy of the American free-market system seems sound enough. But to anyone who is familiar with the economies of America's main competitors, an entirely different — and immensely troubling — explanation for the U.S. shift into postindustrialism is suggested: by dint of far-sighted economic policies, these competitors have been consistently preempting the world's most exciting new manufacturing opportunities. Thus, a great many American entrepreneurs have been lavishing their talents on postindustrialism merely as a passive adjustment to other nations' behavior. In essence, therefore, the U.S. postindustrial drift is driven by foreign nations' industrial policies — policies that often represent the very antithesis of laissez-faire. As we will see, these policies are highly effective thanks to complexities in the real economy that are utterly overlooked in the postindustrialists' simplistic laissez-faire model.

The basic error in the laissez-faire model is that it greatly overemphasizes the interests of capital over those of labor. This bias has always been there, of course, but in modern "global" conditions countervailing forces that in former times tended to curb it have now been largely eliminated. Hence, the characteristic pattern of postindustrial society — large profits for a tiny elite and low wages for the broad mass of the workforce. The postindustrialists, of course, argue that profits are a good thing. Up to a point, this is certainly true, but we can have too much of a good thing, a point that is notably apparent in many parts of the Third World. After all, if a disproportionately heavy bias toward profits were really a formula for superior economic performance, we would expect nations like Mexico and the Philippines to be economic titans. By the same token, if low profits were a recipe for economic dysfunction, nations like Germany, Switzerland, and Japan would be paupers.

The most obvious way in which America's competitors systematically preempt manufacturing opportunities is via subsidies. These are most apparent these days in "strategic" industries. Aerospace is a notable case in point. The spectacular growth of Europe's Airbus consortium, for instance, has been driven in large measure by subsidies. So successful has government support been that, after less than three decades in business, the consortium had drawn abreast of Boeing in market share in large commercial jets as of 1998. Of course, subsidies are supposed to be banned under international trade rules these days, but since the rules are largely unenforceable, subsidies are likely to remain a factor in world economic competition for a long time. Certainly they are becoming an increasingly significant factor in such promising fields as renewable energy and high-speed rail systems. One thing is certain: Europe is unrepentant about using subsidies to build its aerospace industry. In its own eyes, Europe has merely been emulating the United States, which, in an earlier era, established a large lead in aerospace with an unabashed program of direct and indirect government supports.

Beyond subsidies, other nations use a plethora of less obvious devices to promote the growth of promising new manufacturing industries. Many nations, for instance, protect their home markets and thereby provide their manufacturers with a profitable sanctuary from which to attack foreign markets. Of course, in the view of laissez-faire advocates, trade protection is counterproductive because it feather-beds weak companies and bad managers. Although this is indeed sometimes true, there is another side to the story: where protection is structured intelligently with an eye to boosting the national interest as opposed to the sectional interests of individual businesses, it can serve powerfully to invigorate a nation's industries. As long as an appropriate system of rewards and penalties is in place to induce corporations to plow their large domestic profits back into improving their production technologies, worker productivity levels are bound to increase accordingly.

Besides subsidies and nontariff barriers, manufacturing companies in many advanced economies also enjoy the advantage of much greater access to outside capital than do their American counterparts. This reflects a fundamental macroeconomic fact: most advanced manufacturing nations now boast considerably higher savings rates than the United States. Of course, for believers in the simplistic logic of laissez-faire, the perennially weak U.S. savings rate should no longer be a handicap for American manufacturers. After all, capital markets around the world have supposedly become "globalized" in recent years; thus, in theory, savings now flow freely from nations with a surfeit of capital to nations with a capital shortage. In the real world, however, things are different: even in these days when billions of dollars of capital can be moved across an ocean at the click of a mouse, most of the world's savings flows continue to be invested close to where they are generated. This comes as a surprise to the postindustrialists. Blinded by their laissez-faire models, they forget that, in the real world, bankers are not mathematical algorithms but people with families and friends — factors that tend to encourage them to invest in manufacturing businesses close to home. Even David Ricardo, the ultimate nineteenth-century advocate of laissez-faire, considered it only natural that people prefer to invest at home rather than abroad. As he pointed out, at bottom, investors like to keep a close eye on their money. They fear the unknown and are therefore naturally reluctant to invest in foreign lands, where the rules and customs are not fully familiar.

Of course, the world has shrunk since Ricardo's day, but human psychology has not changed much in the meantime. After all, contrary to their globe-trotting image, modern bankers are no more likely than anyone else to enjoy living out of a suitcase. It is surely natural that they should prefer to deal with borrowers with whom they share strong cultural ties. The closer these ties are, the smoother and more productive the banking relationship is likely to be.

The tendency for high-saving nations to invest in their own manufacturing industries is generally bolstered by government policies. As Richard J. Barnet and John Cavanagh have pointed out, this is particularly so in the case of such formidable manufacturing economies as Japan and Germany. Indeed, much financial regulation around the world is specifically aimed at boosting investment in local manufacturing. Certainly, financial regulators tend to ensure that the lion's share of the local banking market is reserved for local banks. In Japan, for instance, Japanese banks enjoy a market share of fully 98 percent of the local savings deposits. Moreover, even where American banks have access to significant savings flows in foreign financial markets, they are under considerable regulatory pressure to lend the money locally rather than make it available to manufacturers in the United States.

Another factor that has contributed to the relative decline of manufacturing in the United States is an imbalance in the flow of trade secrets and other proprietary know-how. Here again, this is a factor that is utterly overlooked in the postindustrialists' laissez-faire models. If the postindustrialists think about these matters at all, they imagine that know-how flows freely in both directions. In reality, however, governments around the world try to ensure that the flow is almost entirely one-way. On the one hand, they pry as much advanced know-how as possible out of the United States. On the other hand, they make sure that few if any of their own corporations' leading-edge manufacturing technologies leak abroad. Of course, as we have already noted, nations like Germany and Japan are increasingly transferring considerable amounts of know-how abroad, but such transfers generally involve midlevel technologies that have already been superseded at home.

All the evidence suggests that a well-organized nation can be highly persuasive in inducing American corporations to transfer their most advanced production technologies to factories within its borders. Its trump card typically is access to its markets. An American company will be presented with a choice. If it tries to export into these markets from its factory in the United States, it will probably face significant trade barriers. But if it chooses instead to manufacture within the nation concerned, it will not only enjoy privileged access to the local market but will probably also be offered many other important benefits, such as investment grants and tax concessions.

The really troubling aspect of this pattern for the American national interest is that in time the production technologies concerned may be entirely lost to the American economy. Once American corporations transfer their production technology to a foreign subsidiary, they may find that it makes sense to concentrate all future production in this subsidiary. Such a decision typically is made when the corporation faces heavy investment costs in jumping to the next stage of the technology concerned; it rarely makes sense to continue to maintain two production facilities turning out the same product. Thus, the obvious choice is to close the original American factory — obvious, that is, because American workers are much easier to fire than their foreign counterparts, who, thanks to tough labor regulation, usually enjoy considerable protection against layoffs. Thereafter, all the crucial learning-by-doing know-how that is the essence of advanced manufacturing accumulates in the overseas subsidiary, to the benefit of the productivity of its workers.

Why don't American executives fight harder against the pressure to transfer their production technologies abroad? Because they see little reason to do so. After all, they can assure themselves that they are not losing a technology merely because it is migrating to one of their foreign subsidiaries. This is the spirit of globalism, and almost everyone in corporate America's boardrooms these days is a true globalist.

Of course, from the point of view of American workers, things look very different. Clearly it is hard for American workers to achieve world-beating productivity rates if their employers do not equip them with world-beating production technologies.

The whole trend of wages over the last fifty years underlines the importance of pivotal production technologies in the world income league table. In the 1950s, when the most advanced production technologies were typically deployed only within the United States, American manufacturing workers were the world's highest-paid, earning about six to eight times as much as their counterparts even in Japan and Germany. By the 1980s, however, Japan and Germany had caught up in production technologies. Wages in these nations duly passed American levels and have stayed ahead ever since.

Since American labor is not represented in American boardrooms, the real losers from technological globalism have no say in the matter. Moreover, workers' interests count for so little these days that American corporate executives openly proclaim their commitment to utopian globalism without the slightest fear of embarrassment. The pattern was memorably exemplified a few years ago by a Colgate-Palmolive executive who told the *New York Times:* "The United States does not have an automatic call on our resources. There is no mindset that puts this country first." A similarly outspoken disregard for the interests of American labor was apparent in a remark by NCR's president, Gilbert Williamson, some years ago when he said: "I was asked the other day about the United States' competitiveness, and I replied that I don't think about it at all. We at NCR think of ourselves as a globally competitive company that happens to be incorporated in the United States."

Many other examples could be cited of how far the real world diverges from the narrow world of the postindustrialists' laissez-faire models. Suffice it to say that the world is far from a level playing field in trade, let alone in finance or flows of advanced manufacturing technologies. Many of the distortions tend to promote manufacturing outside the United States, while the American economy, constantly propelled by the pursuit of short-term profits, drifts ever deeper into postindustrialism.

The worst part of it is that free-market dogma has tended to obscure from Americans how far the United States has been falling behind its principal competitors in recent years, most notably Japan. All press reporting to the contrary, Japan has not ceased to challenge the United States for leadership of the global economy. Far from it. As we will see in chapter 8, Japan has continued to gain on the United States in the 1990s in most of the ways that matter to top policymakers on both sides of the Pacific.

For now, let's merely mention the crucial matter of trade, where Japan's performance has been even stronger in the 1990s than almost anyone has noticed. The result was that in the first eight years of the 1990s, Japan's current account surpluses totaled $750 billion. That was more than two and a half times the total of $279 billion it recorded in the first eight years of the 1980s.

When we remember that (1) Japan runs a large surplus in almost every tradable manufactured product, (2) Japanese manufacturers pay some of the highest wages in the world, and (3) nations with lower wage costs, like the United States, are rapidly increasing their trade deficits with Japan in high-tech goods, it is surely obvious that the Japanese economy is one of the strongest in the world, particularly when judged by the yardsticks that matter to Japanese policy makers.

Japan's very different economy should be judged by Japanese objectives, not Western ones. And here we get to the crucial point: whereas the American economy, faithful to the dictates of laissez-faire economics, is generally run to boost the short-term welfare of the American consumer, the Japanese economy is run to boost Japan's long-term ability to project economic power abroad.

Measured by this latter criterion, the 1990s have been years of spectacular progress for the Japanese economy. Remember that every dollar of current account surplus a nation receives adds an extra dollar to its foreign assets. Japan in the 1990s has been growing its net foreign assets faster than any nation since the United States in the golden years of expansionism in the 1950s. The result, entirely overlooked by the Western press, is that Japan more than tripled its net overseas assets in just the first seven years of the 1990s.

Before looking in detail at postindustrialism in the following chapters, let's sum up the story so far. The argument of this book revolves around many points, but one is paramount: all conventional wisdom to the contrary, modern manufacturing industries are difficult to enter — thus, those nations that achieve early leadership in them are remarkably well insulated against future challenges from lower-wage foreign competition. Modern manufacturing industries require large amounts of both capital and proprietary production know-how — resources that are generally difficult for low-wage countries to acquire.

By contrast, postindustrial services are relatively easy to enter. They typically require neither large amounts of capital nor much proprietary know-how. In fact, most of the necessary know-how can be acquired from public or semipublic sources.

In sum, this book turns upside down the standard presentation of postindustrialism as a more economically desirable activity than manufacturing.

II

Postindustrialism's Drawbacks

2

A Hard Look at Computer Software

Computer software is the quintessential postindustrial business, and as such it is undoubtedly the ultimate test of the postindustrialists' claims. After all, when postindustrialists cite examples of postindustrial opportunities, computer software is typically at the top of their list.

It has blossomed from a niche business that served just a few hundred mainframe computers in the 1950s to one that today is literally ubiquitous. While computer software is most familiar as the programs we run on our personal computers, it is also installed in everything from cars and telephones to video cameras, vacuum cleaners, and even refrigerators.

Looking to the future, the industry's potential to boost American prosperity seems to the postindustrialists to be almost limitless. So much for the hype. Now for the reality.

Microsoft's success: a very special case

For all the euphoria about software, the industry's image of fabulous success is remarkably narrowly based. In fact, this image is largely attributable to just one company, Microsoft. The enrichment of Microsoft's founders has powerfully supported the myth that the information economy is a latter-day El Dorado. The press seems to assume that, just as any young American boy or girl can aspire to become the president of the United States, any new software company can aspire to become another Microsoft. In reality, Microsoft is a very special company, one whose growth has been driven almost entirely by its monopolistic role in setting standards for computer operating systems. Microsoft inherited this role from IBM in the 1980s; as was abundantly apparent from IBM's famously fat profit margins in former times, the ability to set the computer industry's standards amounts to a license to print money. In the words of the American consumer activist Ralph Nader, Microsoft's position is the functional equivalent of "owning the alphabet."

By contrast, other software companies enjoy no such all-embracing franchise — and no such license to print money.

In any case, the Microsoft story is misleading in another way. Although the company is portrayed as a latter-day Leviathan, it is still a relatively modest business in most respects. In fact, it counts as a giant on just one rather dubious measure, its stock market valuation. Measured by its peak stock price in the summer of 1998, Microsoft was worth an astonishing $325 billion — or almost as much as the gross national product of India! More meaningfully, this valuation was a phenomenal twenty times the company's annual *sales* — a truly unsustainable ratio that will one day be looked back on with the same sort of disbelief with which we now regard the Dutch tulip bulb mania of the seventeenth century. Its stock valuation apart, Microsoft is no colossus by most other measures. In fact, as of 1998, ranked by sales revenues, it was little more than a middleweight positioned a lowly number 400 in *Fortune* magazine's league table of the world's 500 largest companies. On the crucial yardstick of jobs, Microsoft compares even worse. As William Greider has pointed out, as of 1997 its American workforce of about 15,000 was only one-twentieth that of Ford Motor.

Even Microsoft Chairman Bill Gates has gone to some lengths to emphasize how *small* his company is. Speaking to ABC Television, he pointed out that even if the company succeeds in its growth plans, it is unlikely to employ more than 40,000 by 2002 — and that would be just one-fifth of IBM's total workforce as of 1997. Perhaps the most telling indication of Microsoft's relative economic insignificance is that its workforce accounts for only about 1 percent of all employment in the American computer software industry. Thus, when the media talk about the famously large compensation levels at Microsoft, one should remember that 99 percent of the industry's workers work for less successful employers.

Those well-paid software jobs: only the best need apply

Judged by the amount of cyberpower in the room, it was a press conference to end all press conferences. There in plain view was Bill Gates of Microsoft and Andrew Grove of Intel. Other notable digerati who turned out included Eric Schmidt of Novell, Gordon Eubanks of Symantec, and Carol Bartz of Autodesk. They were present in their capacity as leading supporters of the Business Software Alliance, a Washington-based industry group. With a mission to increase the industry's lobbying clout in Washington, the digerati and their helpers were intent on doing their damnedest to underline the software industry's importance to the American economy.

Their strongest card was jobs. The industry, they maintained, was not only one of the nation's largest employers but one of the best. Citing survey results, they stated that the industry's sales in 1996 totaled $103 billion. On a value-added basis, therefore, software ranked third among American industries after automobiles and electronics — up from fifth place in a 1995 study. Thus, in the space of just two years, software had leapfrogged two major industries — aircraft and pharmaceuticals. Between 1990 and 1996 the industry had grown at an annual rate of 12.5 percent, nearly two and a half times faster than the American economy as a whole.

The Business Software Alliance went on to emphasize the industry's contribution to the U.S. job base. Measuring indirect as well as direct employment, the industry was already employing 2,065,000 by 1996 and was projected to boost its contribution to the U.S. job base by 66 percent to account for nearly 3 percent of the entire American workforce by 2005. And the best part of it was the pay levels. People employed directly in the industry earned $57,300 a year on average. Workers in the packaged software section of the industry did even better, averaging $64,500.

"The average wages are phenomenal," said Robert Damuth, director of policy studies for Nathan Associates, which conducted the survey on behalf of the Business Software Alliance. "The incomes are extraordinary because software is a knowledge-intensive industry that is thriving and workers are getting compensated for their skills."

It all looks wonderful. So what can possibly be wrong with this picture?

First, let's be clear. There is no question that there is much to be admired in the American software industry. Its achievements are legion. That said, the industry's contribution on the jobs front is distinctly double-edged. The software industry's high wages, for instance, are just the obverse side of the most obvious drawback of postindustrialism — exclusionist hiring. The industry recruits from the cream of the intellectual crop, and Bill Gates for one is not shy about saying so. Gates has publicly confessed that he is "very elitist" in hiring only engineers with extraordinarily high IQs. Of course, few other software companies can afford to be quite so choosy as Microsoft in hiring people who — in *Fortune*'s words — are "geniuses or near-geniuses," but the industry's message to job seekers is brutally blunt: workers of average intelligence need not apply.

In the circumstances, the surprise is not that the industry pays high wages but that its wages are not even higher. Although software workers rank well up among the intellectual elite, their wages are typically only slightly more than the average Japanese wage of $21.01 an hour.

So what are we left with? The industry recruits bright people and pays them wages that are not overly generous compared to their intellectual capabilities. Meanwhile, less intelligent workers who cannot make the grade are left out in the cold. Given the increasing polarization of American society in recent years, the software industry's elitist job structure is clearly not helpful.

And this is just the beginning of the problems with the software industry.

Culture, piracy, and the pursuit of exports

As we have already noted, the software industry is a surprisingly weak exporter. In truth, there are good reasons for this.

For a start, there is the problem of piracy, which deprives software companies of a large share of their rightful revenues in many foreign markets. Piracy is so widely accepted in China, for instance, that popular Western computer software programs such as Microsoft's Windows are sometimes illegally copied in computer stores in full view of the customer. Bootleg copies of Windows are also much in evidence in Taiwan, Russia, Thailand, and many other potentially important markets.

Many other American software products suffer similarly curtailed export revenues because of piracy. According to a study by International Planning and Research, a consulting firm based in Redmond, Washington, about 46 percent of all business software used globally in 1995 was pirated. The resulting losses to copyright holders totaled $13.1 billion, an increase of 9 percent on 1994.

All the evidence suggests that the piracy problem will get worse before it gets better. There is a deeply rooted unwillingness by consumers almost everywhere to pay up for the authentic product — not just in the Third World but even in some of the world's richest regions. Take super-rich Hong Kong, where per capita incomes rival those of the United States. As reported by Joshua Fellman of the Bloomberg news agency in 1997, Hong Kong's top intellectual property official washed his hands of the software piracy problem, saying that any effort by the Hong Kong government to shut down stores that sold bootleg software would not be supported by the general public.

Also undermining software's export potential are various cultural barriers. These are problematical in many of the most visible types of software, not least in "shrink-wrap" personal-computer software, which often needs considerable adaptation to take account of local cultural norms in different markets around the world. In general, the more user-friendly a personal computer program is, the more heavily it needs to be adapted to sell in foreign markets. Known as localization, this adaptation process is often a managerial and cultural nightmare. For the Indian market alone, Microsoft now produces its products in eight different languages!

American software companies usually do their localization outside the United States, typically in the foreign market concerned. Thus, the costs of localization can dramatically cut the exporting company's net foreign exchange receipts — and by extension U.S. export revenues.

Word-processing programs are perhaps the most obvious example of how cultural barriers inhibit the progress of even the most dominant software makers. In trying to sell localized versions of its Word software, Microsoft, for instance, has encountered entrenched opposition in foreign markets. A notable case in point is the Korean market, where as of 1998 a tiny local company, Hangul & Computer, still had an 80 percent market share. Even in the lucrative Japanese market, where Microsoft has used all its marketing muscle to stage a long-running and particularly fierce fight for market leadership, Word has faced stubborn competition from Ichitaro, a locally developed program sold by Tokushima-based Justsystem Corporation. Word finally achieved market leadership in Japan only in 1998. Even then, its success was attributable in large measure to special factors, most notably the company's practice of giving away Word with other programs.

For American software companies that lack Microsoft's enormous market leverage and financial staying power, the struggle for foreign markets is often an unequal one. For one thing, local software developers often reverse-engineer — that is, emulate features from — leading American versions of popular programs, and because they are faster at getting these features into the local market, they can maintain their market share for years against strong American products. Reverse-engineering, which is generally legal, is pandemic in the industry.

In fact, legal protection for software ideas is so poor that many of the greatest U.S. software inventions — what Ann Wells Branscomb has rightly described as "the crown jewels of the information economy" — have proven impossible to patent effectively. Not only are they unprotected in foreign markets, but they cannot even be protected in the American home market. The industry's history is full of great ideas that were "borrowed" by rival companies. IBM in particular has suffered from this sort of borrowing. Take the "relational" software structure that is now almost universally incorporated in database programs. This structure, which enhances speed in searching, was invented by the IBM researcher Edgar Cobbin in the late 1960s but was quickly commercialized by other companies, most notably Ingres Corporation and Oracle Corporation. Now it has been widely copied by software developers around the world — and for the most part such foreign usage of the concept yields no royalties or other revenues to the United States.

Another American company whose pioneering software work has been enthusiastically plundered by software developers around the world is Xerox. Xerox is credited as the ultimate source of, for instance, the font software that controls the look of the alphabetical characters used on computer screens and in printouts. Xerox was also the source of various revolutionary ideas that propelled the growth of Apple Computer. These ideas included screen icons, mouse-activated pull-down menus, and overlapping windows of onscreen text. Of course, Apple's ideas have in turn been reverse-engineered by countless other software companies, most notably Microsoft. In fact, Bill Gates once acknowledged the ultimate source of the ideas behind the Microsoft Windows operating system in a famous witticism. Gates joked that both he and the founder of Apple, Steve Jobs, had lived next door to a rich neighbor called Xerox, and when he broke in to steal the television set, he found that Jobs had already taken it! Of course, both Microsoft and Apple are American companies, so there was no net loss of revenues to the American economy as a whole from this "theft." Less visibly, however, many foreign companies have also exploited Xerox's innovations without paying a penny in royalties to the United States.

American software developers are now pressing hard for tougher intellectual property laws to protect their world-beating ideas. But they have a long battle ahead of them. In the meantime, the world will continue to help itself for free.

All this explains why the software industry is a notably disappointing contributor to U.S. export revenues. But this fact is less well understood than it should be because press reporters often talk airily about the industry's supposedly superlative export performance without checking the facts. The press rarely quotes specific numbers for U.S. software exports, and when it does, its estimates are often exaggerated. In fact, the press often conflates the American industry's exports with something quite different: overseas sales. There is a crucial distinction here: overseas sales include sales of products that are made largely or entirely abroad. Thus, although there may be a flow of dividends and royalties back to the parent company in the United States, most of the revenues generated by foreign subsidiaries stay in the markets concerned.

Microsoft provides a good example of the distinction. Its exports from the United States accounted for only 25 percent of its total sales in 1996. This no doubt will come as a surprise to many Americans, who are under the impression that Microsoft's exports are much larger than this. They confuse Microsoft's overseas sales with its exports. As of 1996, its overseas sales contributed more than 60 percent of total sales. But more than half of such sales came from added value generated largely in its overseas subsidiaries. Only a small proportion of the resulting revenues flows back to the United States. Most of the money goes to pay salaries and other expenses in the overseas subsidiaries. (Workers employed outside the United States account for fully 32 percent of Microsoft's total workforce.)

In any case, as we have already emphasized, Microsoft is a truly exceptional company, and few other software companies enjoy even remotely as advantageous a position in global markets. For the American industry as a whole, exports represent a low proportion of total sales revenues. No reliable official figures are available, but a reasonable guesstimate is that exports represent less than 10 percent of the industry's total revenues.

In sum, it is clear that the perennially troubled American balance of payments is getting a poor return from its most brilliantly successful postindustrial businesses. It is little short of tragic that so many talented people are engaged in an activity that does little to advance America's long-term position in global competition. And then there is the problem of rising software imports.

The coming threat to American software jobs: imports

If culture limits America's opportunities to export software, doesn't it, by the same token, protect the United States from imports? Hardly.

For a start, though many software products are indeed highly culture-specific, many others are not. Major software projects conducted on a contract basis for specific large corporate customers, for instance, generally entail a relatively small proportion of culture-specific work. Even such culture-specific software as the applications programs sold in American computer stores can be written in part by foreign programmers. In fact, the only element of such programs that requires detailed cultural knowledge is the user interface. Most of the rest can be parceled out to skilled programmers anywhere in the world.

Given that programming wages are generally lower abroad than in the United States, American software companies have a clear incentive to rely more and more on foreign labor, and in so doing, they inexorably add to the soaring U.S. import bills. In fact, this incentive increases all the time thanks to a technology-induced sea change in the industry's economics. For one thing, cheap personal computers have replaced expensive mainframes as the main tools for developing software. At a stroke, therefore, the industry has swung from being a highly capital-intensive industry to a highly labor-intensive one. In fact, the capital required to establish a new software business these days is minimal. Virtually the only equipment needed is desks, telephone lines, and personal computers. Thus, for a software entrepreneur in a low-wage country, the capital cost per job can be as little as $10,000, a reduction of more than 90 percent from the mainframe era. This figure is well within the reach of software subcontracting companies in low-wage countries — and far less than is needed to get started in even the least sophisticated areas of manufacturing.

Another factor that has powerfully boosted the competitiveness of foreign nations in exporting software to the United States is the big fall in international telecommunication costs in the last twenty years. This drop has opened the door to many cross-border collaboration projects in which leaders based in the United States can coordinate large teams of programmers working in one or more low-wage foreign countries. Ominously for American software jobs, the impact of modern communications has been particularly dramatic in Third World countries, where satellite communications and cellular phones have suddenly liberated local software contractors from the acute limitations of primitive terrestrial telephone services. Given that at least half the world's people still live more than two hours' travel time from the nearest telephone, we are as yet in only the early stages of a major proliferation of opportunities for the developing world to expand its software exports to the United States.

But how good can a programmer in the developing world be anyway? The answer is — very good indeed. As we pointed out in chapter 1, there is no reason to believe that citizens of poor nations are inherently lacking in the sort of creativity needed to succeed in postindustrial services. But in any case, creativity is not the most important mental faculty required in routine programming of the sort that accounts for most of the software industry's jobs. Rather, as the author Robert X. Cringely has pointed out, the key faculty is merely an excellent short-term memory — the ability, for instance, to remember long strings of numbers. Whereas most people can memorize a seven-digit telephone number, good software writers have the sort of memory that can readily memorize strings of fifteen or more digits.

Microsoft's Bill Gates himself exemplifies in high degree the sort of mind that succeeds in the software industry. He reportedly can recall the telephone extension numbers and car license plate numbers of countless Microsoft employees. According to the authors James Wallace and Jim Erickson, even as a child he displayed amazing memory skills. In particular, he won a local parish contest by memorizing and reciting the entire Sermon on the Mount. The passage is the equivalent of nearly four standard newspaper columns of type. Among the hundreds who participated in the contest over the years, Gates, who was then only eleven, was the only challenger who ever succeeded in reciting the entire passage without stumbling or missing a line.

Recall of this sort is rare, but it is clearly a God-given talent, not a uniquely American cultural attribute. There is no reason that other nations couldn't boast as high a ratio of talented software engineers as the United States.

Of course, the idea that other nations are capable of going head to head with the United States in software seems to be belied by the evidence of the American software market. After all, as even the most casual observer can see, virtually all the software in American computer stores is home-grown. But this actually proves little because personal computer software is a specialty in which cultural factors happen to be particularly important in protecting American software makers from foreign competition.

Even the fact that most of the world's computers now run on operating systems produced by an American company — Microsoft — rather than, say, a German or Japanese one offers little support for the idea that Americans enjoy a special franchise in the software industry. The fact that an American company proved dominant in operating systems was more or less preordained given that the United States enjoyed unquestioned leadership in hardware when the IBM personal computer was launched in 1981. By the late 1980s, when it became apparent that computer users and hardware manufacturers worldwide wanted a single world standard to ensure global compatibility, Microsoft's huge installed base ensured that its operating system was the obvious choice.

One thing is for sure: all talk of a special American edge in software to the contrary, other nations assuredly can make good software. Take the Japanese. Although the postindustrialists often maintain that the Japanese cannot write software, this is contradicted by the fact that thousands of Japanese software engineers work in Silicon Valley and are indeed highly prized there for their talents. Among the more notable admirers of Japanese software writing talents is none other than Microsoft Chairman Bill Gates. In his search for world-beating software talent, he has included six Japanese universities among twenty-five top universities worldwide where he likes to concentrate Microsoft's recruiting efforts. Gates should know about Japanese software talent given that one of his closest friends and confidants in his early days was the Japanese software engineer Kazuhiko Nishi. Before they had a falling-out in the mid-1980s, Gates described Nishi as "my best guy ever."

Not only are individual Japanese citizens noted for their software skills, but Japan-based software companies also are no slouches in the industry. They are particularly active in producing software that leverages Japan's strengths in manufacturing. A good example is computer games, in which the Japanese have had no difficulty developing superb software to go with their ultra-fast hardware. Although not all such software is written in Japan (much of it is written in the United Kingdom, where wages are much lower than Japanese levels), the process is directed from Japan, and much of the most creative thinking is done there. The Japanese are also in a league of their own in writing automation software for their factory robots. Their skills are readily apparent too in the elegant and foolproof "imbedded" software that guides the operations of Japanese electronic products. Such software is often highly complex: a Sony Handycam, for instance, contains as much software as a 1960s-era mainframe computer — and infinitely fewer bugs.

Another nation whose software prowess has also been absurdly underestimated by postindustrialists is Germany. Granted, like Japan, Germany does not export much personal computer software. But it has achieved great success in areas where it has a clear shot to compete on equal terms with the Americans. An example is SAP, a highly sophisticated software house based in Walldorf near Heidelberg. Founded by former executives of IBM's German subsidiary, SAP makes so-called enterprise resource planning (ERP) programs, which enable major corporations to integrate their worldwide accounting, marketing, and production operations into one seamless system. On the strength of serving the global software needs of hundreds of giant European, American, and Japanese corporations, its sales have been growing by 30 percent a year. At last count, SAP (whose name is an acronym for Systems, Applications, and Products) ranked among the world's five largest software companies and had achieved a dominant share in major world markets. In the United States and Canada, for instance, SAP's market share was 34 percent as of 1996 — way ahead of Redwood City–based runner-up Oracle, whose share was a mere 10 percent. In other important world markets, SAP's share ranges as high as 70 percent.

Perhaps the ultimate symbol of its leadership is that its so-called R/3 software has been selected by many software-savvy computer companies as the backbone of their global administrative systems. Companies that rely on R/3 include IBM, Motorola, Texas Instruments, Intel, Hewlett-Packard, Digital Equipment, and — accolade of accolades — Microsoft.

That said, the Germans and Japanese obviously pose no great threat to American software jobs, for the simple reason that their wages generally exceed American levels. In any case, the governments of both Germany and Japan are clearly more interested in promoting manufacturing activities than software and other postindustrial services. But the story is very different for many low-wage nations now breaking into the software business. In truth, lower-wage nations are full of potentially highly capable and productive software workers — workers who need only an appropriate technical education to compete successfully in the world market for software labor. They don't even need to have received any prior training in writing software given that in recent years more and more software employers around the world are happy to provide comprehensive on-the-job training for raw recruits. Moreover, it should be noted that even in some notably poor Third World countries, the appropriate education — in mathematics or science — is readily available to the middle classes, and the standard of educational achievement in those countries often compares surprisingly well with that of the United States.

With the spread of personal computers around the world, the opportunity to acquire hands-on experience in programming is now widely available even in many poor nations. Moreover, the rise of the

Internet has made it possible for software engineers in the Third World to learn of the latest American software-writing techniques just as quickly as their counterparts in the United States. In fact, virtually all of the most important know-how needed to make good software can be transmitted around the world quite legally in informal Internet communications.

The speed with which software know-how leaks out of the United States these days is hard to exaggerate. As William J. Holstein has pointed out, many American software innovators hold an "ardent belief" that pioneering work should be widely disseminated in Usenet groups and Internet chat rooms. Writing in *U.S. News & World Report* in 1998, Holstein cited university researchers who had been engaged by a software company to help develop an important new program. Not only did these researchers not guard the resulting intellectual property from competitors, but they published full details of their work on the Internet before the company could bring the program to market.

One thing is certain: the software business is already a remarkably cosmopolitan one. Even within the American software industry, foreign-born engineers are highly visible. As reported by Pete Engardio of *Business Week,* there are already probably more than 100,000 foreign-born engineers in Silicon Valley alone. Chinese-born engineers in particular are extremely numerous there. Even at the very top of the American software industry, foreign-born engineers are now much in evidence. Take 3-Com, a sensationally successful Santa Clara–based networking software company: its chief executive is the Algerian-born Eric Benhamou. The founder of NexGen is S. Atiq Raza, a native of Pakistan. Indians constitute probably the most visible nationality of all; in some estimates, they account for nearly one-fifth of all the world's programmers. Research by Raman Mishra of MIT indicates that there are more than 5,000 Indian-born engineers working for Microsoft alone. In fact, the core team that created Microsoft's Windows 98 operating program was largely composed of Indian-born engineers.

The point is not just that engineers from low-wage countries can play to win within the American software industry; it is also that more and more social networks are in place that help low-wage nations increase their software exports to the United States. After all, many key foreign executives now holding down high-level jobs in the United

States retain links with friends and college classmates in their home country, and such links not only help low-wage nations to keep in touch with the latest American software trends but give them an inside track in bidding for the American software industry's outsourcing work.

The significance of such links is notably apparent in the case of Ireland. Formerly an agriculture-based economy, Ireland in recent years has built up an important software export business, and increasingly it is exporting to the United States. Ireland has benefited in several ways from the fact that many Irish engineers moved to Silicon Valley in the 1970s and 1980s. In particular, it has enjoyed a reverse brain drain: Irish-born software engineers are increasingly returning from the United States to put their talents — and perhaps more important, their contacts — to profitable use within the Irish software industry.

Ireland's official economic development agency has stimulated the trend and used it to persuade several American corporations to establish important software operations in the country. Among the most notable of these have been Microsoft, IBM, Novell, EDS, Oracle, Motorola, and Symantec. These operations in turn have trained countless more engineers, many of whom have broken away to establish their own software start-ups in Ireland in recent years. Perhaps the most spectacular example is Iona Technologies, which started with just one full-time employee in 1991. By 1997, after it was listed on the NASDAQ market, it was valued at more than $500 million.

Another small nation whose software industry has also benefited greatly from its citizens' personal ties with the United States is Israel. Such major American corporations as 3-Com and Bay Systems have already located some of their most advanced software operations there. Israel is also noted for its strong indigenous software companies, many of which are world leaders in communications. Some, for instance, have made important breakthroughs in asynchronous transfer mode, which is a high-speed, wide-band standard for data communications. Others are leaders in a technology known as wireless LAN (local area network), which, among other things, enables a company's notebook computers to communicate with one another by radio or infrared signals. Still others are advanced in video compression, a key technology in digital television. As of 1997, four Israeli makers of Ethernet switches had won the highest rank accreditation by the U.S.-

based National Software Testing Laboratories, a prestigious testing organization.

As a result of successes like these, it is hardly surprising that Israel, even more than Ireland, has become an important exporter of software to the United States. Of course, because these countries are small and their wages are not much below American levels, their export growth has done little to undermine American software jobs. But they are the thin end of what could prove to be a very large wedge. Certainly their success in exporting to the United States and other leading economies has not been lost on many larger nations, not least such low-wage nations as India, the Philippines, and Malaysia.

Today these new contenders generally participate in the world software industry merely as sources of cheap labor for local subsidiaries of American software companies. But in the long run their own indigenous companies may grow to become major players in the global software industry.

A key point here is that the managerial challenge of running a software company is not nearly as daunting as is generally imagined, and it is certainly modest compared to running an efficient manufacturing business. Whereas the production flow in a modern First World factory may have to be coordinated on a split-second basis (think of the just-in-time inventory control system in the automobile industry), software work generally involves few truly critical deadlines; typically there is just one, the deadline by which the entire program must be finished. Thus, although the success of top manufacturing companies like Toyota and Daimler-Benz stems in large measure from a sophisticated management culture that has taken several decades to hone, software firms need no similarly deep management tradition to succeed.

In short, as the Silicon Valley venture capitalist Donald Valentine has pointed out, software is "a simple business." Given that Valentine helped create such phenomenally successful ventures as Cisco Systems, Oracle, and 3-Com, he should know. Speaking of his habit of investing large amounts of money in software start-ups run by untried young entrepreneurs, Valentine says of the software industry: "Twenty-three-year-olds can figure it out. If it were a complicated business like a steel mill, with unions and all this material coming all the time and two shifts, I might want older people with experience."

Even Microsoft, big as it is by software-industry standards, illustrates the point. According to Michael A. Cusumano and Richard W.

Selby, authors of *Microsoft Secrets,* Microsoft operates on remarkably simple management structures that are reminiscent of the administration of the Roman army. Microsoft ensures that interdependent aspects of a program are kept to a minimum, thus enabling software development managers to function like Roman centurions who "go off on their own and report back only occasionally." What the Roman army could do two thousand years ago, many software start-up companies in the developing world can undoubtedly emulate today.

In fact, a rapidly increasing proportion of software used in the United States is already being imported from low-wage countries. CrossComm of Massachusetts, for instance, has been sourcing important software from Poland. Among other East European countries that are exporting to the United States, Russia is a major player. As reported by Bloomberg News, California-based Sun Microsystems is distributing advanced data-encryption software developed by Elvis+Co., a Russian company created by former Soviet scientists. The software is among the most secure encryption software programs available anywhere in the world because it sustains encryption keys as much as 128 bits long.

Perhaps the ultimate accolade for Russia's prospects as a software exporter has come from Microsoft's Bill Gates. Speaking to reporters in Moscow in 1997, Gates said that a strong education system positioned Russia to become one of the world's three largest software exporters. He added: "Russia has a very bright future as a country developing software, and we are definitely seeing the beginning of that."

Even mainland China is now targeting software as a major export industry. It has already scored a spectacular success with Founder Group, a firm that makes typesetting and desktop publishing systems for East Asian users. Launched in 1976 by a husband-and-wife team of mathematics professors, Founder has now captured 80 percent of the market worldwide for Chinese-language typesetting software. The company serves large publishing companies in Hong Kong, Malaysia, and Taiwan. The company has also developed a system for the Korean language and is participating in Malaysia's ambitious plan to build an export-oriented software industry in the so-called Multimedia Super Corridor near Kuala Lumpur. As of 1996, Founder's sales had hit $482 million, making it one of the developing world's most successful high-tech companies.

Founder's latest gambit has been to target the huge Japanese market, the world's second-largest market for desktop publishing after the United States. Founder has already signed a contract worth several million dollars to supply Recruit Company, a major Tokyo-based magazine publisher. As reported by the *Nihon Keizai Shimbun,* the contract symbolizes corporate Japan's growing recognition of China's rapid progress in software. According to Recruit, Founder's system provides more diverse editing and layout functions than the American software companies that had previously dominated the Japanese desktop publishing market. The Chinese system is also considerably cheaper than comparable American systems.

As yet, China has done little exporting to the United States, but that may be changing. The recent trend of software programs being designed as a series of discrete components has been helping Chinese software companies overcome cultural barriers in exporting software to the West. Already an IBM affiliate in China is showing the way. The firm, Advanced Systems Development Company, a joint venture with a top Chinese science university, is developing a sophisticated range of component software called Java Beans. This is a series of interchangeable software modules designed for commercial users of the Internet. As described to Bloomberg News by the general manager, Ling Rui-ji, the new modules are free of the cultural specificity of previous generations of software. Thus, Chinese programmers can develop software for, say, a clinic in the United States without knowing anything other than the end-user's basic requirements. Perhaps the most surprising — and for American software workers, the most ominous — aspect of IBM's Chinese affiliate is that it is pioneering a new work shift system linking several low-wage countries. When the Chinese programmers finish each evening, they pass their work on to Latvia and Belarus, where other IBM engineers continue working on the modules during the Chinese night. No wonder Bloomberg News commented: "The tilt in software design towards more basic, interchangeable products is good news for countries like China with armies of talented programmers." Given that IBM has laid off thousands of programmers in the United States and other Western countries in the last five years, the message could hardly be clearer: the software industry's spread into the Third World has already begun — and a challenge to the West's software job base is imminent.

Probably no nation illustrates the strength of that challenge more vividly than India, which, as we will now see, is well on the way to becoming one of the world's great software exporters.

Morning in Madras: the rise of the Indian software industry

In their book *The Judas Economy,* William Wolman and Anne Co-lamosca tell a provocative story of how a top executive of the Caterpillar bulldozer company once pulled rank in negotiations with some Indian officials. In an effort to underline India's deficiencies in manufacturing, he flung a cigarette lighter across a conference table with the comment, "When you guys can make one of these things, let me know about it."

Although in the thirty years since this incident took place the Indians have made no noticeable progress in manufacturing cigarette lighters, it is hard to imagine any American executive displaying such hubris these days. For all India's shortcomings in manufacturing, it has made remarkable progress in an industry that to most Americans is more impressive than manufacturing — and that industry is, of course, computer software.

In fact, since India began targeting software as a key element of its economic growth strategy in the mid-1980s, its software exports have been growing at a compound rate of more than 40 percent. Of course, India started from a tiny base and is still a relatively minor player in the global industry. Moreover, it remains an easy country for foreigners to underestimate. For a start, there is the problem of India's overly bureaucratic style of administration. In contrast with Northeast Asian governments, which have generally played a positive role in their nations' economic development, the Indian government can't seem to get out of its own way — or anyone else's.

India's image problem is not improved by the poor quality of official promotional brochures handed out to would-be foreign investors in the Indian software industry. Such brochures are typically printed on cheap glossy paper that betrays a grayish/brownish tint. The typefaces are unfashionable, and the pictorial content consists mainly of faded photographs of satellite dishes in dusty, not overly scenic locations.

Various Indian regions competing for direct investment from foreign software houses add to the amateurish tone with their slightly ridiculous jockeying for attention. As reflected in an official press pack sent out in 1997, no fewer than three Indian states — Karnataka, Gujarat, and Orissa — made mutually contradictory claims to the title of "India's Silicon Valley."

The less than sophisticated image is not surprising given that, with a per capita income of just $362 a year at last count, India remains one of the poorest countries on earth. Little wonder, therefore, that when the government first targeted the software industry, few in the United States took notice. As Dewang Mehta, executive director of the Indian software industry's trade association, has admitted, even Indians themselves originally scoffed at the idea of their country becoming a software powerhouse.

The software industry, however, is a natural choice for India in these days of ultra-cheap intercontinental telecommunications. "Improvements in the telecom infrastructure have meant that the United States and other developed markets are on India's doorstep, not on the other side of the globe," says Iain Allison of Marlin Partners, a Bombay-based consulting firm. "No other Indian industry has this factor favoring it."

India's prospects are also helped by the happy fact that the industry's capital needs are so modest. Just how modest is apparent in the case of Infosys, a software company founded in the mid-1980s by N. R. Narayana Murthi on an investment of less than $1,000. From that tiny acorn, Infosys has now grown into a world-girdling giant that has won important contracts from such notable American clients as AT&T, Nordstrom, Citibank, and General Electric.

Moreover, in targeting software, India enjoys an important fundamental advantage in its education system, which educates the middle class to a level broadly comparable to that of the United States and the United Kingdom. Indian schools tend to be particularly strong in mathematics, a fact that reflects a long tradition of mathematical scholarship dating back to ancient times. The concept of negative numbers, for instance, was used by the Hindu astronomer Brahmagupta in the seventh century — more than nine hundred years before its first recorded use in Europe. Moreover, our so-called Arabic numeral system has its ultimate origin in India.

Thus, India was positioned for takeoff in software even before the government began targeting the industry for growth in the early 1980s. In fact, the industry's true beginnings go back surprisingly far — to 1968, to be exact. That was the year when a firm called Tata Consultancy Services (TCS) was launched as a computer service offshoot of Tata Sons, a giant Bombay-based conglomerate that makes everything from steel to cosmetics.

For the first few years TCS concentrated on the domestic Indian market, serving affiliates in the Tata group as well as other Indian-based clients. In the early 1970s it began testing the water in export markets, and in 1975 it achieved a major breakthrough by securing a contract from a British-based subsidiary of the Burroughs Computer Company. After successfully completing that contract, TCS went on in 1976 to forge a continuing relationship with Burroughs.

Since then TCS has been growing at a compound rate of more than 30 percent a year, and as of 1997 its workforce had expanded to 8,500. Other major Indian software makers, such as HCL Corporation and Tata Infotech — which, like TCS, is an affiliate of Tata Sons — have enjoyed similar growth. The result is that, according to the HCL executive Ashok Syal, the Indian software industry's total workforce quadrupled to 160,000 in the ten years to 1998.

As India's software houses have grown, they have simultaneously honed their skills to the point where today they claim to do leading-edge work in many of the software industry's most important subdisciplines. They pride themselves, for instance, on the speed with which they have adopted the latest software-writing techniques, such as object-oriented programming, a technique by which programs are designed as a series of discrete modules rather than as one large whole. They are also experts in CASE (computer-aided software engineering) and graphical user interfaces.

Recently Indian software houses claim to have pioneered important new approaches to the management of software projects. In particular, they are proud of having introduced an element of forward planning into an industry that had previously been notorious worldwide for false starts and radical midway changes of direction. In an effort to underline their commitment to rigor and precision in the production process, Indian software leaders even talk about their companies as "software factories." As Shiv Nadar, the charismatic chairman of HCL Corporation, points out, the factory concept is intended to conjure up associations with Japan's highly organized mass-production approach in manufacturing.

> We have chosen deliberately to distance ourselves from the image of software development as a "creative activity." Instead, we see it as a process-driven activity. Creativity and problem-solving skills are encouraged during an initial period of "head-butting" or discussion by the project team. But once the project gets going, the teams go in for strict project management using mature development methodologies.

Other Indian software executives draw an analogy with the construction industry. Tata Infotech's Sreenivasan Mohanagopal, for instance, says:

> Our approach requires us to plan ahead, rather like an architect who plans the whole of a building before a single brick is laid. Builders do not alter the basic structure of a building halfway through the construction process; equally in our approach to software engineering, we do not make basic changes to the structure of a software program midway through the production process.

All this is music to the ears of customers around the world because it promises something they particularly value and all too rarely receive: a surprise-free software product delivered on time. In the software industry surprises are generally unpleasant ones, and on-time delivery is a rarity (even mighty Microsoft is noted for missing its own publicly announced deadlines).

The proof of the pudding is in the eating, of course. How well does the Indian software industry live up to its marketing promises? By all accounts, quite well. Certainly the industry has built a long list of satisfied clients in major overseas markets. The industry has been particularly successful in the United States, which now takes fully two-thirds of all Indian software exports. Delhi-based HCL alone boasts a customer list that reads like a *Who's Who* of American business — names like Boeing, AT&T, Citibank, Merrill Lynch, Novell, Cisco, Compaq, IBM, and Sun Microsystems. Its customers also include many of Japan's most prestigious companies, including NTT, NEC, Hitachi, and Toshiba.

As reported by the *Financial Times* of London, Indian software companies are particularly strong in applications for the transportation industry. Indian firms created, for instance, the administrative systems of Swissair and American Airlines, the train scheduling system for the London Underground, and the reservation system for the Holiday Inn motel chain.

All such achievements pale, however, in comparison with the success of Tata Consultancy Services a few years ago in a showcase contract for the Swiss securities industry. The project involved creating a securities trading system that would reduce the settlement time for trades from ten days to just one. It was a contract of national importance for Switzerland — all the more so because a few years earlier the massive task of writing the London Stock Exchange's proposed new Taurus trading program had become so bogged down in unmanageable complexity that it was never completed.

The Swiss project was developed and executed by Nirmal Jain, an intense electrical engineer who typifies the sort of firm leadership now driving the Indian industry. Jain, who earned a doctorate from the University of Hawaii in the 1970s, worked in the American electronics industry in Dallas before returning to India to work for TCS.

When Jain learned that the Swiss were seeking bids for a new trading system, he immediately recognized a chance for TCS to leap into the big leagues. Leaving nothing to chance, he dispatched a team of ten people to Switzerland for six months in advance of bidding on the contract. This move not only enabled him to develop an exceptionally detailed proposal but impressed the Swiss with TCS's seriousness. In the end there were just two finalists, and TCS was one of them. The other was Chicago-based Andersen Consulting, one of the most trusted names in the world of software contracting. Then the word came through from Switzerland that TCS had beaten out Andersen. For the whole of the Indian software industry, it was a moment to remember. And for the American software industry, it was a watershed of sorts. The demanding Swiss had been persuaded that Third World India could deliver the relevant quality standards; thus, TCS's price, at reputedly little more than half of Andersen's, had been the clincher.

There is a special irony in the fact that this most prestigious of contracts was carried out in the southern city of Madras. Even by Indian standards, Madras is an unprepossessing location for a leading-edge business. There could hardly be a more telling illustration of how much more competitive Third World companies can be in software than in hardware, for Madras's success in exporting software to the West contrasts starkly with its distinctly limited export potential in manufacturing. Just how limited is that potential? One of the city's more notable manufactured products is rickshaws.

American software jobs: the coming shakeout

Given the rise of vigorous software-exporting industries in India and other cheap-labor countries, a question arises: why isn't the American software industry running scared?

It is a good question. After all, not only has the American software industry continued to boom in recent years, but as of the late 1990s it seemed to be even more confident than ever.

A key reason for the American industry's sense of invulnerability is that demand for software has exploded in recent years. As a result, there has generally been more work available than people to do it. This state of affairs, however, is unlikely to last forever. It is clear that many of the forces driving the industry's growth in the 1990s are now running out of steam. First and most obviously, there is a question mark over the personal computer industry's ability to maintain its phenomenal growth rate. Sales of personal computer software have boomed in the 1990s, but as Microsoft acknowledged in its 1995 annual report, the industry has now entered a mature phase. Many standard application packages have been around so long that further enhancements add remarkably little value. Word-processing is a good example: though word-processing packages in the late 1990s are much more complex and elaborate than those of ten years earlier, they offer at best only marginally better performance to most users. Spreadsheet and database programs are also entering a mature phase.

Another factor that has greatly added to the false sense of endless prosperity has been huge demand for software in the financial services industry. This demand has been fueled in part by deregulation, which has entailed a great deal of restructuring of financial services; one consequence has been vast investment in new computer systems, not only in the United States but in many other countries. But the trend toward deregulation has now reached a mature phase, and there may be little more milk in this cow.

The financial services industry's demand for software has been further inflated by the introduction of the euro, the new pan-European currency, which has required countless banks and corporations around the world to reengineer their information technology. According to Andersen Consulting, the cost for a typical multinational corporation works out to the equivalent of between 1 and 3 percent of annual sales. Germany's Daimler-Benz alone has spent $110 million on euro-related software.

As if the personal computer boom and the financial services boom were not enough, software demand has been further inflated by the infamous year-2000 problem — the problem of rewriting computer software to take account of the move to the twenty-first century. In typical commercial software, date fields occur on average about once in every fifty lines of code. Unfortunately, the task of locating the relevant lines is extremely tedious because the code is often written in obsolete languages and the original program documentation has long since been lost. Software users have therefore had no alternative but to hire teams of engineers to root out the problem line by tedious line. As of 1997, BankBoston, for instance, was deploying a 40-person task force to test and fix 60 million lines of code in 200 applications. At Merrill Lynch a team of no less than 80 engineers has been working in shifts, 24 hours a day, 7 days a week. The effort is expected to cost the company $200 million.

Abroad, too, the millennium problem has tied up thousands of software workers. In the United Kingdom, for instance, as estimated by the chief of the British millennium task force, Robin Guenier, companies are spending about $50 billion to fix the bug. As for the total worldwide cost, an estimate of as much as $600 billion has been bandied about by the Gartner consulting firm. Although this figure is inflated by costs that would have been incurred in any case in routine upgrading of computer hardware and software, it seems reasonable to believe that the millennium bug has produced a windfall demand for software services totaling about $200 billion. Given that most of this money is being spent on the remuneration of software engineers and consultants, the employment effect is evidently huge — creating enough work for perhaps 300,000 people for up to three years.

What happens after the computer software industry works its way through the millennium problem and the other major tasks in its recently overfilled in-tray? No doubt, new opportunities will emerge, but the pace of growth in demand is likely to slow significantly at just the moment when Third World software exporters look likely to start making serious inroads in the American market.

American software industry workers imagine they are well prepared for the coming onslaught. After all, they have already been going head to head with Indian labor for many years thanks to the development of the so-called body-shop business. Body-shops are recruitment agencies based typically in India that dispatch highly qualified Indian engineers to the United States on short-term visas. Although these engineers work on the premises of American clients, they are often paid wages that are closer to Indian norms than American ones. Not surprisingly, therefore, body-shopping is regarded as a thinly veiled legal stratagem to pay Indian engineers working in the United States less than the American minimum wage. But although the body-shops have created troubling headlines in the trade press — there have even been reports of attacks on Indian workers in Oregon and California — they have done little to undermine American software wages. American software workers, therefore, can be forgiven for imagining that they have similarly little to fear from rising imports of software from the Third World. But the truth is that the scale of the challenge from cheap imports is massively larger than that from the body-shops. After all, the body-shops account for only a small proportion — almost certainly less than 10 percent — of all American software jobs. In fact, typically only relatively few American workers have been displaced by body-shop labor. One of the most significant cases reported in the press, for instance, was the displacement of 250 American programmers by body-shop workers at American International Group.

Numbers like this are clearly small by comparison with the potential pressure on American jobs that would result if such low-wage software exporters as India, China, and Russia hit their stride. One indicator of how big the import challenge could grow has come from the World Bank, which has predicted a twentyfold increase in global trade in data processing and allied services between 1994 and 2005. Given that software wages are several times higher in the United States than in the Third World, there can be little doubt about which nation will be doing the lion's share of the importing.

One thing is clear: many of the Third World countries now targeting the industry have the potential to ramp up their software workforces very rapidly. Take India. According to India's *Economic Times,* 1,700

Indian colleges and institutes produced a total of more than 60,000 graduates in computer science and similar disciplines in 1997 alone.

Given the attractions of the industry to bright young Indian graduates, we can expect a rapidly increasing number of them to choose a career in software in the future. The main attraction is, of course, pay. Although pay rates in the Indian software industry do not seem high by Western standards — they run only about one-third of American levels — they are sensationally high by comparison with other sectors of the Indian economy. In round numbers, a typical Indian software engineer earns about twenty to thirty times the national average wage. In the longer run, the potential for India to increase its share of the world software market is almost limitless, given that it boasts an educated class of nearly 200 million people.

All this helps explain why one American software industry expert, Christian Byrnes, has suggested that India is on the way to becoming a software superpower. Byrnes, an executive of Meta, a Connecticut-based consulting firm, told *Financial World* magazine: "Just as the Japanese took over America's leadership in manufacturing through superior quality processes, the U.S. must now face the challenge of India becoming the world's No. 1 software producer in the next decade."

Perhaps the ultimate irony here is that even for India, the long-term rewards from developing a major software export industry may prove disappointing. As computers become more sophisticated, they may increasingly write their own software — and thus pose a threat even to Indian software jobs. This point may not be that far off. If Bill Gates is to believed, we may reach it as early as 2010. All in all, it is hard to see how the United States can retain its long-term competitiveness if it continues to bet so heavily on an industry whose long-term economics are at best so questionable.

Software and the productivity paradox

So far our account of the economic fundamentals of the American software industry has been one of almost unrelieved gloom. But aren't we overlooking some important positive factors that should be entered into the balance? After all, the early rise of such a vigorous U.S. software industry has at least ensured that the United States has been consistently in the vanguard in applying the benefits of computerization throughout industry.

In the view of postindustrialists, this is self-evidently an unmitigated blessing. And at first sight, they seem to have an important point, given the computer's legendary ability to improve productivity in a host of industrial applications. But has America's early embrace of computerization really been such a good thing? Actually no. Far from it. In fact, a large body of evidence suggests that America's embrace of computers has been too hasty — so hasty in fact that it has proved a net *disadvantage* in competing with nations like Japan and Germany. These latter nations have been generally slower to computerize their industries, and they are often roundly scorned on this score. But what looks like "backwardness" to the postindustrialists should in many cases more correctly be seen as prudence. Where computers are concerned, the watchword in these nations has been "Look before you leap." The truth is that early computerization involves many hidden pitfalls.

Thus, although postindustrialists often celebrate the fact that American businesses spend much more on software than their foreign counterparts, careful academic studies suggest that a large proportion of the huge investment involved is wasted. So marked is the tendency for business software to produce disappointing results that the phenomenon has become widely known as the computer productivity paradox. This paradox has been authoritatively documented by, among others, the Morgan Stanley economist Stephen Roach, the sociologist Paul Attewell, and the former Xerox computing chief Paul Strassmann.

That a good portion of the U.S. investment in computerization has been largely wasted is, of course, hotly contested by the postindustrialists. And every time U.S. productivity figures experience a temporary acceleration — as they did in 1997–99 — the postindustrialists rush to proclaim that America's huge investment in computer software is finally producing large economic returns. But invariably subsequent events show that this was wishful thinking. Perhaps the most accessible account of the productivity paradox has come from Thomas K. Landauer, a top software designer. In his book *The Trouble with Computers,* he points out that the United States has suffered an acute case of diminishing returns as it has attempted to computerize more and more aspects of its economy. On the one hand, computers have generally been highly successful in the kinds of tasks they were first applied to in the 1950s and 1960s. They have been far less effective in later applications, however, and in some cases their performance has been so disappointing that, when all the costs are included, they have produced on balance a negative return on investment for society.

Typical examples of successful early applications — let's call them type 1 applications — include the control of production machinery, the routing of telephone calls, and the automation of utility billing systems. Later applications — type 2 applications — include inventory control and general office administration programs. Type 1 applications are clear-cut and self-contained, whereas type 2 applications are flexible and open-ended. Most type 1 applications require little interaction with human operators, and whatever interaction is necessary can generally be carefully choreographed in advance. Type 2 applications, on the other hand, involve extensive, unstructured interaction with human operators and thus require that the programmer write in a whole host of "if . . . then" sequences to try to anticipate the general fallibility and almost infinite unpredictability of the human mind.

Type 1 applications are typified by foolproof programs that make full use of the computer's great fundamental advantages of speed, tirelessness, and accuracy. The result has been an impressive contribution to productivity in many industries.

Later attempts to extend the benefits of computerization to type 2 applications, however, have been stymied by the complexity of the tasks involved. The most obvious challenge has been to create user-friendly user interfaces. Unfortunately, user-friendliness is generally neglected in the software industry, and this tendency is exacerbated by the fact that the user interface is typically one of the last aspects of a program to be written. Its quality is therefore often sacrificed when software developers are racing to meet a tight deadline.

The result is familiar to every computer user: if a user interface is badly written, the program may hang or crash in response to minor keystroking errors. Confronted with complaints about such problems, the software industry typically adopts a "blame the customer" stance: the hapless user is scolded for not having read the user manual properly. But as Landauer points out, the fault lies not with the user, who cannot be expected to memorize the entire contents of a weighty user manual, but rather with the software developer, whose job it is to anticipate common user errors and provide appropriate safeguards against them.

Even just the everyday task of making sure that a corporation's various computer systems can talk to one another is often traumatic and typically requires heavy running costs in maintaining a large information technology department. Another hidden drawback is the need to keep buying program upgrades. If you don't buy the upgrades, you risk being left behind as your data are stored in an increasingly obsolete format. Yet, as Clifford Stoll has pointed out in *Silicon Snake Oil,* most upgrades are poor value for the money. They may, for instance, include many new commands that superficially add functionality but on closer examination turn out to be no more than marketing gimmicks. Unfortunately, new commands add greatly to a program's complexity because they tend to interact with one another in ways that increase the number of lines of programming code almost geometrically. The result generally is more bugs — and less user-friendliness. As Steven Levy has pointed out, the worst part of it is that program upgrades place heavy demands on users, who must constantly take time out from their busy schedules to keep current with the technology.

Another part of the explanation for the productivity paradox is that corporate America feels tempted to use the computer's dazzling capabilities just because they are there. Once a computer system is in place and all of a company's inventory, sales, and expense data are available for electronic manipulation, the opportunities for analysis are dizzying. Landauer comments: "Every manager now gets reports measured in stack-feet per month. Nobody can read it all or digest what they've read." The result is, of course, acute information overload. As Landauer points out, the information technology industry has found it far more difficult to provide the *right* information than to provide lots of the wrong information.

A major part of the problem is that corporate America's top executives have not been monitoring their information technology departments as closely as they should. As Paul A. Strassmann has pointed out, the millennium problem, for instance, is stunning evidence of "managerial laxity." In his book *The Squandered Computer,* Strassmann comments: "There is absolutely no justification for allowing this condition to burst to executive attention at this late stage."

According to Strassmann, a former chief information officer of

Xerox Corporation, the computer software industry should have started getting ready for the new millennium by the early 1970s, if not the mid-1960s. He gives short shrift to the software industry's excuse that the millennium bug arose because programmers were legitimately concerned about economizing on computer space. He maintains that such economizing was justifiable only in the very earliest days of computerization, the era of punched cards, which ended in the mid-1960s. "The insistence on retaining for more than thirty years a calendar recording system that everyone knew would fail after December 31, 1999, is inexcusable management," he says.

Worse, the managerial myopia demonstrated in the millennium affair is, he maintains, only the tip of the iceberg.

> A typical programmer can make hundreds of such myopic decisions in each project. The only reason that the year 2000 "insufficiency" has attracted so much attention is that it is ubiquitous and has a deadline when its effects will become visible. There are millions of other bugs just as negligent as this, but they pop up randomly, one location at a time, to be squashed with as little publicity as possible.

Strassmann issues this stunning verdict: "Very soon the decades-long infatuation with spending money freely on information technologies will come to an end. It will become acceptable to admit that organizations were spending too much money because operating executives were afraid, unwilling, or untrained to manage it, while abdicating that role to technical experts."

Another notably double-edged factor driving the software industry's growth in the United States has been government regulation. As computer power has grown, government agencies have placed increasing demands on corporations to report ever more minutely on their compliance with regulations on pension fund administration, equal opportunity employment, environmental protection, and a host of other matters. Strassmann himself conducted a study that indicated that, in the 1994 tax year alone, tax-paying corporations incurred paperwork costs totaling $98 billion to pay taxes totaling $175 billion.

Perhaps the most ludicrously wasteful use of information technology has been in finance. As Landauer points out, the financial services industry has been second to none in its enthusiasm for information technology over the years. In particular, the industry has displayed an almost insatiable appetite for trading software. This is notably evident, for instance, at Barra, a Berkeley-based firm whose sales of software for trading stocks and derivatives have been growing by a phenomenal 30 percent a year in the 1990s. Overall, thanks to heavy investment in computers and software, the financial services industry's investment per employee has risen sixfold in real terms since the 1950s. Yet the industry's record in boosting productivity in recent decades has been deplorable. In effect, the financial services industry has used computers primarily not to reduce its costs but to increase the complexity of its products. As we will see in chapter 3, the end result has merely been to bamboozle customers in ways that tempt them to trade far more often than is necessary. This may do wonders for the financial services industry's profits, but clearly the implications for society as a whole are hardly positive.

The ultimate evidence against computers is in the overall U.S. productivity statistics. As the editor of *Challenge* magazine, Jeff Madrick, has pointed out, although American businesses have been increasing their investment in computers by more than 30 percent *a year* since the early 1970s, the rate of growth of productivity has fallen from an average of 2.85 percent a year in the decades before 1973 to about 1.1 percent a year since. No wonder the Nobel Prize–winning economist Robert Solow has commented: "You can see the computer age everywhere but in the productivity statistics."

Given that the United States has invested more than $4 trillion in computerization since 1960, the scale of the waste is staggering. The American love affair with information technology reminds one of Dr. Samuel Johnson's characterization of remarriage: the triumph of hope over experience.

3

Finance: A Cuckoo
in the Economy's Nest

As we noted in chapter 1, the financial services industry ranks second only to computer software in the extent to which it is extolled by postindustrialists. And true enough, at first sight, the postindustrialists' enthusiasm for financial services seems to make sense. After all, pay levels in financial services are generally well above average. Moreover, many kinds of financial services have shown extraordinarily rapid growth in recent decades, not least in the two leading postindustrial economies, the United States and the United Kingdom.

But on closer examination, such apparent strengths turn out to be distinctly double-edged. Take the industry's high salaries and bonuses. These are simply a reflection of the fact that, like computer software, the financial services industry hires disproportionately from the cream of the intellectual crop. Given that many top financial professionals clearly possess superb entrepreneurial skills, it is not hard to imagine them enjoying similarly large rewards running high-growth companies in exciting new fields of advanced manufacturing. Their attraction instead to a career in finance deprives the manufacturing sector of vital leadership and thus undoubtedly contributes directly to the serious deterioration in manufacturing competitiveness that the United States has suffered in recent decades. In this respect, the United States is merely following in the footsteps of the United Kingdom, whose deindustrialization in the early part of the twentieth century was driven in part by a similar trend: the cream of the intellectual crop preferred

careers in finance and other high-prestige service industries over manufacturing careers.

Now for the financial sector's growth. Clearly seen in terms of its
increasingly significant role in depriving the manufacturing sector of
leadership, such growth is far from the unmitigated blessing the postindustrialists imagine. Worse, many of the financial sector's fastest-
growing activities turn out to be utterly unproductive and even positively destructive from the point of view of the general public good.
As we will now see, much of what the financial sector has been doing in recent years has been feathering its own nest at the expense of
the great investing public. Growth of this sort is the economics of the
cancer cell, and in praising it, the postindustrialists have made their
biggest mistake of all.

First, some faint praise

Let's be clear at the outset: much — perhaps most — of what the
financial services industry does even these days is of considerable value
to society. Banks, for instance, make a vital contribution not only in
facilitating the transmission of money (via checks and bank wires) but
in providing a store of value (via savings accounts) and in financing
business expansion. Insurance companies enable individuals and businesses to minimize their risk of loss from accidents and other instances
of bad luck. Foreign exchange dealers facilitate trade between nations.
Even the securities industry, whose many excesses we discuss in detail
later, makes a vital and important contribution to prosperity to the
extent that it facilitates *long-term* investment in stocks and other risk
assets.

Yet for all the talk of the supposedly beneficial effect of financial
innovation in recent years, the financial sector's economically productive services are almost all old, established ones that had already
reached a high degree of maturity more than a century ago in both the
United States and the United Kingdom. In fact, there really have been
few truly useful major innovations in financial services since then.

It is chastening, therefore, for today's financial professionals to look
back to that time. For it is an amazing fact that the financial sector
preempted vastly less labor then than it does now. Even the London
financial services industry got through the day with a total of no more

than 30,000 clerks, scriveners, and messenger boys — less than half
the workforce of a typical major Wall Street firm today. Yet London
was then by far the world's largest financial center, functioning as it did
as the clearinghouse not only for the United Kingdom's internal
finances but for most of the world's international transactions. Today,
by comparison, the London financial services industry needs more
than 500,000 people to conduct a much smaller share of the world's
financial transactions.

A question arises. Why do financial services preempt so much more
labor today than in former times? A large part of the answer is, of
course, that fundamental demand for financial services has soared in
step not only with expanding world trade but with increasing personal
wealth, and rising populations. Meanwhile, various minor but highly
useful new services, such as credit cards and travelers' checks, have
also contributed to the growth.

But there is something else going on here beyond an increase in
demand for useful services — something that is best called financialism. The term refers to the increasing tendency for the financial sector
to invent gratuitous work for itself that does nothing to address society's real needs but simply creates lucrative jobs for financial professionals. The financial sector can get away with this because the people
ultimately paying the bill usually don't know they are doing so. The
beneficiaries of big pension funds, for instance, rarely have any knowledge of, let alone control over, how their money is invested. Financialism has probably always been with us, but it has grown rapidly in
recent decades, in step with the progressive deregulation of financial
markets. In painting a euphoric picture of further fast growth in financial services, the postindustrialists are in the main merely projecting
forward into the future the continuing proliferation of wasteful financialism.

The essence of financialism:
trading for trading's sake

Probably the greatest factor driving the financial sector's growth in
recent years has been an explosion in financial trading. It has also been
probably the most undesirable; as such, it is the very essence of corrosive financialism.

It is difficult to exaggerate the scale of the trading explosion. In aggregate, financial trading in the United States grew more than thirty-fold in real terms between the early 1970s and the mid-1990s. And in some specialist areas, the growth has been even more spectacular. Take trading in foreign securities. As reported by Nicholas D. Kristof of the *New York Times,* such trading has grown one hundred times faster than the American economy as a whole in the last quarter of a century.

The major driver of all this growth has clearly been deregulation, which, in turn, has been driven by the widespread belief among conventional economists that the freer a financial market is, the more "efficient" it is — that is, the more accurate it is in valuing financial assets. Such accuracy is important to the general health of the economy in that it serves to ensure that capital is channeled to those uses that are most likely to result in high economic growth.

The problem is that there is no evidence that deregulated financial markets do in fact value assets more accurately than regulated ones. Rather, the reverse may be true: the evidence is that as deregulation has proceeded, markets have become increasingly volatile and are therefore valuing assets more and more irrationally.

The all-time classic example of how deregulation has served to increase market volatility was the New York stock market's infamous "Black Monday" plunge of 22.6 percent on October 19, 1987. If share prices are supposed to reflect a rational consensus on the future prospects for corporations, this move was utterly inexplicable. There was no significant development in the real economy that day that presaged serious trouble ahead for American business. In fact, as the Yale economist Robert J. Shiller has pointed out, the only significant economic news on Black Monday was the news of the crash itself. Based on a survey of nearly 1,000 investors soon after Black Monday, Shiller concluded that the collapse was an utterly irrational outbreak of crowd psychology in which 40 percent of institutional investors experienced "a contagion of fear from other investors." This conclusion was handsomely vindicated in the following year, when not only did the American economy boom, but New York stocks bounced back spectacularly to recover all their losses and more.

The important point for our purposes here is that the Black Monday crash — the biggest one-day fall ever — took place in what free-market theorists considered the most "efficient" market in financial history. Thanks in large measure to deregulation, countless new financial instruments had been introduced in the previous decade that had dramatically increased trading volume — and thus were supposed to forestall precisely the kind of monumental irrationality so apparent on Black Monday.

Among these financial instruments, perhaps the most devastatingly counterproductive was so-called portfolio insurance. Portfolio insurance is a system of program trading in which an investment fund automatically sells more and more of its holdings as share prices drop. In principle, it closely resembles the "stop-loss" orders favored by many unsophisticated small-time stock speculators. Stop-loss orders are widely considered by intelligent investors to be a loser's strategy, and for good reason: they run directly counter to the basic logic of sensible long-term investment, which is, of course, to buy low and sell high. According to the Brady Report, an official inquiry into the incident, between $60 billion and $90 billion of equities were subject to portfolio insurance in mid-1987 and were thus poised to be dumped as the market fell. The result was what Robert Kuttner has aptly described as "mindless freefall."

The tendency for increased trading to breed ever more irrational volatility has also been notably apparent in currency markets, where trading volume has been soaring at a compound rate of 20 percent annually in recent years. The irrationality has been particularly apparent in the case of the tempestuous relationship between the Japanese yen and the American dollar. By the standards of conventional economics, the yen-dollar market should be one of the world's most efficient and, by extension, one of the most stable. After all, the fundamental determinant of exchange rates is each nation's relative competitiveness in tradable goods. Given that divergences between different nations' levels of competitiveness change only very slowly over the years, the yen and the dollar should probably move within a band of no more than a few percentage points against one another in any one year.

In practice, however, the yen-dollar exchange rate has become ever more irrationally volatile since the mid-1980s. In that time the yen has doubled in dollar terms on two separate occasions — first in the mid-1980s, and again in the first half of the 1990s. Then, in the second half of the 1990s, it was the dollar's turn to soar: between the spring of 1995 and the summer of 1998 it jumped more than 80 percent against the yen. To cap it all, the market then immediately reversed itself, with the yen soaring more than 30 percent in less than two months, one of the fastest recoveries in currency market history.

There might have been a modicum of method in all this madness if each currency had risen or fallen as its home economy's fortunes waxed or waned. But if anything, the pattern of the last fifteen years has demonstrated the opposite principle. Several times when the American economy has done badly, the dollar has soared on currency markets — most notably in 1980, 1982, 1990, and 1991. Similarly, in several years when the Japanese economy has done badly, the yen has soared — most notably in 1986, but also between 1992 and 1995. Conversely in 1996, a year when Japan recorded the best growth of any major nation, the yen lost more than 9 percent of its value.

It is hard to see any purpose in all this financial churning — other than, of course, to create lots of jobs for currency traders. The consequences are doubly negative for society at large: not only are such traders' talents wasted on a useless activity, but the volatility created by the trading explosion generates dangerously misleading signals for business executives trying to plan ahead. In the early 1980s, when the dollar was wildly overvalued, American business executives made major decisions to move production offshore — only to find that with the subsequent fall in the dollar these decisions looked distinctly questionable. Perhaps the most farcical example was a decision by IBM in the early 1980s to initiate a major expansion of its production operations in Japan to take advantage of the then-low exchange rate for the yen. In pursuit of that strategy, IBM moved hundreds of key American and European executives into Tokyo in 1984 and 1985. Most of these executives had families who had to be transplanted to Japan at vast expense in terms of moving costs, real estate commissions, and initial charges for joining exclusive Tokyo clubs. Yet no sooner had the expenses been incurred than the yen suddenly rocketed on foreign exchange markets, thereby pulling the rug out from under the entire plan. Within three years the yen had doubled — and an embarrassed IBM was forced to sound an ignominious retreat, in the process incurring additional large expenses extricating the bemused families from Tokyo!

If the irrational volatility of financial markets were the only evidence we had to indict the trading explosion, our case would be damning enough. But there is much more. Take, for instance, the contribution of the ever growing army of well-paid analysts and other "experts" whose views drive so much trading these days. When Wall Street analysts turn positive on a stock, institutional investors rush to buy. Then a few months later, when the analysts inevitably turn cool, the institutions dump the stock by the million.

For Wall Street securities firms, this is a wonderfully profitable merry-go-round — which is, of course, the whole point. But for society at large, the vast amount of intellectual energy expended on all this churning is almost entirely wasted. For the fact is that Wall Street securities analysts are notoriously unreliable. In a study in 1997, David Dreman and Eric Lufkin found that Wall Street analysts' forecasts of corporate earnings were "written in sand." In the first seven years of the 1990s, a typical analyst's forecast of corporate earnings was off by a shocking 48.7 percent — an even worse performance than was revealed in similar surveys carried out in the 1970s and 1980s. Writing in *Forbes* magazine, Dreman issued this resounding condemnation: "The inaccuracy of these forecasts shows how dangerous it is to buy or hold stocks on the basis of what analysts predict for earnings. In a dynamic, competitive worldwide economy there are just too many unknowables for such pretended precision."

So much for the securities industry's efforts to predict corporate earnings. Some of its other efforts to provide investment advice are even less intellectually respectable. Take, for instance, the activities of Wall Street's "chartists." These are analysts who ignore corporate fundamentals such as earnings trends and instead try to predict future stock price movements based merely on studying a stock's past trading patterns. Yet for all the millions of man-hours the chartists expend on analyzing stock charts, it is a well-known fact, proven in careful academic studies, that chart-reading simply does not work. The ultimate indictment of the chartists has come from the economist Burton Malkiel, who in a famous study many years ago asked students to construct bogus stock charts based on flipping coins. He then presented these charts to several chartists. Sure enough, the chartists professed to read into the random zigzags significant patterns that they believed would help them make money on future price movements of the "stocks" concerned.

Given advisers like these, it is clear that most fund managers are adrift in a sea of make-believe and self-delusion. And the proof is in the pudding. All the evidence is that fund managers in aggregate consistently fail to match the performance of the market averages. In fact, the shocking truth is that American portfolio managers, aided as they are by an army of advisers, a globe-girdling network of computers, and a cornucopia of new financial instruments, are likely to underperform the random choices of a chimpanzee throwing darts at the stock pages.

As reported by Edward Wyatt of the *New York Times,* barely 10 percent of all diversified mutual funds outperformed the Standard & Poor's 500-share index in the five years to 1998. Nor was this an unrepresentative period. As far back as 1968, Michael C. Jensen showed that mutual fund managers failed to outperform relevant market indexes. According to a survey in 1992 by Ravi Shukla and Charles Trczinka, no less than 200 subsequent studies generally supported Jensen's conclusions.

A detailed analysis by John C. Bogle, chairman of the Vanguard group of mutual funds, has shown that in the ten years to 1995 the annual return on diversified funds lagged the index by fully 1.8 percent a year. Yet to produce this disappointing result, the mutual fund industry had employed a veritable army of highly paid portfolio managers in identifying and buying stocks believed to enjoy better-than-average prospects. As a result, the funds incurred expenses totaling about 1.7 percent of total assets each year.

The conclusion is that portfolio managers are engaged in what is at best a zero-sum game; to the extent that they incur any significant expenses, it becomes a negative-sum game. Not surprisingly, therefore, most first-rate independent advisers tell savers to steer clear of the standard heavily advertised mutual funds and invest instead in so-called index funds, whose portfolios mirror the makeup of a relevant market index and therefore guarantee a performance close to that of the index. As index funds require virtually no ongoing trading or stock-picking, they can therefore promise to keep expenses to as little as 0.2 percent of total assets under management.

Of course, this is not to deny that *some* investors can beat the market. But all experience shows that such people are rare, and not unnaturally they prefer to apply their talents to managing their own money — or at least to managing investment vehicles in which they themselves are major investors. In essence, the typical run-of-the-mill investment manager who runs mutual funds and other widely marketed investment vehicles is wasting his time. One is reminded of the old adage, "Those who can, do; those who can't, teach." In the matter of picking winning stocks, those who can, make profits for themselves; those who can't, lose money for other people.

Perhaps the ultimate irony is that some of the world's most successful investors are outspokenly scornful of both the recent explosion in financial trading and the deregulation that has spawned it. Take, for instance, the speculator-turned-philanthropist George Soros. Having built a fortune of several billion dollars by taking advantage of the irrationality of other investors, he can probably claim to understand better than almost anyone how *inefficiently* today's deregulated markets value financial assets. In recent years he has become a vociferous advocate of a move back to greater regulation of financial markets as a way to "stop the market destroying the economy."

Perhaps even more devastating for the postindustrialists is the testimony of Warren Buffett, the Omaha-based stock investor who is ranked by *Forbes* as second only to Microsoft founder Bill Gates among the world's richest individuals. Buffett never tires of mocking the proliferation of new financial services. His message is that those Wall Street gurus and advisers who come up with new techniques for evaluating shares and other financial assets are — not to put too fine a point on it — snake oil salesmen.

As for new financial instruments, he flatly rejects Wall Street's self-serving view that these do the work of Adam Smith's "invisible hand." Rather, in Buffett's view, such instruments are "an invisible foot kicking society in the shins." He sees traded stock options as gimmicks that do nothing to create real wealth but merely ensnare financial professionals in playing futile zero-sum games with one another. He has been particularly scornful of portfolio insurance, labeling it an "Alice-in-Wonderland practice," and he has been perhaps the single most influential voice in blaming it for the Black Monday crash of 1987.

The ultimate tragedy is that all the money to keep this charade on the road comes from millions of ordinary American savers. They pay high fees for the management of their pension and mutual fund assets, and less visibly, they pay the stockbrokers' commissions and other costs incurred in the ever quickening pace of financial trading.

A key to understanding why this charade continues unchecked is marketing. Mutual funds and other investment products are sold, not bought. The more an investment company spends on marketing, the more business it can expect to garner. Various techniques have been honed over the years to take advantage of savers' emotions — and particularly their gullibility and greed. The time-honored method of catching unsophisticated savers, for instance, is persistent foot-in-the-door salesmanship. At a higher level, the formula that works is more subtle: mahogany-paneled offices, Persian rugs, British hunting prints, and an army of well-tailored sales executives drawn mainly from the upper ranks of society. But either way, what wins business is the right marketing strategy, not the best investment record. This is abundantly apparent in, for instance, the fact that, as recorded by the investment columnist James K. Glassman, those fund management houses that charge the highest fees actually produce by far the worst investment performance. The simple truth is that such houses don't have to perform well so long as they can continue to charge the hefty fees that fund their vast ongoing marketing efforts.

The end result of all this excessive marketing and trading is that the American investment management business is costing the United States probably at least $50 billion a year more than it should. This represents enormous waste by any standards. Yet in large part because the workings of the modern financial services industry have been so enthusiastically endorsed by the postindustrialists, it has never been subjected to any serious reality checking.

American financial exports: myth versus reality

American savers are, of course, not the only potential customers for the American financial services industry. There is a whole world of foreign savers out there, many of whom have huge amounts of money to invest. This point has encouraged the postindustrialists to imagine that the United States can make a fine business exporting its financial services to "less financially sophisticated" nations around the world.

At first sight, this seems to be one of the postindustrialists' stronger cards. After all, to the casual observer it would appear that American financial companies are already huge exporters. In fact, in their public relations activities, American financial organizations never tire of boasting about their "global reach." As any American who travels on business can testify, American financial organizations seem to have long ago appropriated much of the prime office space in such important foreign financial capitals as London, Hong Kong, and Tokyo.

But how globalized are American financial organizations really? The truth is profoundly disappointing for the postindustrialists.

Take a look, for instance, at the operations of a typical "globalized" financial firm such as Merrill Lynch. To judge by its self-evaluation, Merrill Lynch is the sun around which the world's financial system revolves. Rarely has this message been more powerfully conveyed than in the firm's 1996 annual report. As one leafs through the pages, the clichés of financial globalism fairly tumble out. The report opens with a parade of picture-postcard views that would do justice to a travel agent's brochure: a camel seated in front of an Egyptian pyramid, a fleet of Neapolitan gondolas, a little Japanese girl in a traditional kimono, a turbaned Indian boy, a troupe of African dancers. Later pages are decorated with a snowstorm of exotic foreign banknotes, plus enough national flags to outfit a Miss World contest.

The report makes much of various awards the firm's international operations received in the year under review: "Best Debt House in Asia," "No. 1 Latin American Research House," and five other similar mouthfuls that in their grandiloquent territorial claims would do justice to Ozymandias himself.

In view of the apparently vast scope of Merrill Lynch's foreign activities, one would have been forgiven for assuming that the firm was a major contributor to America's invisible exports. A look at the fine print, however, shows that its contribution was actually negligible. In fact, for all the globalism of the firm's annual report, fully 76 percent of its revenues in 1996 were generated within the plain old United States of America. Moreover, little of the 24 percent of revenues generated abroad constituted American exports. Remember that for a service to count as a U.S. export, it must not only be paid for by foreign customers but be performed within the United States. Most of Merrill Lynch's foreign revenues, however, arose from services performed offshore by foreign personnel working in foreign offices. After deductions for foreign salaries and other foreign expenses, there was little left to be remitted to the United States. Take, for instance, a typical service provided by the firm's Tokyo branch — a purchase order from a Japanese client for stock in a Japanese company. Typically such a trade is handled by a Japanese employee working in a Japanese office. The employee's salary, the office rent, the telephone bill, and countless other expenses are paid in yen and represent value added that accrues entirely to the Japanese economy. In fact, the American economy's balance of payments is likely to benefit only to the extent that the Tokyo branch makes a profit on the trade.

In reality, the aggregate amount of profit remitted to the United States by Merrill Lynch's overseas subsidiaries is tiny and probably represents less than 3 percent of the firm's total revenues in a typical year.

Similar analysis shows that other supposedly globe-girdling American financial services companies make equally disappointing contributions to the U.S. balance of payments. Take American Express. In many ways, it is better equipped than any other important financial services company to compete in foreign markets. After all, having introduced the traveler's check in 1891, it was a highly globalized company before World War I, and with the subsequent development of the American Express card it went on to establish a network of offices in more than 160 countries. Thus, American Express enjoys probably a greater global reach than any other financial services company, and it certainly boasts one of the strongest brand names in the global financial services industry.

That said, American Express's contribution to the U.S. balance of payments is quite disappointing. Of the company's total revenues of $16.2 billion in 1996, fully $12.0 billion came from within the United States. Thus, little more than one-quarter of the company's business was done abroad. Yet fully 40 percent of its workforce — a disproportionately large share of the total — was employed outside the United States, and many of the company's other foreign expenses were also correspondingly large. When the company's various foreign expenses were deducted, the company's net contribution to the American balance of payments was probably less than $500 million — or about 3 percent of the company's total revenues.

Clearly, from the point of view of the American balance of payments, a fundamental problem with financial services is precisely that they are services and thus for the most part must be performed close to the customer. But this is far from the only reason financial services tend to make a poor contribution to a nation's export prowess. Another key reason is that almost all the world's financial markets are tightly regulated in a way that inevitably limits opportunities for great American financial institutions.

This is particularly true in East Asia, which happens to be precisely where the great bulk of the world's savings surpluses arise these days. The financial markets of most continental European countries also offer disappointingly few export prospects for American banks. Take Germany. As the world's third-largest economy after the United States and Japan, Germany could be a lucrative market for American banks. In reality, the vast German banking market remains a secure fiefdom of Germany's Big Three banks, Deutsche Bank, Dresdner Bank, and Commerzbank. In particular, Germany's great industrial corporations generally entrust the Big Three with most of their banking business. This is not an accident: much of the stock in major German industrial corporations is owned or controlled by the Big Three.

Opportunities for American banks are similarly curtailed in most other parts of the developed world. In truth, banking is considered almost universally by government officials to be a "strategic" industry that wields potentially enormous power to shape a nation's economy. Thus, nations naturally prefer that their bank industry stay under the control of their own nationals.

But even in areas of the financial services industry where politics is less likely to be a major concern than in banking, American players are still firmly blocked in their hopes of expansion abroad. Take the American discount brokerage industry. In theory at least, its services ought to be of great interest to countless investors around the world. After all, as the Tokyo-based economist Kenneth Courtis has argued, the low commission rates they charge make them highly competitive compared to brokers in other parts of the world. Take a typical example, a purchase order for one hundred shares of Microsoft. As Courtis has pointed out, this would cost a Japanese investor around $500 in brokerage and other transaction costs if it were carried out in Tokyo, but as little as $3 if carried out over the Internet by an American discount broker.

Yet Japanese investors do virtually no business through American Internet brokers. The reason, of course, is that there are many barriers blocking the expansion of American Internet brokers around the world. One obvious obstacle is the requirement that American brokers obtain local regulatory permission to advertise their services in foreign markets. As John Tagliabue of the *New York Times* has pointed out, such permission is generally withheld when a brokerage firm provides its services from a location beyond the reach of the financial regulators of the nation concerned. The inability to advertise may seem like no more than a minor hindrance, but in practice it is a major barrier because investors tend to prefer to deal with organizations whose names are well known to them.

Even English-speaking nations known for their strong support for the theory of globalization are notably inhospitable to the American discount brokerage industry. Take Canada. Before it allowed E*trade, a California-based online broker, to do business within its jurisdiction, it insisted that the firm set up a branch on Canadian soil. Australia and New Zealand also set similar conditions. As *The Economist* pointed out, such conditions largely negate the basic advantage of online trading, which is that it obviates the need to maintain the costly physical infrastructure necessary in pre-cyberspace days.

Perhaps even more startlingly, the United Kingdom has given U.S.-based Internet brokers a chilly reception. Again, E*trade's experience has been instructive. When E*trade first applied to do business in the United Kingdom, British regulators insisted that, among other things, it locate its computers on British soil. In the end, E*trade finessed the problem by announcing plans to provide its services through a British partner — but this arrangement, of course, meant that the service would be performed largely or totally by workers in the United Kingdom, not by U.S. workers. The contribution to the U.S. balance of payments is therefore likely to be negligible.

The most significant aspect of the United Kingdom's attitude is that it is likely to provide cover for other nations that have consistently dragged their feet about opening their financial markets. If even the enthusiastically globalist United Kingdom is not prepared to exempt American online brokers from local regulatory oversight, few other major nations are likely to roll out the red carpet for them. And in fact, as of the summer of 1998, most European governments were adamantly refusing to allow the American discount brokerage industry to advertise for business within their territories.

To apologists for postindustrialism, the fact that so far most foreign financial markets are largely closed to American financial organizations represents no more than a temporary problem. In their view, other countries have merely been a little slower than the United States to recognize the supposed win-win advantages of deregulation and globalization. Thus, the apologists confidently look forward to the day when other nations will deregulate and therefore open themselves to the American financial services industry. This expectation, however, overlooks the strategic view that other nations take of their financial systems. For a start, most other nations see tight financial regulation in part as a vital tool in deterring their wealthier citizens from hiding hot money in foreign bank and brokerage accounts. Moreover, governments tend to regard their nations' savings as a national resource that should be applied in the first instance to boosting their own industries and jobs. Even the supposedly open financial capital of Singapore insists that its citizens put much of their long-term savings money in the government-controlled Central Provident Fund. Needless to say, this fund favors Singaporean jobs in its investment policies. A similar, if much more subtly expressed, concern that national savings be mobilized for the benefit of local job creation can also be discerned in several rich European countries, most notably Germany and Switzerland.

U.S. aspirations to sell financial services abroad are further frustrated by a fundamental weakness of the modern American economy — a low savings rate. In the space of a single generation, the United States has gone from being the world's biggest exporter of capital to the world's biggest importer. Since capital is the scarce raw material of financial services, the hidden leverage that the United States once enjoyed over world financial markets has long since disappeared. The unfortunate truth is that the United States no longer sets the rules of world finance.

A question of ethics: finance as rotten apple

If the expansion of financial services in recent years resulted merely in the frittering away of the talents of many top Americans on a negative-sum game, it would be bad enough. But another lamentable dimension to the financial services explosion cries out for attention: the deterioration it has fostered in the nation's ethical standards.

As turbo-charged new investment vehicles such as derivatives have proliferated, illicit opportunities for financial criminals to enrich themselves at the expense of the general public have increased dramatically. Perhaps even more important, the risk of detection is decreasing all the time. It has become vastly more difficult to police financial markets in these days of radical deregulation in which miscreants have ready access to the secrecy of foreign bank accounts and can dress up their finagling in a dense thicket of complexity.

At issue here are not the cruder forms of financial crime, such as selling worthless penny stocks to elderly widows and other vulnerable members of society. Today, as in the past, heartless villainy of this sort is practiced by only a tiny minority. At issue instead are much more subtle practices that are likely to prove tempting to a much broader range of financial professionals, most of whom would never stoop to the bare-faced blackguardism of the penny-stock promoters.

One such practice is insider trading, which, if the Securities and Exchange Commission's caseload is any guide, has grown dramatically in recent years. As reported by Paul A. Gigot of the *Wall Street Journal,* the SEC at the end of 1997 was investigating more than twice as many cases as it had been a decade earlier. Moreover, given that financial scams are now more difficult to detect than ever before, the SEC's caseload is probably no more than the tip of the iceberg.

One of the fastest-growing financial crimes is a maneuver known as "front running," which involves buying a stock ahead of a major buying program by a big fund management house. A few days later, after the buying program has sent the stock price soaring, the front runner can hope to cash out at a handsome and almost risk-free profit. Another form of insider trading that has probably burgeoned in recent years is illicit buying by influential stock analysts for their own accounts before they issue a bullish view on a stock.

Other financial crimes can be a lot more subtle. Take, for instance, a technique known as selective allocation. The key to this is that many portfolio managers act for several different portfolios in their stock-purchasing activities. They often allocate their purchases to their various portfolios only at the end of each day — by which time many trades may already be showing significant profits while others will be showing losses. By selectively allocating the profitable trades to some portfolios and loss-making ones to others, they can greatly favor some beneficiaries at the expense of the rest.

As Steven D. Kaye has documented in *U.S. News & World Report,* favoritism in allocating winning trades can pay dividends for fund managers in many circumstances. In one blatant case uncovered by the SEC a few years ago, Kemper Financial Services (a firm now renamed

Zurich Kemper Investments) allocated winning trades to an in-house account, while allocating less profitable trades to two Kemper mutual funds that managed money on behalf of the ordinary investing public.

In a less blatant version of the technique, fund management houses may allocate winning trades to portfolios run for large corporations and other sophisticated clients. Such clients are generally much more demanding than small investors in expecting good performance and are much faster to vote with their feet when the performance is sub-par. Thus, a fund management house has a strong interest in keeping such clients happy, even if this means penalizing the mutual funds and other portfolios run for the benefit of small investors. Many variations are possible. In one example of alleged impropriety reported by the SEC, a California-based money manager was accused of allocating profitable trades to certain accounts that paid high management fees based on performance, while allocating less profitable trades to other accounts that paid no special reward for good performance.

The development of increasingly complex derivatives in recent years has been a particular boon to financial criminals. In a typical pattern, securities firms deliberately concoct instruments that are so complex that most institutional investors cannot fully understand them. Moreover, the market in any particular type of instrument is typically extremely thin, and thus prices can be readily manipulated by the securities industry. Devastating accounts of Wall Street's profits from the derivatives game have been written by, among others, the former Salomon Brothers executive Michael Lewis and the former Morgan Stanley executive Frank Partnoy. Partnoy in particular has been coruscating in his criticisms of the securities industry's practices. After alleging in his book *F.I.A.S.C.O.: Blood in the Water on Wall Street* that Wall Street makes huge profits by "trickery and deceit," he adds for good measure: "Everyone I knew who had been an investment banker for a few years, including me, was an asshole." Referring to his time as a derivatives salesman, Partnoy commented: "The way you earned money on derivatives was by trying to blow up your client."

Of course, the securities industry has never been famous for its high ethical standards. But the problem today is not only that the scale of the finagling is larger than before, but that thanks in no small measure to the postindustrialists, the industry enjoys much more prestige than formerly and its ethical standards have thus proved contagious. Prominent Americans in other walks of life see how money is made in a highly regarded industry and reckon that similarly opportunistic, if not illegal, tactics are acceptable in their own less exalted fields.

The contagious effect of Wall Street's low ethical standards is particularly apparent in, for instance, the increasingly manipulative way that industrial executives now use executive stock options to line their own pockets — often by engaging in short-term financial maneuvering that they know is damaging to their companies' long-term prospects. As early as 1989 the MIT Commission on Industrial Productivity reported that there was "no shortage" of executive incentive plans geared to a company's profit performance over just one year or even a mere six months. As the commission pointed out, a chief executive whose compensation is geared to such short-term measures is likely to take an even more shortsighted view than the stock market. The worst part of it is that short-term executive incentive programs tend to encourage outright gambling by corporate executives in their frantic efforts to manipulate their companies' profits. Such gambling is in fact a no-lose proposition for the executives themselves. On the one hand, if a gamble pays off, they can obviously cash out quickly at huge profits. Less obviously but even more controversially, if the gamble fails, they always have another chance to play the game. And this time, because the stock price has undoubtedly fallen in the meantime thanks to the previous year's losing gamble, executives can reset the buying price for their options at a much lower level, thus putting themselves in line to benefit hugely from even the most modest recovery in their companies' profits.

All in all, it is clear that the financial services industry has played the role of pied piper in leading American society toward a general lowering of standards in the last thirty years. The consequences are hard to measure but are clearly significant for economic efficiency, not to mention for the general spiritual health of the nation.

Yet as we have seen, the apotheosis of American finance in recent years is based on an utterly wrongheaded reading of the role that finance should play in an economy. Forgetting that services should *serve* people, the financial services industry has come to regard itself as somehow superior to society — an attitude that the postindustrialists have clearly done nothing to discourage.

Our conclusion, therefore, is that finance is an essential service without which the economy could not function. But it should not be raised on a pedestal above the rest of the economy. Still less should it be considered a driving force of the economy's future prosperity.

Stripped of rhetoric, most of the new financial activities the postindustrialists extol feed parasitically on the rest of the economy. What we have is not a goose that lays golden eggs but a different feathered vertebrate entirely: a cuckoo in the economy's nest.

4

From Cyberspace
to Tinseltown

Besides computer software and finance, other businesses that are often regarded as important elements in the American postindustrial future include consulting, the media, direct mail, database information services, think tanks, and the management of "designer" brands. The story in these businesses is broadly similar to that of software and finance: most of these businesses make significant contributions to society, but their economic shortcomings in virtually every case are typical of postindustrial services generally — an unbalanced mix of jobs, a high degree of labor-intensity, poor export prospects, and little opportunity to build up a national reserve of proprietary know-how. In most cases, these shortcomings are so obvious that they need no elaboration. In concluding our look at postindustrial services, therefore, we will confine our comments to a few activities whose shortcomings are less obvious — activities, moreover, that figure particularly prominently in the hopes of postindustrialists.

First we look at the communications revolution of the 1990s, particularly the Internet. Then we move on to an analysis of the entertainment industry.

The Internet: everyone's gone surfing

The jury is out on the Internet. On the one hand, the postindustrialists, like most other observers, regard it as an epochal breakthrough that promises almost boundless prosperity for the United States in the years ahead. On the other hand, a skeptical minority persists in debunking the Internet as little more than a gimmicky, if amusing, system for transmitting "garbage at light speed."

So which is it — seminal breakthrough or overhyped toy? The truth clearly lies somewhere in between. While the Internet boasts many dazzling, almost magical capabilities, such capabilities do not necessarily add up to an economic revolution.

One thing is certain: much of what the postindustrialists say in hyping the Internet is the sheerest nonsense. Take, for instance, the New Age guru Bran Ferren. Speaking in apocalyptic terms on ABC Television's *Nightline* program in 1997, Ferren rated the Internet as perhaps the human race's most significant discovery since hominoids first began to speak. It is a sign of the times not only that Ferren felt no need to elaborate on this extraordinary statement, but that the presenter, Forrest Sawyer, felt no need to challenge him.

Or take Barry Howard Minkin, a futurologist who has predicted that 97 percent of all new jobs in the United States will soon come from "knowledge work." In his book *Future in Sight,* he waxes enthusiastic about the economic possibilities of the Internet and the wider telecommunications revolution it epitomizes. But exactly what benefits will this revolution bring? Minkin seems notably short of ideas. He mentions video telephones and home shopping — two applications that have been heralded for decades by previous generations of futurologists. But beyond these, most of his ideas are comically trite. One such idea is the possibility of more polished sales presentations. Minkin sees these as particularly valuable to "smaller companies that need to create the impression that they are more substantial." He could have added that the Internet offers many other possibilities for people to pretend to be something they are not — but in pre–New Economy days, misrepresenting oneself was rarely considered a service to society!

Another Minkin idea is "blur-mercials" — hybrid video broadcasts that blend advertising and editorial content. He expects them to "flood the airwaves" and create "significant consumer demand." But what sort of themes will blur-mercials focus on? Minkin's suggestions are notably underwhelming. He foresees, for instance, blur-mercial sequences combining information about "the how and why of exercise, food-making equipment, as well as ways to become a millionaire."

Conspicuously absent from Minkin's vista is any mention of the damage the blur-mercial concept could do in undermining the media's editorial independence.

Minkin is also highly enthusiastic about the role that the telecommunications revolution will play in improving corporate America's labor relations. Corporations will increasingly use video instead of print, he believes, to communicate with employees. This will enable them to provide graphic video coverage of employee outings, including "softball game highlights" accompanied by choruses of baseball songs. Very entertaining, no doubt — but what the American economy needs is not more ways to amuse office workers but higher white-collar productivity levels.

Does all this add up to the biggest technological revolution since hominoids first started fine-tuning their vocal chords? Clearly not. In fact, the views of people like Ferren and Minkin constitute classic examples of the sort of cyberbabble that the Internet-debunker-in-chief Clifford Stoll has derided as "silicon snake oil."

Before taking a closer look at the downside of cyberspace, let's first dispose of one of the most important positive developments promised by the ongoing telecommunications revolution: video telephones. Predicted for decades, they now finally look set to take off in a big way early in the next century. The video telephone clearly promises to add significantly to the consumer's quality of life, particularly for anyone wanting to keep in touch with far-flung friends and relatives. But for advocates of postindustrialism, this innovation is cold comfort because it represents an opportunity mainly for manufacturers, not for postindustrial businesses. After all, there are only two critical blocks to the wide use of video telephones: (1) the techniques for the mass-production of video telephone equipment have not yet been developed, and (2) the high-capacity telephone lines they require have not yet been laid. As manufacturers become more efficient in making the transmission infrastructure and receiving equipment, the price of video telephony can be expected to plummet. Then, in a pattern similar to the way earlier communications technologies such as radio and television were commercialized, demand will explode, bringing about further price cuts and increases in volume.

Video telephones apart, most of the excitement surrounding the telecommunications revolution is clearly based on a false historical analogy. As the science writer Robert Pool has noted, countless Internet boosters draw an implicit or explicit parallel between the Internet and the invention of printing. They imagine that just as printing utterly transformed the world five hundred years ago, the Internet will work a similarly large economic miracle in the years ahead. The argument is superficially persuasive, but a moment's thought reveals that it is nonsense. Remember that, before printing, the task of replicating and transmitting written information was wretchedly slow and expensive. Just to produce a single copy of a new book took a scribe — one of the most skilled and brilliant workers of his era — many months or even years. Then, with the invention of movable type, information-industry productivity suddenly soared several hundredfold. Within fifty years of Gutenberg's technological innovations, the total number of books in Europe had jumped from a mere 30,000 volumes to 9 million. And this was only the beginning: cheap books, in turn, brought a sea change in the structure of society as more and more of the population acquired an education.

Those who imagine that a similarly historic transformation is afoot today forget that in its most economically significant applications, the Internet offers at best only a marginal improvement in productivity. Take, for instance, electronic mail. Used intelligently, e-mail clearly offers cost and efficiency advantages over its nearest rival, the fax machine. But just as faxing did not really change the world very much (after all, before we had faxes, we could transmit urgent messages by telephone or telex), e-mail is having only a minor effect in boosting the economy's fundamental efficiency. By comparison with e-mailing, using a fax machine may seem cumbersome and expensive, but the savings offered by e-mail are not significant compared to the total cost of the message (of which the sender's time is typically the major element). In fact, according to Michael L. Dertouzos, head of MIT's computer science laboratory, fully 95 percent of e-mail activities and other computer-driven communications these days represent only a minor advance on the efficiency of the telegraphy age a century ago.

Moreover, the benefits of e-mail are reduced by some notable drawbacks. Specifically, the convenience of e-mail has generated an electronic version of Gresham's Law: frivolous and time-wasting users are driving out serious and welcome ones. In the five years since e-mail became widely used in American business, many American office workers have seen at least a threefold increase in the daily volume of mail. But how much of this increase is desirable? Probably very little.

Certainly there is no question that most of the increase comes from nonessential users, among whom self-publicists, office comedians, pranksters, and other nuisances seem to be greatly overrepresented. Moreover, the fact that sending e-mail costs practically nothing has fostered the proliferation of a whole new, and almost universally unwanted, industry: electronic junk mail.

The rising problem of e-mail overload has provoked alarm among information-industry experts. Michael Dertouzos, in his book *What Will Be,* sounds a note of outright despair: "Opening your door to e-mail is not far from opening the front door of your home and shouting to everyone: 'Come right in when you wish, and as you wish! I will see you and hear you out.'"

Not surprisingly, e-mail recipients are increasingly resorting to mass deletion of unread messages when in-boxes get overloaded. If a few grains of informational wheat must inadvertently be sacrificed in deleting all the chaff, so be it. In fact, so acute has e-mail overload become that some people are beginning to automate the deletion process via so-called bozo filters. A pioneer in this regard has been Steve Ward, an MIT professor who decided to take drastic action some years ago after he began routinely receiving more than one hundred e-mail messages a day. He designed a filter program that automatically rated each message for relevance (based on such criteria as the sender's name, the number of people on the copy list, and the presence in the text of words of special interest to him). Senders whose messages failed to score high enough were automatically told that their message had been deleted and that if they wanted to end-run the computer's verdict they should contact Ward in person — via that miracle of nineteenth-century communications, the *telephone.* If the telecommunications revolution keeps racing ahead at this pace, pretty soon we'll be back to carrier pigeons!

Of course, the Internet offers more than a mere e-mail service. It is extensively used, for instance, as a research tool. As such, it seems at first sight to provide a tremendously useful and efficient service. But does it? Certainly the Internet contains an embarrassment of information on virtually every topic under the sun. But when this information is judged on its *quality* as opposed to its *quantity,* its value is often a lot more debatable. By quality we mean, among other things, relevance. The truth is that much of the information turned up in an Internet search tends to be irrelevant. And the more specific and targeted your quest for information is, the less useful the Internet tends to be. If one is seeking a particular fact — even something as simple as, say, the address of a specific foreign company — the Internet can be a disappointing waste of time. The pattern is that it serves up everything but what you want. This writer discovered this the hard way when he was planning a business trip to Germany and urgently needed to establish which of the companies he had short-listed for a visit were located in which parts of the country. One of these companies was a much-publicized solar energy subsidiary of a major German electrical combine. Its address should have been easy to find, but after a fruitless ninety-minute search he was forced to throw in the towel. He then went back to researching the matter the pre-cyberspace way. In a matter of five minutes (and at the expense of a local telephone call to the nearest marketing office of the German combine), he had turned up the information.

Perhaps this is an extreme example, but in general the Internet proves disappointing for seekers after truly useful business knowledge. It could hardly be otherwise. After all, if you think about it, the sort of information that businesses disclose to the public is almost by definition more chaff than wheat. The one exception is the financial disclosure that a corporation is required to make by law — but as business researchers have long had easy access to such disclosures, the Internet provides little added value in this respect. As for other business information, corporations are naturally reluctant to release anything that would be of value to competitors. In fact, the more valuable a piece of economic information is, the more likely it is to be jealously withheld from the public. Think, for instance, of the formula for making Coca-Cola. It is very valuable information. How likely are you to turn it up in a Net search? To ask the question is to answer it. In reality, of course, the Coca-Cola formula is so closely guarded a secret that it is kept in a vault of the Trust Company of Georgia.

A great deal of the business information one can download from the Internet is mere public relations material, and as such, it is designed to serve the provider's interests, not the recipient's. Known to the cognoscenti as "brochureware," such material generally conceals more than it reveals and is sometimes quite misleading or even mendacious. On the Internet, as elsewhere in life, you get what you pay for — and free information downloaded from the Internet is rarely worth more than the paper it's not written on!

Of course, not all information is free. Surely in the case of paid-for information, the Internet provides a service of value? Not really. Information sold over the Internet typically consists of newspaper clippings and other material that already exists elsewhere in the public domain and is thus easily accessible, for the most part, via a good business library. For almost anyone who has a serious need for business information, the Internet provides at best an element of convenience.

In any case, the value to business executives of information culled from the press is, to say the least, controversial. Such information is often subject to significant spin control and thus is often at best highly misleading. In fact, the press has a distinct habit of letting its readers down at precisely the moment when they most need reliable information. Any review of the record shows that the press has often been years or even decades behind the times in spotting trends that have crucially affected the American economy. Take, for instance, the rise of the Japanese steel industry. The press failed to spot the trend in the early days when an intelligent look at the Japanese industry would have sounded a timely warning for the complacent giants of Pittsburgh; instead, the press took notice only when the layoffs started. By then, of course, it was far too late for warnings.

Japan is, of course, a famously hard nation to read, but even in covering crucial developments nearer home, the American business press is often a treacherous guide for business executives. Take the press's generally fawning coverage of IBM in the 1980s. This was a time when journalists should have been alerting their readers to the near-fatal mistakes IBM had made in ceding to Microsoft and Intel control of the future of the personal computer industry — mistakes that in the 1990s redrew the map of power in the computer industry.

Even when press information is accurate and timely, its value to a busy executive may be highly debatable. Often, as the famed quality control expert W. Edwards Deming pointed out a few years ago, executives who spend too much time monitoring the media just exacerbate their already huge information-overload problems. In his book *The New Economics,* he commented:

> Many of us deceive ourselves into the supposition that we need constant updating to cope with the rapidly changing future. But you cannot, by watching every moment of television or reading every newspaper, acquire a glimpse of what the future holds. To put it

another way, information, no matter how complete and speedy, is not knowledge.

Perhaps the ultimate comment on cyberspace as a source of information has come from the feminist author Germain Greer. Writing in the *Guardian* newspaper, she delivered this resounding verdict on the Internet: "95 percent of what is on it is wrong, 3 percent is criminal and the other 2 percent is useful, if of course you can find it."

So much for the information revolution as seen by users of information. But how does the revolution look to information providers — the companies that stand to profit from the growing market for information? The truth is that for them too the Internet, so far at least, has been a distinct disappointment. In the words of Mark Landler of the *New York Times,* media companies have been "resoundingly unsuccessful" in squeezing a profit from the World Wide Web.

Beyond economic information, the Internet is a conduit of scientific information. Here, in contrast to business information, the Internet can be of great value. But even so, the Internet does remarkably little to benefit the American economy. To the extent that valuable technological information can be downloaded from the Internet, the main beneficiaries are America's foreign economic competitors. Leading American scientists and engineers have always worked within easy reach of first-rate scientific libraries that stock the relevant journals and papers, but their foreign counterparts have hitherto been greatly hampered by a lack of similarly comprehensive library facilities. For many Americans, the availability of scientific papers on the Internet at best merely obviates a pleasant ten-minute stroll to a campus library. For foreigners, by contrast, the ability to download American scientific papers via the Internet may save the time and cost of an intercontinental flight to the United States.

So much for the Internet's information potential. Perhaps its most important other possible use is as a new medium of commerce — a sort of global electronic shopping mall. Although this application is the subject of much heady discussion among New Age commentators, the prospects for electronic commerce seem a lot less exciting to business executives. In fact, most business executives are distinctly skeptical of the Internet's potential. Typical is Nathan Morton, chief executive of the Computer City superstore chain, who recalls that previous

New Age marketing ventures have proven to be expensive flops. "Back in the 1980s, when the Home Shopping Network first came online, I can remember people on Wall Street saying, 'Retail is dead and everyone will be buying through their television sets,'" he told Saul Hansell of the *New York Times*. "Well, that has not happened."

Most shoppers still prefer to buy even computers from a traditional store rather than over the Internet. According to Forrester Research, only 2 to 3 percent of computer hardware sold in 1997 was bought online. Meanwhile, America Online reported that only 12 percent of its members had ever made a purchase from any of the many merchants included in its service.

Of course, it is early days yet. But as Rupert Murdoch, among others, has suggested, to the extent that Internet commerce succeeds, it will cannibalize more traditional forms of marketing and distribution such as print advertising and direct mail. In the long run, the press in particular stands to lose. As the *Newsweek* economics commentator Robert Samuelson has pointed out, certain advertisers, such as innkeepers in holiday resorts, find that the Internet is an enormously more cost-effective way to reach prospective customers than advertising in newspapers and other traditional paper-based media. All this is good news for the world's dwindling forests. But otherwise, the rise of Internet-based marketing probably promises a lot less of an improvement in economic efficiency than the public has been led to believe. And as Samuelson, among others, has suggested, the tendency for the Internet to undercut more traditional forms of advertising could lead to a drastic reduction in the quality of the American mass media.

Some postindustrialists have postulated the possibility that American Internet merchants may be able to harness the medium's global reach to boost U.S. exports. To say the least, this idea seems premature. There are many practical barriers to be overcome before the Internet can ever serve as a major global marketing medium. For one thing, as U.S. Trade Representative Charlene Barshefsky has pointed out, many U.S. trading partners are less than enthusiastic about making the necessary deregulation moves to enable their citizens to import foreign goods freely over the Internet. In any case, the many local distribution partners through which American exporters operate in foreign markets will use their deeply entrenched political and operational power to fight cross-border Internet commerce.

Besides these institutional and political barriers, there are also fundamental economic problems with Internet commerce. Many products need local service support, and this must generally be provided by a network of local distributors in foreign markets. In markets like Japan, such distributors are expected to meet extremely high standards in both quality of service and speed of response. All this has to be paid for — and the money comes from the higher prices generally charged in such markets.

As the Internet commerce expert Mary Cronin has pointed out, a wish to maintain different prices in different markets is a key reason why, as of the late 1990s, the long-predicted explosion of Internet-based international commerce had not happened. She cited the example of Millipore, an American company that supplies equipment to semiconductor manufacturers and scientific laboratories around the world. Noting that Millipore's website was being visited by 40,000 computer users every month, she commented that, on a superficial analysis, the company seemed to be a prime candidate to conduct international commerce via the Internet. Nonetheless, Millipore's website did not include pricing, product availability, ordering, or payment facilities — the so-called four horsemen of electronic commerce. In effect, Millipore's website was no more than an elaborate electronic advertisement. A key reason Millipore had balked at supplying price information was that its prices vary considerably in different markets abroad. Putting prices on the Internet would have stirred up a hornet's nest of problems with overseas customers and distributors. Moreover, the company did not want to disclose information on product availability to competitors. This concern is shared, of course, by many other companies operating in fast-moving markets.

Cronin reported that online payment ranked lowest among the services desired by customers in a survey of online commerce. She commented: "Despite the hullabaloo over E-commerce, customers may not even want it."

In the end, as the *New York Times*'s Saul Hansell has pointed out, a fundamental problem for Internet commerce is that typical shoppers still want to see and feel merchandise before they buy it. There are exceptions, of course. As Amazon.com, for instance, has convincingly demonstrated, books can be sold with great success over the Internet. In fact, the Internet can provide enormous added value to many book buyers — particularly scholars and other discerning readers for whom the searchability and interactive capabilities offered by Internet-based bookstores are a vital aid in identifying exactly the right purchase. And as the New York–based publisher Jason Epstein has pointed out, Internet bookstores are a godsend for many publishers who have found that most traditional booksellers are ill equipped to sell specialized books that are of interest to only a small segment of the reading public. That said, even in the case of books, the Internet represents no more than an additional outlet; for as far ahead as we can see, the great bulk of books will probably continue to be sold in traditional stores, which should have no problem maintaining their competitive edge in ambience and the serendipity that has always been associated with book buying.

Books apart, many of the most conspicuous success stories of Internet commerce pack a distinctly double-edged message. Take electronic junk mail, which, according to *U.S. News & World Report,* is one of the relatively few Internet businesses that has already become profitable. As of 1997, one firm alone, Pennsylvania-based CyberPromotions, was claiming already to be spewing out between 15 million and 20 million electronic junk-mail messages a day.

Then there is the notorious proliferation of sex-related sites on the Web. As estimated by the makers of Cyber Patrol, a software program designed to prevent children from gaining access to pornography on the Internet, there were already 20,000 sites unsuitable for children on the Internet as of 1997. According to the Web-tracking service Relevant Knowledge, the ten most popular sex-related websites were visited by a total of 9.6 million people in the space of just one month in 1998. No wonder that, as reported by Daniel S. Greenberg, editor of the Washington-based *Science and Government Report,* smut is now the leading revenue producer on the Internet.

Another undesirable activity fostered by the Internet is medical quackery. The anonymity of cyberspace has afforded crooks and charlatans a new way to prey on the gullibility and desperation of the sick. A basic problem is that those who seek medical help via the Internet often don't know who they are dealing with. Most cybersources are, of course, bona fide — but not all. The trouble is, it is often difficult to tell the difference. One problem is that many sites that give perfectly good advice have links to sites where the advice is self-serving or even dangerous. Thus, at the click of a mouse, the unwary Internet surfer can enter a medical twilight zone. In a 1998 *Fortune* account of cyberquackery, David Stipp told of the ordeal of a twelve-year-old Chicago girl who was dying from a rare type of bone cancer. With the help of an Internet search, the girl's parents had discovered an Iowa-based cancer advisory service, which in turn referred them to an alternative-medicine clinic in Mexico. When the clinic demanded an up-front fee of $2,000, the desperate couple paid up without a quibble. After bringing their daughter to the clinic, however, they quickly concluded they were dealing with quacks. They promptly returned to Chicago, where their daughter died a few days later. The Iowa-based advisory organization refunded a $200 membership fee it had charged, but the couple never recovered the $2,000 fee paid to the Mexican clinic.

Another controversial industry that seems to have achieved more than average success on the Internet is gambling. According to Sue Schneider, chairman of the Interactive Gaming Council, an organization that seeks to set guidelines for Web gambling, there were about thirty gambling sites on the Internet as of 1997. These sites now offer gambling services ranging from casino-style games like video poker, baccarat, and roulette to wagers on sports events. Most such sites are based offshore in places like Australia, Asia, and the Caribbean, thus evading American regulations designed to ensure fair play.

According to Joseph Paravia of California-based Virtual Gaming Technologies, the early experience of Internet casino operators has shown that Web gambling can be "wildly successful." Members of the Interactive Gaming Council expect the industry to be worth at least $8.5 billion by 2000.

Clearly, from society's point of view, such an explosion of online betting is a mixed blessing. For a start, business productivity may suffer if, as the Internet gambling expert Elio Masie has suggested, many workers are being induced to gamble during office hours. And of course, the lack of regulation of Internet gambling is a major concern. The state of Wisconsin in particular has been vociferous in condemning Web gaming as a "very bad bet." Jim Haney of the Wisconsin attorney general's office has commented: "You don't know who you are dealing with. You have no assurance that the games are fair and not manipulated. You don't know where to go if you are scammed."

Of the more useful businesses spawned by the rise of the Internet, most are still amazingly small. Even Netscape, the Web browser maker, achieved sales of a mere $448 million in 1998, and America Online, the big information provider, achieved a mere $2.6 billion. Moreover,

Amazon.com, the Internet bookstore regarded by many as the most successful example so far of an Internet-based sales organization, had sales of just $610 million.

Then there is Yahoo!, the most successful Internet search engine company. Thanks to the postindustrialists' hype, Yahoo! is now regarded as a New Economy colossus — so much so that already by July 1998 its stock market valuation had soared to $9 billion. That was more than twice the value of the old, established Dow Jones & Company. But the reality is that Yahoo! boasted sales of just $67 million in 1997 and employed just 386 people. By comparison, Dow Jones had sales nearly forty times larger and employed more than thirty times as many people.

Of course, to be set against their small size is the fact that many online businesses have been growing extremely fast in recent years. But even if the postindustrialists' most optimistic hopes are borne out, one point should not be forgotten: the Internet will require vast amounts of hardware to realize its potential and thus will provide a bountiful source of high-wage manufacturing jobs for the world's richest manufacturing nations.

The unimportance of being virtual

For many postindustrialists, one of the most exciting prospects promised by the telecommunications revolution is virtual reality. Certainly virtual reality will have many interesting applications, but it is far from the panacea it is sometimes portrayed to be. For the most part, virtual reality will be confined to narrowly defined niches for many years to come. It will be useful, for instance, in enabling people to work by remote control in dangerous or inaccessible places, such as nuclear power stations, the ocean floor, outer space, burning buildings, and deep mines. It will also be an important tool in engineering, scientific research, and entertainment.

That said, much of what is expected from virtual reality is the sheerest moonshine. Take, for instance, the euphoric views of Newt Gingrich. In his book *To Renew America,* he suggests that the United States could harness virtual reality to become an export superpower in medical services. Noting that doctors may one day be able to operate remotely on patients in other countries via cyberspace, he predicts:

"American doctors will be called upon to operate on people in India. We will be able to sell our services in every corner of the world. . . . We have a dramatic opportunity to increase our foreign exchange earnings."

Referring to the problems of the American health care system, Gingrich triumphantly adds: "What we regarded as a huge liability may turn out to be our biggest asset. That is what comes from taking problems and turning them into entrepreneurial solutions."

Maybe, but to others, Gingrich's vision seems less a matter of entrepreneurial solutions than of glib assumptions. First, Gingrich is on notably shaky ground in assuming that virtual reality will be widely accepted by surgeons, let alone patients. As the medical educator Austin Leahy has pointed out, the medical world regards virtual reality mainly as a potentially useful aid in teaching surgery. Virtual reality may soon, for instance, allow medical students to hone their fledgling surgical skills on imaginary patients in much the same way that would-be pilots safely learn to fly by using flight simulators.

One thing is certain: it will be a long time before patients come to trust virtual reality medicine. And if MIT's Michael Dertouzos is to be believed, their reservations will be amply justified. Referring to virtual reality medicine in *What Will Be*, he comments:

> The reliability of complex systems that combine computer hardware, software, and communication links would be far too shaky to be trusted with people's lives. Even NASA's computers, designed for maximum reliability, are known to fail every few launches. . . . No matter how far technology advances, we should — and undoubtedly will — always feel free to exercise our human prerogative by saying No.

In any case, even if by some technological miracle the risks of virtual reality medicine could be eliminated, there are other fatal problems with Gingrich's vision. For one thing, he blithely assumes that other countries' health regulators will throw their markets open to the American medical profession's virtual reality exporters. To say the least, this seems unlikely. After all, national regulators regard it as one of their most important duties to control entry to the medical profession. The task of checking out the credentials of their nationals is daunting enough without having to check out the credentials of countless cyberspace practitioners operating outside their jurisdictions.

Moreover, any effort by cyberspace practitioners to globalize the medical services industry will be opposed by national medical guilds, whose express purpose is to minimize competition for their members.

Perhaps the most devastating flaw in Gingrich's logic is an economic one: he overlooks the simple fact that trade is a two-way street. If the United States is to sell medical services to the rest of the world, the rest of the world will want a similar right to sell medical services to the United States. Thus in any future global market for virtual reality medicine, American doctors can expect to face stiff foreign competition. The truth is that the United States has no monopoly on good medicine. Doctors and medical technologists in other countries have repeatedly shown that, given similar levels of funding, they can match their American counterparts in ingenuity and originality. In fact, many key medical developments in recent decades have been pioneered outside the United States. Examples include the development of heart pacemakers (invented by Siemens of Germany in the 1950s), the first heart transplant (performed in South Africa in the 1960s), and the first cloning of an animal (performed in Scotland in the mid-1990s).

This is not to disparage American medicine, which is rightly noted for its pioneering doctors. Certainly, if virtual reality is ever accepted as a routine medical tool, some top American doctors will carve out a lucrative niche for themselves providing "virtual" treatment to plutocratic foreign patients. But given that many lower-wage countries boast fine surgeons who charge less than equivalently skilled American surgeons, it is easy to guess which way overall U.S. trade in virtual reality medicine would run.

Gingrich's analysis overlooks the fact that American health care costs are greatly inflated by a dysfunctional American legal system. In an attempt to ward off disingenuous malpractice suits, American doctors not only must invest in exorbitantly expensive insurance but are forced to waste much precious time and resources on medically unnecessary tests and procedures. Foreign doctors who are not subject to such burdens clearly have a major competitive edge. Thus, if the American health-care market were ever opened up to foreign competition, demand would create its own supply. Encouraged by the prospect of earning huge American fees, foreign doctors in such Old World centers of medical excellence as London and Vienna could afford to invest in the best education and the most advanced equipment and still dramatically undercut their American counterparts. In the long term even the Europeans might find themselves being undercut as, thanks to the dissemination of the latest medical techniques via cheap modern communications, poorer countries got into the act.

There are similar problems with most other proposed efforts by Americans to sell services abroad via virtual reality. The result is that, in almost every case, a global free-for-all would result in more American imports than exports.

Entertainment: it's only rock and roll

Entertainment has been one of the fastest-growing of all American industries in recent decades. In fact, it has grown so large that it is now regarded by postindustrialists as a cornerstone of the American economy.

But is the entertainment industry living up to the postindustrialists' hopes? It certainly is in the case of feature films, which we will consider separately in the next section. As for other sectors of the American entertainment industry, which in combination probably account for ten times as many workers as the feature film business, there are major concerns about the economic and — still more so — the social value of the industry's contribution.

The concerns are particularly justified with respect to television, whose growth has accounted for an utterly disproportionate share of the industry's human resources. This growth has been driven by a fivefold expansion in the number of channels available to most American viewers in the last three decades.

Are television viewers getting a better service today than they did thirty years ago? Probably. But are they getting an increase in satisfaction commensurate with the expansion in the industry's scale? Almost certainly not. One thing is certain: the explosion in the production of television programming in recent years contrasts markedly with an extremely modest increase in the American public's television viewing. As measured by the A. C. Nielsen market research organization, the typical American increased his or her viewing by less than 5 percent between 1981 and 1997. Clearly, therefore, the major consequence of the increased supply of programming has been that each broadcaster's share of the available audience has almost inevitably fallen dramatically over the years. One notable casualty has been CNN, whose market share in the United States fell to just 0.39 percent in 1997 — half its level of a decade earlier. The big networks have also suffered badly. The proportion of adult Americans who regularly watched the networks' nightly news programs, for instance, fell to just 38 percent in 1998 — down from 60 percent in 1993.

As the president of Sony Corporation of America, Howard Stringer, has pointed out, all this audience-splitting naturally has strong negative implications for the quality of the viewer's experience. "As you go from thirty-five channels to seventy-five, you diminish the audience for everything," he says. "That makes it harder to generate the advertising revenue for quality programming."

That said, from the postindustrialists' point of view, the quality of the American entertainment industry's output is less relevant than the industry's export prowess. In the postindustrialists' view, this is a trump card. Although they rarely if ever present authoritative figures to back their case, they claim that the entertainment industry is now a huge contributor to the U.S. balance of payments. But here again, they are guilty of misleading the American public. The truth is that, in relation to the amount of labor they preempt, most sectors of the American entertainment industry are quite small exporters.

Even the recorded music industry is a much less powerful contributor to the American balance of payments than is sometimes supposed. The reason should be obvious: trade in music runs two ways. Although the United States exports a lot of recorded music, it is also imports a lot. The United States is probably close to balanced trade in music with Europe. After all, several key record companies are based in Europe, most notably the largest of them all, PolyGram. Other huge European players include London-based EMI and the Bertelsmann group's BMG subsidiary.

Elsewhere, American export opportunities are curtailed by the fact that in most of the non-Western world recorded music is local or regional in origin. Language and taste see to that. Apart from a few mega-stars like Elvis Presley and Frank Sinatra, most American musicians have little appeal outside the Western world — and certainly derive at best only puny revenues from non-Western nations. This helps explain why in East Asia, for instance, music by local artists accounts for about 70 percent of revenues from sales of recorded music.

The export story is hardly much more encouraging in the case of television programming. American talk shows and game shows, for instance, are generally too culture-specific to have much appeal outside the United States. But even in the case of the minority of American television programs that could generate good sales abroad, foreign trade barriers conspire to limit U.S. export revenues. Even the United Kingdom, which itself is probably the world's second-largest exporter of television programs after the United States, has dragged its feet in opening its television market to American programming. For many years foreign programming was limited to just 15 percent of the British market. After the U.S. government pressed for liberalization, the British relaxed their barriers somewhat, but even today broadcasters in the United Kingdom, in common with those in other EU countries, are required under European law to ensure that at least 50 percent of their programming originates in Europe.

Nor are such trade barriers to American entertainment exports likely to disappear anytime soon. On the contrary, they may well become an even greater stumbling block in the future. The governments of many key nations are becoming increasingly hostile to American entertainment exports, as was notably apparent in the summer of 1998 when officials from twenty nations gathered in Ottawa to consider measures to protect their nations' culture. Among the nations playing important roles at the meeting were such American allies as the United Kingdom, France, Sweden, Canada, and Mexico. Although these nations generally favor global free trade in everything else, they saw no ideological embarrassment in making a special exception for cultural products. Nor was there any doubt about whose cultural exports they wanted to exclude. Their target was, of course, the United States. This was made pointedly clear in the fact that American representatives were allowed to attend the meeting merely as "observers." Anthony DePalma of the *New York Times* described the treatment of the United States as an "obvious slight"; certainly the attitude of many influential participants at the meeting bodes ill for American hopes of establishing a true global free market in entertainment products.

Trade barriers apart, U.S. entertainment exports face many other problems in foreign markets. A key one is, of course, piracy. This is often thought of as a problem mainly in the Third World, but even solvent countries such as Taiwan, South Korea, and Greece have a record of lax enforcement of Western intellectual property rights. True, some progress has been achieved in recent years. After decades of stonewalling, Japan, for instance, has now agreed to raise its period of protection for copyrighted musical recordings from twenty-five years to the Western norm of fifty. As a consequence of Tokyo's previous stance, music by such best-selling artists as the Beatles, the Beach Boys, the Rolling Stones, the Berlin Philharmonic, and the New York Philharmonic was sold in Japan mainly in unauthorized local bootleg versions. But the fact that Japan has now toed the line on copyright hardly presages a general improvement in the protection of Western intellectual property rights in export markets. Far from it. Japan's change of heart was stimulated at least partly by enlightened self-interest: Japanese corporations now have important investments in such key Western music labels as CBS Records and MCA, and thus Japan's interests now lie increasingly with the gamekeepers, not the poachers.

The West faces much tougher problems in eradicating copyright abuse in other markets. Emerging economies in particular typically feel entitled to help themselves to the talents of foreign artists for free. Their attitude has deep roots in history. Even the United States was once notorious for freeloading in this respect. Up to 1891, foreign authors and songwriters had no copyright protection under American law — a fact that famously infuriated British novelists like Charles Dickens as well as such titans of British music as W. S. Gilbert and Arthur Sullivan.

These days China is one of the biggest offenders. Reporting in 1995, Louis Kraar of *Fortune* alleged there were twenty-nine factories in China turning out 75 million bootleg CDs a year for sale at prices as low as $1.70. Under pressure from the United States and other Western nations, Beijing authorities subsequently clamped down on piracy, but the net effect was merely to transfer the problem to China's so-called special administrative region, Hong Kong. According to the International Federation of the Phonographic Industry (IFPI), CD manufacturing in Hong Kong was expected to total 400 million units in 1998, up from a mere 60 million in 1997. The city was producing about twenty-three times more CDs than were sold legitimately within its territory. In reality, most of the production was coming from pirates and the output was destined for sale in mainland China.

We have already noted that there are no reliable figures for the American entertainment industry's exports. But a look at the financial statements of a few typical American entertainment conglomerates is suggestive. Take, for instance, Viacom, which, with some justification, describes itself as "one of the world's largest entertainment and publishing companies and a leading force in nearly every segment of the international media marketplace." The worldwide scale of Viacom's activities is indeed impressive. Besides Paramount Pictures, these activities include:

- MTV: Reaching 281 million homes in seventy-nine countries and territories in 1997, MTV has been described by *Time* as "second only to God in omnipresence." Certainly among the world's cable networks, it is the most widely distributed.
- Nickelodeon: This is one of the world's largest producers of children's programming.
- Blockbuster entertainment stores: Blockbuster receives more than 1 billion customer visits a year worldwide and claims to open a new store every eleven hours somewhere in the world.

Clearly Viacom's reach is indeed global. But how much does this contribute to U.S. exports? The numbers are startlingly disappointing. Even with the help of a large contribution from Paramount (whose movie library includes 2,500 titles), Viacom's exports from the United States came to a mere $283 million in 1996. That represented just over 2 percent of Viacom's total revenues of $12 billion.

Viacom's disappointing export performance is less surprising when we take a closer look. Although it does considerable business abroad, most of this represents added value that is created abroad and therefore does not contribute in any significant way to the American balance of payments. Virtually all that the United States receives is a thin trickle of dividends and royalties.

The story of the MTV group, for instance, is revealing. As of 1997, it was operating fifteen major services abroad, but in virtually every case it originated most of the added value in the foreign markets concerned. Fully ten of the overseas services were broadcast partly or totally in a language other than English — most notably German, Swedish, Spanish, Mandarin, Hindi, and Portuguese. Moreover, in several cases Viacom was operating with local partners; as a result, even the dividend income from these businesses in large measure stayed in the nations concerned.

At other major American entertainment companies, the export story is equally disappointing. Take the Walt Disney Company. Although the company's core movie business is a muscular performer in overseas markets, the fact is that movies account for only a small part of the company's total business. And as with Viacom, Disney's non-movie entertainment businesses are generally poor exporters. A glance at these businesses reveals why: they include the ESPN sports channel as well as various cable channels, not to mention the ABC Television network. It is hardly surprising that the company's exports of $746 million in 1996 represented less than 4 percent of total sales.

Many other examples could be cited, but the point should already be indisputable. In sum, there has been an explosion in the size of the American entertainment industry in recent decades, but it has not generated a noticeable return in terms of the two economic criteria that really matter: consumer satisfaction in the home market and export success overseas.

Of course, as we have noted, there is one area of the entertainment industry that is solid gold. It is time to look at the movie industry.

Hollywood: merchandising the American Dream

Making movies is a great business for the United States. In marked contrast to most other postindustrial businesses, Hollywood visibly creates a balanced mix of jobs — a relatively few jobs for directors, actors, scriptwriters, composers, and other brilliant creative types, plus thousands of jobs for more ordinary mortals such as makeup artists, electricians, carpenters, painters, and drivers. Moreover, it is a growth industry, given that in the space of just seventeen years, the number of people employed in movie production and related activities in the United States nearly tripled to total 242,000 as of 1997.

Even better, wages in the movie industry are notably high. In fact, if a survey by the Motion Picture Association of America in 1997 is to be believed, movie industry wages run about 70 percent higher than the California average — making them the highest to be found in any industry in the United States.

True, as Andrew Pollack has pointed out in the *New York Times,* some movie production has migrated abroad in recent years. But most Hollywood jobs are well protected from foreign competition. After all, Hollywood movies are typically set in the United States, and this fact naturally determines where the bulk of the production work must be done. Thus, unlike running shoes or computer software programs,

American movies cannot be readily outsourced to cut-price studios in Malaysia or Belarus.

And, of course, the industry's trump card is that it is a big exporter. After growing rapidly in the 1980s and early 1990s, Hollywood's international box-office gross surpassed the domestic box-office gross for the first time in 1995. In fact, movie exports have grown so large that as of the late 1990s Hollywood seemed poised to pass the aerospace industry as the largest U.S. export earner.

What of Hollywood's future? In the short to medium term, things look great. Certainly Hollywood will remain by far the most successful of postindustrial businesses in the United States. But in the very long term, Hollywood's prospects are more questionable. As Paul Fahri and Megan Rosenfeld have pointed out in the *International Herald Tribune,* Hollywood's leadership of the world movie industry is to a large extent a function of the present dominant position of the English language in world culture. The postindustrialists tend to take that dominant position for granted — but they shouldn't. The English language's long-term prospects are in fact largely a function of the general performance of the overall American economy. If the United States does not succeed in reversing its pattern of long-term relative decline, the English language's prestige is bound to suffer. This would tend to undermine Hollywood's position in many key foreign markets.

Take a market like Japan, which happens to be one of Hollywood's biggest export markets. Although fewer than 5 percent of the Japanese people speak English fluently, a much larger proportion has some knowledge of the language. Thus, it is almost a foregone conclusion that when Japanese moviegoers have a choice between an American movie and, say, a Polish one, the Polish one will come off second-best. The truth is that American movies appeal to the autodidact in moviegoers in many foreign markets because, by reading the subtitles and listening to the original sound track in English, non-English speakers can hope to enjoy themselves while painlessly improving their English-language skills.

Hollywood's fortunes are tied to those of the overall American economy in another way: with its abundance and its tradition of boundless economic opportunity, the United States has long been regarded by moviegoers around the world as an idealized version of what they would like their own societies to be. At least, the affluent side of

American society is so regarded. By contrast, as Sharon Waxman has pointed out in the *International Herald Tribune,* movies about the poverty of American inner-city life tend to be distinct losers in foreign markets. The side of America that foreign moviegoers want to see is the American Dream. Thus, movies featuring affluent American heroes and heroines tend to enjoy a special aura of universality in the eyes of foreign moviegoers. And even though foreign moviegoers may find many of the nuances of daily life in the United States remote or puzzling, their ability to share vicariously in the American Dream helps bridge the culture gap. It is notable that British movies also benefit from a similar ability by foreign audiences to empathize with British culture. British movie directors tap into this phenomenon most successfully when they set the action in the nineteenth or early twentieth century — a period when, by no coincidence, the United Kingdom was regarded as the world's leading society.

Thanks to the American economy's domestic wealth and overseas influence, there is a huge potential market out there that justifies Hollywood's famously extravagant production budgets. The budget for just a run-of-the-mill feature film these days typically exceeds $50 million, and many Hollywood directors work with budgets several times this. James Cameron's 1998 blockbuster *Titanic,* for instance, cost $200 million, and Kevin Costner's *Waterworld* cost $175 million. Budgets like these are vastly larger than anything available even to the best directors working in the French, German, or Japanese movie industry. Of course, Hollywood's big budgets do not always translate into box-office revenues (as the notoriously unsuccessful *Waterworld* demonstrated). But in the hands of the right director, a Hollywood budget makes possible a degree of quality in casting, props, and special effects that effortlessly outclasses foreign competitors.

Clearly, therefore, if the United States loses its central position in the world economy, Hollywood will lose the various special competitive advantages it has hitherto enjoyed by virtue of its American base. And in fact, there is some evidence that the rot may already have set in. Certainly, as Samuel P. Huntington has pointed out, the reduced role of the United States in the world economy has already led to some decline in the once-unrivaled status of the English language as the world's second language. The German language, for instance, has been making inroads in continental Europe, particularly in the former East Bloc countries of Central Europe such as Poland and the Czech Republic. Meanwhile, both Chinese and Japanese are clearly gaining ground as second languages throughout East Asia.

Moreover, as other countries catch up with the United States in incomes, American society will lose some of its charm as a setting for movies. Already for many of the world's moviegoers there are other cities nearer home that compete in glamour and excitement with New York and Los Angeles. Take Hong Kong. Given that it has already drawn level with the United States in per capita income, it now boasts a patina of sophistication similar to that of the most glamorous American cities. As such, it is an exciting setting for countless Chinese-language movies turned out by the Hong Kong movie industry for distribution throughout East Asia.

For now American movies continue to do well in East Asia, not least in Hong Kong itself (where *Titanic*, for instance, was by far the biggest box-office draw in 1998). But in the long run, the Hong Kong industry seems set to match Hollywood's budgets as the Chinese movie market grows. Clearly plots about Chinese-speaking heroes and heroines set against a Chinese cultural backdrop and presented in original Chinese sound tracks have as strong a market advantage in East Asia as English-speaking movies about American characters have in the United States. (It should be added that in competing in China culture is not the only barrier to American movie exports. A variety of trade barriers imposed by the Beijing authorities have consistently marginalized Hollywood's offerings in China.)

Looking to the future, it seems likely that Hollywood is going to face stiffer competition in export markets. In addition to Hollywood's dwindling cultural and linguistic advantages, there is the simple fact that as other countries become rich, their local moviemaking industries can afford to aim for higher standards.

All in all, however, Hollywood will probably continue to dominate the world movie industry for decades to come. And in fact, the net effect of American economic decline thus far has actually been to *increase* Hollywood's export revenues. This is because the main manifestation of American decline has been a weak dollar. When foreign box-office receipts are translated into dollars, they tend to rise strongly in dollar terms over the years even though they may show little or no increase measured in the local currency.

But for postindustrialists, any realistic look at Hollywood's position carries a somber message. Heartening though Hollywood's perform-ance continues to be, the movie industry alone is not remotely sig-nificant enough singlehandedly to sustain America's edge as the world's leading economy. Even if, against the odds, Hollywood contin-ues to maintain and enhance its share of world movie markets, the conclusion quite clearly is that postindustrialism is not enough. There is really no substitute for manufacturing as the main driver of prosper-ity. It is time therefore to take a closer look at the opportunities af-forded by modern manufacturing.

III

Manufacturing's Advantages

5

A Showcase of
Manufacturing Strengths

Postindustrialists often talk as if there were no challenging or interesting manufacturing industries left in the world today. How wrong they are. The truth is that the world's most advanced economies are full of great manufacturing industries — industries that not only pay superb wages to a broad range of workers but are also strong exporters.

Take the car industry. Although as far back as the early 1980s the noted postindustrialist John Naisbitt predicted that carmaking would soon migrate to the Third World, the car industry remains a major engine of prosperity in the First World — most notably in Germany, where it is the veritable backbone of the country's export economy.

Even the U.S. automobile industry, much criticized though it has been by postindustrialists in recent years, is a fundamental contributor to American prosperity. In particular, though it has continued to lose international competitiveness in recent years, it is second to none as a source of high-wage blue-collar jobs, accounting as it does for about one-fifth of all American manufacturing employment.

Equally in Japan, the automobile industry remains a fundamental economic contributor. Although postindustrialists have predicted for years that Japanese automakers would be hollowed out by various lower-wage nations in the East Asian region, they have for the most part more than held their own. They have suffered remarkably little even from the rise of the vaunted South Korean car industry, which ranks second only to Japan's in the East Asian region in size and sophistication. In fact, although the Korean industry has enjoyed considerable success in exporting to the developing world, it has made only marginal inroads into the United States, Western Europe, and other rich markets. The result is that, even with Japanese wages running three to five times higher than Korean levels in the 1990s, Japanese carmakers continue to tower almost effortlessly over their Korean rivals in total revenues. And whereas the Koreans are mere assemblers of cars, the Japanese automobile industry increasingly is switching out of assembly to specialize in much more sophisticated activities, such as making high-tech components, advanced materials, and production machinery. In fact, one of the Japanese industry's biggest customers for both auto components and production machinery has been the Korean industry, and thus the rise of the Korean industry has on balance been a net plus for the Japanese. The Japanese automobile industry's success in defying predictions of decline is a striking demonstration of how the postindustrialists underestimate the contribution of capital intensity and knowledge intensity in enabling the world's highest-wage nations to continue to dominate world markets even in the face of determined competition from low-wage countries.

Many other examples could be cited of how great manufacturing industries contribute disproportionately to the wealth of First World nations. Particularly notable in this regard are aerospace, construction machinery, power-generation equipment, pharmaceuticals, household appliances, and machine tools.

And then there is electronics, which more than any other industry exemplifies the message of this book. In truth, many sectors of the electronics industry have long been unjustly slighted by postindustrialists. As we will see in this chapter, this view goes to the root of the postindustrialists' misunderstandings about how the modern world economy works.

The electronics industry is relevant for another reason as well: it is quite literally the prime mover of world prosperity. The electronics industry's most obvious contribution in this regard has been to supply a rapidly growing torrent of ever more powerful and reliable components for virtually every kind of manufactured product. Sophisticated electronic components are now crucial to the function of most home appliances, for instance. They are used not only in such obvious gadgets as videocassette recorders and television sets but in air conditioning systems, refrigerators, vacuum cleaners, dishwashers, and stoves. In virtually every such application, electronic components have not only cut the cost of the appliance but dramatically improved its performance and reliability.

Electronic components have also clearly made a dramatic contribution to improving the performance of cars in the last thirty years. Electronic fuel injection, for instance, has cut fuel consumption by nearly half. Microchip-controlled airbags have made driving much safer. Various other electronic systems have provided everything from a smoother ride to more effective braking. So important is the electronics industry's contribution that today nearly one-fifth of the entire manufacturing cost of a typical car goes to electronic components.

The electronics industry has made a less obvious but even more important contribution to the world's overall economic progress by enabling other industries to hone their production processes. Computerized production techniques have boosted productivity in a host of manufacturing industries, from shipbuilding to telecommunications. Even in such traditional industries as steel, the effect has been dramatic. As we will see in chapter 6, computerization has been a key factor in dramatically cutting the real cost of steel in recent decades.

In a word, electronics is the mother of modern manufacturing. In the rest of this chapter, we will take a closer look at this bountiful industry and show how it exemplifies the best of what manufacturing can do for a modern economy.

A journey to the source of the electronic Nile

Almost everyone knows that AT&T, Intel, and Microsoft have played key roles in hastening the information age. Few, however, are aware of the important contribution made by the Japanese camera maker Nikon. Even fewer have any inkling of what goes on at Nikon's glassworks in the remote Tokyo suburb of Sagamihara.

But if we trace back the long series of highly sophisticated manufacturing steps involved in making semiconductors, all roads lead to Sagamihara. The Sagamihara glassworks is the repository of highly secret, world-beating techniques that have propelled Nikon to a dominant position in the manufacture of the key production equipment used to make semiconductors. It is hardly an exaggeration to say that Sagamihara is the ultimate source of the electronic Nile.

Outwardly, Sagamihara seems ill cast for its starring role in the electronic revolution. A classic Japanese *bedotaun* ("dormitory town" — the word is a combination of the words "bed" and "town"), Sagamihara is reached from Tokyo by taking the expressway southwest for about twenty miles. You exit into the claustrophobia of a typical Japanese suburb and quickly find yourself on a narrow road that picks its way between a jumble of vending machines, convenience stores, family restaurants, garden shops, and golf driving ranges.

Turning left, you enter an even narrower road, and there just ahead at a T-junction is the Nikon glass factory. All in all, it seems like a remarkably unprepossessing little chemical works. The central building is just two floors high; built mainly of what looks like corrugated iron, it is a classic example of Japan's utilitarian, no-nonsense school of industrial architecture. To the side is a taller, more modern building with various large pipes and flues running here and there.

Apart from a few surveillance cameras and a guardhouse manned twenty-four hours a day, there is not the slightest hint here of Promethean industrial activity. Nevertheless, this plant leads the world in making glass with uniquely powerful optical qualities that are vital in the production of semiconductors. Thanks to this glass, Nikon has come from nowhere in less than two decades to become the world's dominant manufacturer of so-called steppers. Almost unknown to the general public, steppers play as important a role in world manufacturing in the late twentieth century as blast furnaces did in the nineteenth. They are lithographic machines that perform the crucial function of printing circuit patterns on silicon wafers. The printing is done by focusing an image of the circuit pattern onto a photo-sensitive material coated on each wafer. The image is formed by shining a light through a "mask" — a stencil-like metal replica of the circuit pattern — and is progressively reduced through a series of huge lenses. It is then reproduced on the silicon wafer. Because the resolution power of each new generation of steppers is greater than that of the last, the semiconductor industry can print ever finer lines on each new generation of chips. And of course, the finer a chip's lines, the greater its information-processing capacity.

Lithography accounts for about one-fifth of the total manufacturing cost of a typical semiconductor, and thus it is the industry's single most critical manufacturing process. Not surprisingly, therefore, steppers are the mainstays of the semiconductor equipment business — a business that as of 1996 was generating sales of $21 billion a year and, as estimated by the Dataquest market research firm, was set to grow by 14 percent a year in the five years to 2001.

Much of the stepper industry's growth in sales revenues comes from price hikes as each succeeding generation of machines offers ever greater performance. Thus, whereas the first steppers introduced in the 1960s took up little more space than a refrigerator, the new steppers launched in the late 1990s had ballooned to fill a large freight elevator and, at about seven tons, were five times heavier than a New York taxi. In a complicated intertwining of mechanical, optical, and electronic components, the innards of a modern stepper look like a cross between a jet engine and an intergalactic telescope. As of 1998, a state-of-the-art stepper cost more than $5 million. This represented a fivefold increase over Nikon's first steppers in the early 1980s. Moreover, a next-generation stepper, due to go into volume production in 2000, is expected to cost as much as $8 million.

When Nikon entered the business in 1980, the width of the thinnest lines its steppers could print was one micron (one millionth of a meter — or about one-eightieth the width of a human hair). By contrast, its new steppers that went into volume production in 1998 were capable of printing lines of less than one-quarter of a micron.

All in all, the Nikon stepper business is a particularly striking illustration of the ability of great manufacturers to make more with less. Nor could there be a much more convincing illustration of how manufacturing contributes to strengthening a nation's economy. After all, virtually all the added value entailed in making steppers is created in Japan; from a standing start in 1981, the Nikon stepper business's sales had already by 1997 grown to more than $1.5 billion.

For the Japanese national economy, the most striking benefit has been soaring exports. Nikon exports more than 50 percent of its steppers. Moreover, even those Nikon steppers that are installed in Japanese semiconductor plants contribute strongly, if indirectly, to Japan's exports because they are engaged mainly in making semiconductors for export.

The stepper business has also been a great job creator. As estimated by the Nikon stepper executive Hisayuki Shimizu, fully half of Nikon's domestic workforce of 7,000 as of 1997 was engaged directly or indirectly in making steppers. Moreover, the stepper division's employment profile closely matches the job creation needs of Japanese society in that it offers plenty of jobs to workers of average intelligence. Specifically, nearly 50 percent of the stepper division's production workers have had no more than a high school education — a slightly higher proportion than in the Japanese workforce as a whole.

As for pay levels, Nikon ranks well up among the best employers in Japan. As of 1997 its workers earned on average ¥404,900 a month. That was worth about $3,300 at the 1997 exchange rate. In addition, workers received large biannual bonuses that brought their total income to around $55,000 a year. In other words, Nikon's pay levels were comparable to those in Japan's world-beating automobile industry.

One thing is certain: Nikon's factory-floor workers enjoy an especially solid sense of job security. Nikon's stepper division workers are backed by a unique tranche of secret technological know-how that has made Nikon the global leader in semiconductor lithography. With a world market share of more than 40 percent, it towers over the only other significant players in the industry — Tokyo-based Canon, which boasts a share of 24 percent, and Netherlands-based ASM Lithography, with 20 percent. Two American players, SVG and Optimetrix, share a few remaining percentage points between them.

Nikon is unique in that it boasts full in-house control of all the stepper industry's main production technologies, which in addition to optics include photoelectronic sensing and precision mechanics. As Nikon President Shoichiro Yoshida points out, this gives the company great scope to pioneer the development of new technologies in which mechanical and optical components have to be closely coordinated.

Of these technologies, optics is clearly the most important and explains much of Nikon's meteoric rise in the industry. Even before it entered the stepper business, Nikon had become the world leader in advanced optics. By the late 1970s its prowess was notably apparent in making, for instance, the ultra-high-performance lenses used in microfiche machines. Since then it has continued to lead in optical innovation. As explained by Hisayuki Shimizu, by maintaining its own glass factory Nikon enjoys great flexibility in developing new types of glass with superior refraction indexes. "There are various trace elements in glass such as copper and iron, and these affect its optical quality," says Shimizu. "It may take two years to develop a new glass and a further two years to develop a lens using it. Thus, if our competitors want to copy what we are doing, they will trail us by several years."

In precision mechanics too, Nikon boasts a long history of leadership. Here its early experience with so-called ruling engines has been crucial. These are highly sophisticated devices used by engineers and scientists for cutting and marking to ultra-fine tolerances. By the 1970s Nikon was already making ruling engines that could operate within tolerances of a mere 0.1 microns.

The stepper industry's need for highly precise mechanics stems in part from the ultra-demanding level of accuracy required in positioning silicon wafers for the lithography process. If a wafer's position is off by much more than 0.1 microns — little more than one-thousandth of a hair's breadth — the resulting chips may prove fatally flawed.

To understand the full significance of positioning, it is important to remember that microchips are three-dimensional devices. Like the floors in a tall building, layers of circuits are imposed one on top of the other. If each succeeding layer is not precisely aligned over the one below, the circuit connections between the layers will not line up. The mechanical challenge is greatly compounded by the fact that steppers print the same tiny pattern repeatedly on each wafer. Thus, the wafer, which typically measures eight inches across and will later be cut into many separate chips, must be repositioned many times in quick succession to receive each separate printing. (This process has become known as "step and repeat" — hence the name "stepper.") Given that a stepper must typically process each wafer within about one minute, wafers have to be repositioned rapidly between printings.

To achieve the necessary speed and accuracy, the stepper's mechanical parts must be machined to tolerances of hitherto unheard-of fineness — so fine in fact that steppers are said to be the most precise machines ever built. Steppers must be assembled in so-called clean rooms in which dust particles are excluded by elaborate air-filtering systems. Moreover, steppers are so delicate that even slight fluctuations in temperature can fatally disturb their mechanical settings. Thus, Nikon must take special care in transporting steppers: for export orders, for instance, the company insists on using special cargo planes that are normally used for transporting perishable fruit because these planes boast particularly reliable temperature controls.

The story of how Nikon came to dominate the world stepper business is a classic tale of U.S.-Japan rivalry. Like many other advanced products that are now made mainly in Japan, the stepper was invented in the United States. The concept was pioneered by the David W. Mann division of GCA Corporation, which monopolized the industry into the early 1980s. In the time-honored pattern of American business, GCA executives at first greatly underestimated the Japanese challenge and dismissed Nikon's early steppers as cheap copies.

In reality, however, even by the standards of corporate Japan generally, Nikon was a dangerous competitor to underestimate. For a start, Nikon's skills in the stepper industry's fundamental technologies were already at least a match for GCA's. In particular, Nikon was, of course, a leader in optics. In fact, it was already effortlessly ahead of GCA in that department: whereas GCA depended on an outside supplier, Zeiss of Germany, for lens-making, Nikon not only made all its own lenses but made them to world-beating standards of precision.

Moreover, in addition to technological leadership, Nikon enjoyed various commercial advantages by virtue of being a Japanese company. One key advantage was that the Ministry of International Trade and Industry in Tokyo had already targeted semiconductors in the 1970s as an industry of the future. By dint of its linguistic edge as well as the general nature of Japan's tightly integrated industrial infrastructure, Nikon could expect more than its share of the Japanese market. In particular, Nikon could expect to benefit from the fact that it was a top member of the huge Mitsubishi family of companies. This gave it more or less affirmative action status with many notable potential stepper customers.

More generally Nikon's base in Japan gave it a crucial edge in labor quality. This edge stemmed in large part from the Japanese employment system, which discourages job-hopping and has thereby ensured that Nikon captures the full benefit from its worker training programs. Even by Japanese standards, Nikon is a particularly heavy investor in the skills of its workforce. Its new recruits spend up to 70 percent of their time in training programs that can continue for as long as four years. Thereafter, Nikon retrains its workers every two years to keep them abreast of advances in production technology.

Another advantage of the Japanese labor system has been that it protects Nikon from the risk of competitors acquiring its secret production know-how by hiring away its workers. Under the lifetime employment system, Japanese workers are required to give their full loyalty to their employer, and it is unthinkable for them to use their knowledge of an employer's trade secrets to win a big pay increase from a rival employer.

A final benefit of Nikon's base in Japan was a plentiful supply of long-term capital. In particular, Nikon could count on its Mitsubishi connections to ensure that it had privileged access to the torrent of patient capital available from the Mitsubishi group's various banks and insurance companies.

Perhaps the most important lesson of the stepper story is that a flagging, old-line manufacturing company can reinvent itself. Launched in 1917 by Kowata Iwasaki, nephew of the Mitsubishi group's founder, Yataro Iwasaki, Nikon was Japan's first maker of optical equipment. For the next sixty years — through peace and war and then peace again — camera sales boomed. But by the late 1970s the joy had gone out of the camera business as many markets in the developed world showed signs of saturation. Nikon — in common with other Japanese camera makers — needed to develop new products.

Nikon's main rival, Canon, had already established an important beachhead in copiers and used this advantage to achieve leadership in the emerging laser printer business. (Canon supplies the key enabling components in laser printers to companies like Hewlett-Packard.)

Nikon chose to focus tightly on the stepper business. Thus, although to the world at large the Nikon brand name continues to denote cameras, in fact cameras now account for less than 30 percent of Nikon's total sales — down from 54 percent as recently as 1986.

Clearly, had Nikon not boldly entered the stepper business in 1980, it would have faced a future of stagnation, if not decline. Nikon's stepper story is a classic example of how a growth-oriented company can leverage existing manufacturing skills to develop new growth opportunities and maintain stable long-term employment for its workers.

Silicon: one thousand times more valuable than steel

Probably the stepper industry's nearest rival as a fundamental enabler of the electronic revolution is the silicon industry, which is also much overlooked in public discussions of the electronic age. Although the word *silicon* is promiscuously used as a synonym for *electronics,* semi-conductor-grade silicon as a material is perhaps the ultimate example of a highly advanced product that postindustrialists mistakenly assume is a mere "commodity" that can be safely taken for granted.

The truth is that only a handful of highly sophisticated companies are capable of making silicon to the standards required in the semiconductor industry. And just the top three of these companies — Tokyo-based Shin-Etsu Chemical, St. Louis–based MEMC Electronic Materials, and Munich-based Wacker-Chemie — account for well over half the world market.

In one sense, it is perhaps not surprising that people tend to take silicon for granted. As the euphoric prophets of the New Economy point out, silicon is the second most common element after oxygen and, in one estimate, accounts for an astonishing 30.5 percent of the earth's crust.

But there is a big difference between raw silicon as found in nature and the highly refined form used in the semiconductor industry. In fact, semiconductor-grade silicon is produced in only tiny volumes, and in the epitaxial form used for high-performance computer chips, it costs more than $80 an ounce. That is the equivalent of nearly $2.9 million per metric ton — or nearly one thousand times the price of steel.

The task of converting raw silicon into silicon wafers involves more than a dozen complex processes. In the words of Barnaby J. Feder of the *New York Times,* "if digital technology is a mix of mathematics and electrical engineering, then think of wafer production as the molecular chemistry that makes the digital era possible."

The silicon production process begins with quartz sand, which is reduced and refined to produce a material known as polysilicon. This looks like irregularly shaped gray rocks but boasts an almost incredible level of purity — just one foreign atom per one billion. The polysilicon is then melted in combination with minute amounts of "dopant" elements such as boron and phosphorus and converted into cylindrical ingots of monocrystalline silicon. The dopant elements are special impurities that determine the precise electrical properties of the final silicon wafer.

Another crucial stage is the slicing of the ingots into wafers. Since these wafers can be almost as thin as a postcard, the cutting requires extremely precise machinery. Afterward, the wafers are carefully cleaned and polished. In the case of epitaxial wafers, a further key process is necessary as the polished silicon slices are coated with a special layer of ultra-pure silicon of an electrically different character. Chips made from epitaxial wafers generally boast enhanced reliability and make possible more complex designs, such as those used in Intel's high-performance microprocessors.

All this complexity adds up to a great business for the world's silicon wafer producers. This is notably apparent, for instance, at Wacker-Chemie, which accounts for nearly 30 percent of all the world's poly-silicon and about 15 percent of its semiconductor-grade silicon. Founded in 1914 by Alexander Wacker, a German financier and indus-trial pioneer, Wacker-Chemie boasts deep roots in the German tradi-tion of chemical innovation. The company originally made calcium carbide, an intermediate material needed for producing acetylene, which in turn was used to fuel the gas lighting of the early twentieth century. Calcium carbide was made in a complex process that required large amounts of electricity, a commodity that was then far more ex-pensive in real terms than it is today. Alexander Wacker found an abundant source of water power in southern Germany, and harnessing it to generate cheap electricity, he quickly became a major producer of calcium carbide and acetylene. Of course, gas lighting quickly went the way of the buggy whip, but the chemical works he established — near the beautiful medieval town of Burghausen — soon developed other applications for acetylene in various areas of the chemical industry. Later Wacker-Chemie was highly successful in diversifying into vari-ous silicon-based products that kept output on a consistently rising tack. The most important of these at first was silicon carbide, which is used in industrial abrasives. Then came various forms of silicone, which are organic compounds of silicon used in lubricants and var-nishes. Finally, in the early 1970s, the company began making semi-conductor-grade silicon. Along the way, Wacker's Burghausen work-force has consistently burgeoned to the point where today it numbers more than 10,000 people, of whom about 35 percent are engaged in making semiconductor silicon.

As with most manufacturing industries, the silicon business has been highly successful in creating excellent jobs for ordinary blue-collar workers. In fact, more than 80 percent of Wacker's silicon workers are mere high-school graduates. And given that Burghausen is located in one of Germany's most prosperous regions, Wacker necessarily pays notably high wages.

Of course, a glance at the structure of Wacker's business shows that the company can well afford to pay superior wages. The reason is that silicon-making, in common with most advanced manufacturing business, is highly capital-intensive. Wacker's silicon works is full of the latest equipment from such specialist chemical equipment makers as Peter Wolters, Leybold Systems, and CRP Technic. In the crystal-growing process, for instance, one worker looks after as many as ten Leybold "pullers," each of which represents a capital investment of nearly $1 million.

The silicon industry is also notably knowledge-intensive. The crystal-growing process in particular is highly complex, and by dint of trial and error over the years the main producers have accumulated a huge stock of proprietary know-how. Much of this know-how takes the form of patents that the main producers share via extensive cross-licensing of patents. The incumbents in the industry also enjoy a huge edge in productivity over would-be entrants by dint of a large reserve of trade secrets. Even something as apparently simple as the appropriate settings for production equipment are closely guarded trade secrets known only to a few top engineers and other trusted senior executives.

The level of proprietary knowledge required is constantly rising as the industry moves rapidly to ever more sophisticated and varied products. Much of the variation comes from the "doping" process, which can produce many different grades tailored to the precise needs of individual semiconductor makers. As reported by Barnaby Feder, MEMC, an affiliate of the German conglomerate Veba, now makes more than a thousand different types of wafers, each with its own exacting specifications for silicon purity, electrical properties, thickness, surface coatings, and many other characteristics. Typically chip makers spend months testing various types of wafers, but once they decide to go with a particular wafer they tend to remain loyal customers for years to come.

Silicon makers have also had to build up considerable proprietary expertise as they have striven to make ever larger wafers over the years. Starting with a diameter of just four inches in the early 1970s, they have moved three times to successively larger diameters. Each move has required a major leap in technology because the larger the wafer, the greater the difficulty in delivering the sort of dimensional perfection required by semiconductor makers. The standard diameter these days is eight inches, but the industry is preparing for yet another leap, this time to twelve-inch wafers, which are expected to go into mass-production soon after 2000. Larger wafers are a boon to semiconductor makers because the processing of each wafer involves high setting-up costs that are largely independent of the wafer's size; thus, the larger a wafer is, the lower the setting-up costs per chip. Moreover, the larger wafers reduce the proportion of wasted silicon. (Waste results when the final rectangular chips are cut from the circular wafer, rendering a significant proportion of the area along the perimeter of the wafer unusable; the proportion is considerably larger with smaller wafers.)

Given the level of capital and knowledge needed, virtually all the key processes in the semiconductor-grade silicon industry are conducted by high-wage workers in First World factories. Although Malaysia, China, and other growth-hungry East Asian developing nations have been trying to establish a foothold in the industry, they remain marginal players that perform only the least sophisticated processes. As Heinz Herzer, a director of Wacker's silicon-making subsidiary, points out, moving key operations to a cheap-labor location simply does not make economic sense for a leading-edge player like Wacker. "We need to operate in an advanced economy for several reasons," he says.

> For one thing, a reliable supply of electricity is absolutely essential, and this is hard to find in cheap-labor countries. If there is an electricity blackout, our crucibles would be destroyed: the liquid silicon would solidify and expand and the crucibles' heaters would be damaged beyond repair. If we had just one blackout in a year, the costs would be a lot greater than anything we could save by locating the factory in a low-wage country.

Another key reason for locating in an advanced nation is that the silicon business requires notably high-quality labor. Wacker looks particularly for reliability in its workers, a trait that is hard to find outside advanced First World countries like Germany that boast both a superb high-school education system and a long tradition of disciplined labor. Because of the nature of the silicon business, Wacker demands that its workers be highly disciplined in following rules and procedures. Even in such an apparently lowly function as dispatch, the company holds its workers to enormously high standards — and for good reason. As Heinz Herzer points out, sending the wrong wafers to a customer could result in a major business disaster. He explains: "The mistake will probably be discovered only months later, by which time the customer will have not only to write off millions of dollars of finished chips but may have to renege on its promised delivery date to its customers."

All this helps explain why, even though by the late 1990s wages in Germany were the highest of any major country, jobs at Wacker's Burghausen silicon plant — and at an epitaxial operation in nearby Wassenburg — remained notably secure. Even during the wrenching recessions that periodically afflict the electronics industry, Wacker has never had to resort to layoffs. Quite the contrary, Wacker's silicon business has consistently shown strong growth over the years, and its workforce has increased more than tenfold in the last twenty-five years. Similar job growth has been experienced by MEMC in the United States and by Shin-Etsu in Japan. By all accounts, the industry can look forward to many more years of strong growth. In projections by the Dataquest market research company, the silicon industry could sell as much as 6.2 billion square inches of semiconductor wafers by 2000 — an increase of nearly 60 percent on 1996.

Even in 2000, the prospects for further growth will probably be nowhere near exhausted. After all, computer engineers have for years aspired to make machines that come close to matching the capabilities of the human brain. They still have an awfully long way to go. As Wacker-Chemie's managing director, Rudolf Staudigl, points out, the world semiconductor industry's entire output of computer memories in 1996 represented the memory capacity of just two human brains. Great though the electronics industry's achievements have already been, the world undoubtedly has nowhere near reached satiation in its appetite for silicon.

Let's now look at the next link in the chain of advanced manufacturing processes that have made possible the information revolution — and have created some of the best blue-collar jobs in the world. It is time to visit a state-of-the-art semiconductor factory.

Semiconductors: an advance on mushroom farming

When American semiconductor makers were under strong competitive pressure from fast-expanding Japanese rivals in the mid-1980s, a furious policy debate raged in Washington. For many in the Reagan administration, the appropriate response seemed clear: do nothing. Their position was famously encapsulated in a remark attributed to the top Reagan administration economic adviser Michael Boskin: "Computer chips, wood chips, potato chips. What's the difference? They're all chips." Boskin later denied making this comment, but as Clyde Prestowitz, author of *Trading Places,* pointed out, it accurately summarized the Reagan administration's true attitude on the matter. Reaganites believed that the choice of which goods the United States should or should not produce was best left to the unfettered free market. If American companies found quicker, easier profits in making potato chips or wood chips than computer chips, then this was where the nation's best prospects for prosperity supposedly lay.

So much for ideology. In the real world, there were several flaws in this argument, of which the most obvious was that if the American economy was to remain one of the world's strongest, the United States needed not only profitable corporations but good jobs. The strong case that could be made, from a jobs perspective, for questioning the market's wisdom was made all the stronger by the fact that the profit downturn the American semiconductor makers had suffered stemmed from no fundamental slowdown in the industry's phenomenal growth rate but rather from short-term oversupply problems created by the aggressive expansion of notably farsighted Japanese semiconductor companies. These companies had clearly seen that taking short-term losses would pay off in the long run in greater market share — and better, more productive jobs for their workers.

One thing is clear as we look back from the vantage point of the late 1990s: had the United States abandoned the semiconductor business in the mid-1980s, it would have missed out on enormous subsequent growth. In just the ten years to 1996, worldwide sales of microchips multiplied fivefold to total $132 billion. Although there are no reliable figures for jobs in the semiconductor industry, a good guess is that the industry's total workforce doubled in the period.

All in all, the semiconductor industry has been a superb economic performer in recent years. In few parts of the world is this more evident than in Higashi Hiroshima, a medium-sized Japanese town that is home to one of the world's largest and most advanced semiconductor fabrication plants.

Measuring four hundred meters long and about thirty meters high, the plant is located in a semirural setting on the outskirts of the town. This region has seen industrial glory before: it supplied much of feudal Japan's iron and salt. But these days the immediate vicinity is a quiet residential district. Just beyond is scenic countryside dotted with traditional tile-roofed farm cottages. From the workers' canteen, you look out on a picture-window view of woods and mountains. There is not even a hint of other industrial activity in sight. All in all, the area looks more like the setting for a pricey ski resort than for one of the world's most massively capitalized factories.

The plant is operated by NEC, which ranks as the world's second-largest semiconductor maker after Santa Clara–based Intel Corporation. For our purposes, NEC is a more interesting company to look at than Intel because it has based its success almost entirely on world-leading manufacturing skills, whereas Intel's growth has come largely from a so-called market lock-in — its virtual monopoly in making chips for Wintel-standard computers.

When this writer visited Higashi Hiroshima in the summer of 1997, NEC had just finished building a new extension full of state-of-the-art manufacturing technology. The extension, code-named A2, was expected to lead the world in mass-producing chips with lines as thin as 0.25 microns — one-quarter of one-millionth of a meter. This was an important advance on the semiconductor industry's previous mass-production best of 0.28 microns, and it paved the way for NEC to pioneer the production of massively powerful 256-megabit memories. Each of these will have enough capacity to store Shakespeare's complete works four times over. These memories, which are expected to become the industry standard by 2000, will be four times more powerful than the state-of-the-art 64-megabit memories that were just entering the mass-production stage as of 1998.

Perhaps the most impressive thing about A2 is its price tag — a cool $630 million. It is a good example of the pattern for Japanese companies to make their largest investments at home — a pattern reflected in the fact that though NEC operates more semiconductor factories abroad than in Japan, fully two-thirds of all the investment capital it pours into its worldwide semiconductor business each year goes to domestic operations. Given that the additional workforce NEC needs to operate the A2 facility totals just 441, each worker is backed by more than $1.4 million of capital — or about 140 times the investment needed to create each new job in the Indian software industry. And this takes account merely of the capital tied up in physical assets. Additionally, workers at Higashi Hiroshima are backed by billions of dollars' worth of proprietary know-how, which NEC has painstakingly accumulated over a period of two decades at the leading edge of the semiconductor industry.

Clearly the Higashi Hiroshima plant is a classic example of manufacturing's ability to create superb First World jobs. Moreover, in common with other manufacturing operations, the plant has created an excellent range of jobs: nearly 80 percent of NEC's Higashi Hiroshima workers are mere high-school graduates, a considerably higher proportion than in the Japanese workforce as a whole. Perhaps the best thing about the Higashi Hiroshima plant is the pay: a typical 30-year-old worker earns nearly ¥7 million a year, including twice-yearly bonuses. As of 1998, this was equal to more than $50,000, even at the yen's low valuation of ¥135 to the dollar. For a 50-year-old worker, wages plus bonuses came to well over $60,000 a year.

The plant also illustrates the tremendous growth that is possible in a leading-edge manufacturing business. Founded in 1988, the plant has been in an almost constant state of frenzied expansion ever since — an expansion that at last count brought the total workforce to 1,400, up from just 300 initially. Since fully 58 percent of the workforce has been hired locally, the effect has been to transform prospects in the local employment market, where previously agriculture was the fundamental source of jobs. In fact, other than silicon chips, the area's most notable product is *matsutake* mushrooms, which grow under pine trees and are a characteristic flavoring ingredient in traditional Japanese cuisine. The evidence of the 1990s is that the job prospects are better in semiconductors than in mushrooms — not to mention wood chips or potato chips.

Let there be lasers: light as an all-purpose tool

Next to computer chips, the most important enabling components of the electronic revolution are undoubtedly lasers and other high-tech light-emitting devices. In contrast with computer chips, however, the highly advanced and important business of manufacturing laser devices gets little attention in the media. This is perhaps understandable given the laser industry's amazing diversity. There are hundreds of different types of laser devices, made from widely different materials and used in highly varied applications. Even in their physical dimensions, lasers are startlingly varied. Many are tiny, sometimes no bigger than a pinhead. Others are as big as a room — one experimental laser developed at Stanford University in the 1980s, for instance, ran to forty feet in length.

The one thing they all have in common is that they create a highly homogenized form of light. Whereas a ray of sunlight consists of a mixture of widely different wavelengths, a laser emits "coherent" light — that is, light whose wavelengths are contained within one narrow band.

Laser technology has created a host of manufacturing opportunities for high-tech companies in many advanced nations. In Germany, for instance, manufacturers are particularly strong in laser-based cutting devices, which in various forms are now widely used everywhere from shipyards to hospital operating theaters. The Germans are also leaders in laser-based welding devices, which, like the cutting devices, harness the ability of gas-based lasers to concentrate energy in a very focused way. This ability is a major advantage in dealing with metals that boast both high heat conductivity and a high melting point. Aluminum, for example, was notoriously difficult to weld effectively until lasers came along. The problem is that applying heat to any point on a sheet of aluminum is a bit like pouring water into a sieve: the heat dissipates rapidly throughout the sheet, thus making it difficult, with pre-laser welding techniques, to raise the temperature of the area targeted for welding. Lasers are more effective than traditional heating methods because they apply massive amounts of heat very rapidly to the targeted area. Laser welding devices are often huge and typically use such lasing mediums as carbon dioxide or nitrogen. Among German laser companies, notable players include Lambda Physik and Trumpf.

In the United States, too, several high-tech manufacturers have developed important laser-based businesses. A key example is San Diego–based Cymer, which has pioneered the manufacture of the highly sophisticated laser-based etching devices used in state-of-the-art steppers for the semiconductor industry. Spectraphysics and Coherent have established important positions in argon-based lasers. Another notable American player in the laser business is Perceptron, which specializes in making laser-based measuring devices.

To see the potential of the laser industry to full advantage as a source of excellent jobs and strong exports, however, it is necessary to look beyond developments in the United States and Germany to Japan. The Japanese are key players in several of the most important areas of the laser business. They are strong in cutting devices, for instance. They are also leaders in laser-based precision instruments. Tokyo-based Komatsu, for instance, is now challenging Cymer in making lasers for the stepper industry. But perhaps the ultimate success story of the Japanese laser industry is Sony Corporation, whose recent experience with lasers represents a classic illustration of the economic virtues of advanced manufacturing.

Sony's specialty is laser diodes, a product category it entirely dominates worldwide. Laser diodes are tiny devices that are most familiar as the key enabling components in compact disk players, CD-ROMs, and digital video disk players. They are also crucial in laser printers. Even more important, they are key enabling components in the telecommunications industry, where they are used to send pulses of light through optical fiber networks. As Paul Saffo, an analyst with the Institute for the Future in Menlo Park, has pointed out, laser diodes are in fact the ultimate driver of the telecommunications revolution of the 1990s.

In the circumstances, Sony's leadership of the laser diode business constitutes a classic tale of the economic virtues of advanced manufacturing. Sony got its start in the industry as recently as the early 1980s and has been on a path of breakneck growth ever since. On the strength of an estimated threefold increase in its factory workforce, it has expanded its monthly output from less than 300,000 units in 1982 to 14 million units in 1998. This amounts to a phenomenal sixteenfold increase in labor productivity, and it has been powered in large part by Sony's success in maximizing its "yield" — the proportion of flaw-free units in its total production. In laser diodes, as in other electronic components, yield is a crucial determinant in that, in the absence of ultra-strict quality controls, as much as 90 percent of a factory's output may have to be scrapped because of defects. As we pointed out in chapter 1, one well-known technique for improving yield is to filter the factory air to remove all but the most minute particles of dust and other contaminants. But in truth, many of the secrets of improving a factory's yield are highly elusive and can be discovered only by a careful, laborious process of trial and error.

The scale of the difficulties in this field is nicely illustrated by a story often told in the Japanese electronics industry. As the story goes, a semiconductor factory was suffering notably erratic yield levels: sometimes the yield of good products was very high, sometimes very low. The problem baffled engineers for months until a humble factory-floor worker noticed a correlation between poor yields and the local train schedule. Subsequent inquiries proved that minute vibrations from passing trains were periodically playing havoc with the production process. The story may be apocryphal (it is hard to imagine the sort of razor-sharp engineers who run Japan's semiconductor factories not checking for vibrations at an early stage in their investigations), but it illustrates in microcosm the wide diversity of factors that must be considered in identifying the causes of yield problems.

Not surprisingly, the know-how needed to maximize yields is among the most closely guarded secrets in advanced manufacturing. Not only does Sony decline to enter into any discussion of its yield-maximizing know-how, but it carefully restricts entry to its laser diode factories. We do know, however, that a team of top engineers led by the Sony general manager Osamu Kumagai has raised the company's yield to well over 90 percent in recent years. By comparison, the company achieved a yield of less than 10 percent in the early stages of production in 1982. It is probably no accident that Kumagai is one of the world's foremost experts on gallium arsenide, the advanced semiconductor material that is the key ingredient in Sony's laser diodes.

Sony's yield achievement alone accounts for a nearly fivefold boost in labor productivity. On top of this, the company has achieved other major productivity improvements thanks, for instance, to massive investments in robot-driven automation systems.

As a result, Sony has cut its prices by more than 90 percent since the early 1980s. Along the way the company has implemented a major qualitative improvement in its products by both shrinking their size and boosting their performance. The results can be seen in consumer markets around the world. Sony's success in honing its laser diode production know-how helps explain why CD players are now everywhere — not only in the First and Second Worlds but increasingly even in the Third World. They are evidently far more numerous than the record-players they superseded. Since CD players were first sold in 1982, they have achieved total cumulative sales of a phenomenal 550 million units — one for every ten residents of the planet. Moreover,

Sony's success in improving the capabilities of its laser diodes has paved the way for extensions of the product for use in CD-ROMs and digital video disk players (which work off disks that contain more than seven times as much digitized information as ordinary music CDs). The result is that as of the late 1990s Sony had grabbed a 60 percent share of the $4 billion world market for laser diodes.

It is a market that continues to grow rapidly thanks to break-throughs both in finding new applications for lasers and in developing better and cheaper lasers. One major breakthrough recently has been in the manufacture of blue lasers. These had hitherto been available only in huge gas-based versions that cost $50,000 each. Now Nichia Chemical Industries of Anan, Japan, has developed tiny blue laser diodes based on the semiconducting material gallium nitride that are expected eventually to be mass-produced for less than $2 a piece.

For the laser industry, this represents a major landmark because, among other things, blue light has a much shorter wavelength than red, the color of most laser diodes manufactured thus far. A shorter wavelength enables a laser diode to read smaller marks on CD platters; if blue lasers become widely available, they will enable the information industry to pack four to five times as much information onto CD platters. This is just the beginning of the possibilities for blue lasers. Engineers believe that down the road blue lasers may play a crucial role in a host of applications, in everything from color fax machines and copiers to ultra-high-capacity optical fiber networks.

Already blue light–emitting diodes, which are simpler devices than lasers but work off the same basic chemical breakthroughs, are being made in mass-production volumes and have opened a host of opportunities for new products. A key point is that blue is one of the three primary colors. Since cheap green and red lasers are already available, the development of cheap blue light-emitting devices completes the color "palette." One immediate result is to make possible the development of vast outdoor television screens made up of millions of light-emitting diodes.

In another application, arrays of light-emitting diodes that produce white light may soon be used to replace traditional lightbulbs in many applications. As noted by Gerhard Fasol, a Tokyo-based scientist who has coauthored a book on the blue laser with the blue laser inventor Shuji Nakamura, the traditional lightbulb is based on a century-old technology. Unlike its first cousin, the radio valve, the ordinary lightbulb has not succumbed yet to the semiconductor revolution. But with the development of cheap blue lasers and light-emitting diodes, the lightbulb's days may be numbered. One application in which light-emitting diodes are already beginning to replace lightbulbs is in traffic lights. "Bulbs are very inefficient for traffic lights," says Fasol. "The reason is that much of the energy they consume is emitted as invisible infrared rays and is dissipated as heat. In the case of a yellow lamp, perhaps only one-tenth of the energy consumed creates visible light. Light-emitting diodes are more efficient in that more of the energy they use goes directly to creating light."

In Fasol's estimate, a move to light-emitting diodes would cut the energy costs of traffic lights by 75 percent. Moreover, the new traffic lights promise huge savings in maintenance costs because light-emitting diodes last at least twenty times longer than lightbulbs, and at the end of their lives they fade out gradually, rather than failing suddenly. Thus, not only would replacements be needed much less frequently, but they could be organized on a regular schedule that would make much more efficient use of maintenance workers' time.

For now Nichia is claiming the lead in mass-producing the blue laser diode. But other companies are racing to develop rival products, most notably an affiliate of the Toyota Motor group. Either way, it seems that further extensions of the laser diode concept are likely to continue to create jobs mainly in Japan.

In fact, the laser diode business's heavy concentration in ultra-high-wage Japan is perhaps the best illustration of this book's proposition that high wages rarely constitute a significant competitive disadvantage in advanced manufacturing industries. And, of course, other parts of the world where the laser manufacturing business is strong are also noted for high wages. Germany, for instance, is hardly a low-wage location. Neither is Santa Clara, where Coherent, one of the largest U.S. players is based. Ditto for San Diego, home to Cymer.

As for job security, the industry's evidently explosive growth prospects bode well for the future. Certainly new applications are being found for lasers all the time, and most of these applications play to the existing, highly secret know-how of the industry's incumbents.

The last word on the prospects should come from Sergey Krayushkin, a top Russian laser expert. He draws an analogy with the history of magnets. Magnets have been around for many hundreds of years, yet people still keep inventing new applications for them. He comments: "Lasers have been around less than forty years so we are really just at the beginning."

Intimations of the next big thing

So far in our look at the electronics industry we have focused on production machinery, materials, and components. In concluding our analysis, it is time to look at final consumer products. It is the pace of innovation in new consumer products that ultimately is the industry's main engine of growth.

In the last two decades alone, we have seen the introduction of an enormous spate of blockbuster electronic products — most notably videocassette recorders, camcorders, compact disk players, fax machines, and, of course, personal computers.

It is a spate that shows no signs of drying up. As of the late 1990s, a wealth of recently developed products like cellular phones, high-speed modems, and car navigation systems were making the explosive transition from the early-adopter stage to mass-market acceptance. The growth opportunities generated for manufacturers of everything from semiconductor silicon to laser diodes were clearly huge. But in terms of manufacturing opportunities, probably none of the recently developed consumer products packs more potential than digital television. In concluding our review of the electronics industry, therefore, we will take a closer look at the enormous economic possibilities just this one new consumer product presages for the electronics industry.

In its most advanced form, digital television delivers high-definition images that provide four times as much detail as conventional television. The result is wonderfully sharp pictures that promise soon to do to conventional color television what color television did to black-and-white a generation ago. Certainly most experts sense that at the right price, almost everyone will want high-definition television's movie-style picture quality.

That said, the huge potential importance of high-definition television (HDTV) has so far been obscured by some unfortunate missteps in the concept's introduction. In particular, high-definition has got off to a notably disappointing start in Japan. A pioneering version has been operated by NHK, the Japanese national broadcasting company, since the late 1980s, but as of the late 1990s sales of HDTV sets were still languishing at derisory levels. The NHK system's disappointing showing is highly misleading, however, in that it stems from special factors that do not speak to the concept's general potential. NHK moved too early and in so doing backed the wrong technological horse. It went with an old-fashioned analog version of high-definition that had been in development in Japan since the 1960s. Just as NHK launched its system, breakthroughs in video compression in the United States suddenly rendered it more or less obsolete. These breakthroughs made it feasible for broadcasters to abandon analog technology and move decisively into the digital era. Although digital HDTV does not deliver an appreciably better picture than Japan's analog standard, it boasts other advantages that will clearly give it an enormous market edge in the long run. In particular, digital television sets can readily be made compatible with other digital devices, most notably personal computers. Thus, digital HDTV has opened up many exciting opportunities to blend pin-sharp vision with superfast computing. Once the feasibility of a digital approach became obvious around 1990, Japanese television set makers lost faith in the NHK standard. Since then, they have evidently been waiting for NHK to shift to a digital standard before they get serious about pushing sales in Japan.

In the United States too, the development of HDTV has been marked by inordinate delays. A major stumbling block was created by various squabbles between interested parties, notably one dating back to the 1980s about how to share the available broadcast spectrum between the telecommunications industry and the broadcasting industry. As of the late 1990s, however, most of the problems had been resolved and an officially mandated move to digital television had begun.

Even so, as with the introduction of other major technological advances in the American entertainment industry, HDTV will probably take several years to win broad consumer acceptance. In the meantime, several things must happen. Most important, the electronics industry will have to make dramatic cuts in HDTV set prices. In the view of John Stich, a senior marketing executive at Texas Instruments, the industry must get retail prices down below $2,000 before high-definition will break out as a mass-market product. As of 1998, the industry still seemed to be far from that goal: retail prices ranged from $3,300 for low-end 30-inch sets to as high as $20,000 or more for top-of-the-range 60-inch sets. In principle, however, there is no reason the industry could not start reducing prices rapidly once the American broadcasting industry achieves critical mass in the amount of high-definition programming material it puts out. From that point on, increased sales volume would enable manufacturers to spread their fixed costs over more units, thus making possible significant price reductions, which in turn would generate further increases in volume, leading to even deeper price reductions. Given that an exceptionally high proportion of the total cost of making HDTV sets consists of up-front research and development spending, manufacturers enjoy tremendous scope to cut prices once they achieve sufficiently high levels of volume.

Everything depends, therefore, on the American broadcasting industry. As this book was being written, many American broadcasters seemed to be balking at the heavy investments needed to provide a full high-definition service. But the betting was that sooner rather than later competition would force their hand. All it will take is one significant broadcaster in each market leading the way for the others to be dragged willy-nilly into the high-definition era. Given how competitive the American broadcasting industry has become in recent years, there is little doubt that aggressive broadcasters will come forward to lead the industry in a speedy move to the new system.

With luck, therefore, HDTV could reach critical mass in the first years of the twenty-first century. Who, therefore, will garner the lion's share of the spoils? Japanese manufacturers in particular seem well positioned to profit from the changeover. In fact, as reported by Joel Brinkley of the *New York Times,* Japan's Mitsubishi Electric was the only manufacturer whose sets were available in American electronics stores when the official U.S. move to digital television began in late 1998. This came as a surprise to many observers who had earlier portrayed the Japanese as lagging in high-definition. In reality, however, the Japanese lag merely in the standard their own national broadcasting company has chosen for the home market. Japan's domestic standard is largely irrelevant to the Japanese television set industry's export prowess. In fact, Japanese set makers have long been renowned for their ability to tailor their products to meet widely varying broadcast standards in different export markets. In any case, most of the manufacturing work involved is largely the same, irrespective of whether the sets are geared to receive digital or analog signals.

One thing is certain: there will be plenty of business to go around. Already manufacturers in Europe and the United States as well as in

Japan are gearing up for a bonanza. Important opportunities await not only makers of sets and components but makers of materials and manufacturing equipment.

The semiconductor industry alone is set to enjoy a field day. The new sets require not only powerful memory chips and microprocessors but many specialized chips such as digital signal processors. As estimated by Texas Instruments' John Stich, each HDTV set contains at least $250 worth of semiconductors, and depending on the choice of screen technology, higher-end sets may need many special chips, called screen drivers, that will take the total semiconductor cost per set to $350 or more. Thus, as Stich points out, the semiconductor industry is in line to generate fully 60 percent as much revenue from a typical HDTV as from a high-end personal computer. The bonus, of course, is that HDTV is likely to achieve much broader market penetration than high-end personal computers.

HDTV will also create a big new market for makers of miscellaneous components, such as speakers, channel changers, and set-top cable equipment. There is even a likely bonanza here for the laser diode industry. Although laser diodes will not participate directly in the boom (because they are not required in stand-alone television sets), they will benefit indirectly as the crucial enabling components in new high-definition digital versatile disk players. These complements to HDTV sets are expected to achieve major sales.

Probably the most interesting manufacturing opportunities will be for makers of screens. As yet, no manufacturer has come up with a completely satisfactory screen technology to make the most of the new medium. For the moment, the screen technology of choice remains the venerable cathode-ray tube, the technology that has dominated the television industry since the 1940s. This plays directly to the interests of Japanese corporations, which have long dominated the cathode-ray tube industry. Sony and Toshiba in particular have fully mastered the technologies involved in making HDTV-standard cathode-ray tubes. (They have already been making similar tubes for many years for use as high-end monitors in the computer industry.)

But there is a problem here: to savor high-definition in its full glory, the screen should be as big as sixty inches. Although it is technically possible to make cathode-ray tubes that large, they are not an ideal solution because they are too bulky for most living rooms.

The television set industry is therefore working on several less bulky screen technologies. One alternative is the liquid-crystal display, which boasts the key advantage of being a flat panel that typically is only about one inch thick. But given present levels of manufacturing technology, liquid-crystal displays are disproportionately difficult to mass-produce in large sizes. Moreover, they fall well short of the cathode-ray tube in picture quality: not only are they generally less bright, but they are not as effective in keeping up with fast-action images.

In the search for a successor to the cathode-ray tube, therefore, many electronics companies are developing new types of flat-panel displays that do not suffer the disadvantages of liquid crystal. The most advanced contender so far is the so-called plasma display. Like a liquid-crystal display, this is a flat panel. In picture quality, it comes close to matching the best cathode-ray tubes. Unfortunately, however, despite its slim appearance, a plasma display is exceedingly heavy (often weighing as much as two hundred pounds). Thus, it cannot safely be hung on the wall of a typical living room. Its weight is a function of the fact that the screen must be divided into thousands of separately addressed chambers, each enclosed in its own glass housing. Because a plasma display also demands a great deal of power, it emits a lot of unwelcome heat. Moreover, plasma displays, like large liquid-crystal displays, are difficult to mass-produce and thus are extremely expensive. Medium-sized plasma-based HDTV sets, for instance, were priced at around $10,000 as of the late 1990s. Although manufacturers of plasma displays will undoubtedly cut prices as volumes increase, it seems unlikely that they will ever get their manufacturing costs down to the low levels that prevail in the cathode-ray tube industry.

In view of all the problems with the various existing screen technologies, there is clearly a major market opportunity for an innovative approach. The hiatus is seen by American engineers such as Mark Eaton of Kipwee Display, a Texas-based start-up, as a chance for the United States to make a comeback in display technologies after a long fallow spell in which the Japanese have effortlessly led the field in all three proven technologies — cathode-ray tubes, liquid-crystal displays, and plasma displays.

For the foreseeable future, however, the main contender will remain the plain-vanilla cathode-ray tube. Most of the early sets are likely to feature cathode-ray tubes with screens manageably sized in the 30- to

40-inch range. The betting is that this formula will provide an attractive enough picture to propel the early stages of the concept's market acceptance.

How big could the HDTV industry become? If, as seems likely, set makers breach the $2,000 price point well before 2005, the industry could be selling as many as 30 million sets a year by 2010. That would add up to annual revenues of at least $20 billion. Meanwhile, the market for broadcast equipment, satellite dishes, and other ancillary products could add another $15 billion to $20 billion.

Given prospects like these, it is fair to say as we conclude our look at the electronics industry that its best years are still in the future. Of course, this is not to say that all the technologies we have reviewed here are likely to enjoy boundless growth forever. But the electronics industry is nothing if not resourceful, and its incumbents have a long record of success in evolving new technologies when existing ones have run their course. Certainly electronics is a classic growth industry. And given how difficult it generally is to break into this industry (in that its more advanced areas require disproportionately high levels of both capital and know-how), it clearly constitutes a showcase of the economic advantages of manufacturing in creating jobs and highly exportable products.

But as postindustrialists are quick to point out, not all manufacturing industries offer such rosy growth prospects. In fact, many manufacturing industries are quite mature, and their growth prospects are correspondingly curtailed. But are such industries dinosaurs, as the postindustrialists suggest? In most cases, no. As we will now see, some of the oldest manufacturing industries remain pillars of some of the world's richest economies. It is time to look at some golden oldies.

6

Golden Oldies:
Ships, Textiles, Steel

It is often assumed that just as people have life cycles, so too do industries. An industry starts as an infant, grows rapidly, becomes mature — and then it dies. Or so conventional wisdom has it.

But is death really as inevitable for industries as for people? Hardly. In fact, some of the world's oldest manufacturing industries have shown remarkable resilience over the years, and even today, at the end of the twentieth century, they continue to make important contributions to the world's prosperity.

Take the ceramics industry. With a history dating back to ancient China, it is assuredly an old industry. Yet even in the late twentieth century it continues to set a fast pace in product innovation — a pace so fast in fact that several leading ceramics companies have carved out vital positions for themselves in high-tech industries. Kyoto-based Kyocera, for instance, has more than doubled its sales in the last ten years, largely on the strength of a dominant position in supplying high-tech ceramic packaging to the world semiconductor industry. Other ceramics makers have developed new heat-resistant materials that are essential in everything from jet engines to power-station turbines. Ceramics makers are also playing a vital role in the growing pollution control industry, most notably in making the key materials in the catalytic converters that minimize noxious emissions in automobile exhaust gases.

Similarly, with a history almost as old as that of ceramics, the glass industry maintains a steady pace of innovation that has kept it at the forefront of technological progress in the late twentieth century. For example, the special forms of glass used in making steppers, as described in chapter 5, are vital for the semiconductor industry. Elsewhere in the glass industry, the venerable Corning company, among others, has played a key enabling role in the telecommunications revolution with its development of the highly sophisticated forms of glass used in fiber optics.

Another notably mature industry that continues to thrive even in the late twentieth century is printing equipment. Admittedly, this fact has been somewhat obscured by the disappearance of several once world-beating U.S. printing equipment makers. But far from reflecting a general decline in demand for printing equipment, their fate stems entirely from a failure to keep up with changing technology.

Their Japanese rivals, by contrast, have been adept at riding the technological tiger and as a result have gone from strength to strength. A notable example is Japan's Mitsubishi Heavy Industries, which is now a world leader in the huge high-speed presses used in the newspaper industry. In fact, these days even the *Washington Post* is printed on Mitsubishi machines.

Perhaps the ultimate proof of the printing equipment industry's enduring strength is in Germany. The Germans, after all, have been leaders in printing technology since Gutenberg's time more than five centuries ago. They still are. Such German companies as Roland and König & Bauer-Albert are major suppliers of presses to the world's newspaper companies. As the dominant maker of printing presses for magazines, Heidelberger Druckmaschinen ranks as the world's largest maker of printing equipment. Employing 21,000 people, most of them in Germany, it derives more than 80 percent of its sales from foreign markets — and thus is a classic illustration of how strongly manufacturing can bolster a nation's balance of payments. And even in these days of such vaunted "paperless" media as CD-ROM encyclopedias and Internet databases, the chairman of Heidelberger Druckmaschinen, Hartmut Mehdorn, is facing the future with confidence. "The world needs printed goods," he says. "No electronic media will kick printing out. Advertising will go on, packaging will go on, newspapers will go on." Mehdorn believes the industry will continue to show decent growth for many years to come — and will certainly outpace most service industries.

Admittedly, a common characteristic of even the most economically significant of the world's mature manufacturing industries is a pattern of declining employment. But this hardly justifies the postindustrialists' portrayal of such industries as "deadbeats," let alone "dinosaurs." Far from being a drag on the overall economy, these industries are actually, on balance, major contributors to economic growth. And it is precisely because they have reduced their labor requirements in recent years that they have done so much to spur growth. Remember that the key to economic growth is to make more with less; in this respect, reducing the labor input per unit of output is even more important than reducing material inputs. These industries' job cuts are simply the flip side of their success in boosting labor productivity.

Of course, this does not gainsay the fact that the dislocation caused by job cuts can be painful. But in a well-managed economy, the effects of such dislocation can be minimized by, for instance, ensuring that most if not all job losses result from attrition rather than layoffs. And as the Japanese experience has repeatedly demonstrated, attrition is a feasible remedy provided that an industry plans sufficiently far head. But even when layoffs are unavoidable, these are generally preferable to the wholesale abandonment of mature industries advocated by the postindustrialists.

The postindustrialists view their slash-and-burn approach to old industries as "creative destruction," but in fact it is far more destructive than creative. Sacrificing a whole industry because it has become a little overstaffed makes no more sense than chopping down a fine apple tree because it has become a little overgrown.

In the rest of this chapter, we will take a detailed look at the hidden virtues of three mature manufacturing industries that are particularly scorned by the postindustrialists — shipbuilding, textiles, and steel. Let's be clear: these industries have their problems, and they are therefore hardly our strongest examples of the merits of manufacturing. Nonetheless, as we will see, the postindustrialists are utterly wrong in advocating the indiscriminate shutdown of such industries.

Sink or swim?: smart shipbuilders make their own luck

Probably no important manufacturing industry has been written off so often as shipbuilding. Predictions of the wholesale demise of the First

World shipbuilding industry have been a commonplace of Western economic discussions since at least as far back as the mid-1970s. Yet nearly a generation later, the First World continues to account for nearly 70 percent of all new tonnage launched each year — and for close to 100 percent of the world market in many of the industry's most sophisticated subsectors.

Those who have taken a bearish view of the industry's prospects have been misled in large part by a long shipbuilding slump in the latter half of the 1970s and the early 1980s. While this slump was painful, it hardly signaled the industry's demise. The problem was merely a huge hangover of excess shipping capacity built up during the hectic boom that preceded the oil crisis of the mid-1970s. It took several years for the resulting shipping capacity glut to clear. But clear it finally did.

In fact, shipbuilders have been enjoying generally rising demand since the 1980s. And for good reason: the world needs ships. Shipping capacity grows in line with world trade, which in turn grows in line with rising living standards, especially in the developing world. Reflecting quickly rising living standards in developing countries, demand has grown particularly in recent decades for bulk carriers to ship key commodities around the world. Measured in terms of the industry's standard tonne/mile yardstick, coal shipments, for instance, have nearly quadrupled since 1970, iron ore shipments have nearly doubled, and grain shipments have increased by about one-half. The result is that, according to figures compiled by *Fearnleys Review,* an Oslo-based shipping publication, the world's shipping fleet has more than doubled since 1970.

Another factor that has encouraged postindustrial commentators to take an overly cautious view of the First World shipbuilding industry has been the rise of low-wage competition. In particular, South Korean shipyards have been remarkably successful in boosting their market share in the last three decades. To the postindustrialists, this is an indication of how far the shipbuilding industry has "fallen" in terms of industrial sophistication in recent years. But the real message is quite different: in reality, South Korea's rise reflects how far that nation has advanced. Thus, the postindustrialists are profoundly wrong in imagining that South Korea's rise presages a general migration of the shipbuilding industry to the Third World. The fact is that South Korea is the only developing country that has had any success in becoming a significant force in shipbuilding in recent decades. That more developing countries have not broken into the industry is hardly surprising given the formidable barriers that would-be entrants face. Just the most obvious barrier is capital. South Korea raised the enormous amounts of capital needed to get established in the industry by enforcing tough economic policies that few other developing nations would dare to impose on their citizens. Another barrier is that the industry requires large amounts of special production know-how. South Korea was lucky in this regard: thanks to various mutually advantageous partnerships with Japanese shipbuilders, it received important transfers of midlevel Japanese production technology.

In any case, the South Koreans' success is actually much exaggerated. They continue to lag in labor productivity, particularly in comparison with the Japanese, who for years have been investing heavily in highly automated production processes. At the big Kure yard near Hiroshima, for instance, no less than sixteen huge robots work tirelessly handling such major assembly operations as fitting and welding. Thanks to investments like this, Japanese shipyard workers are about twice as productive in welding and four times as productive in cutting and painting as their Korean counterparts. Thus, as recounted by the Tokyo-based shipbuilding expert Seiji Nagatsuka, Japanese shipbuilders require only about half as much manpower to build a typical oil tanker as the Koreans. Given that shipbuilding is a capital-intensive industry in which wages account for only one-quarter to one-third of total costs, the Japanese remain highly competitive despite paying wage rates about three times Korean levels.

Aside from superior productivity, another way in which more advanced nations have met the Korean challenge has been by specializing in the more sophisticated subsectors of the industry, where the South Koreans lack the expertise to compete effectively. Several major Japanese shipbuilders, for instance, lead the world in making ships' engines and components for such engines. This is a great business given that the engine can account for as much as 10 percent of the total cost of a ship. The Japanese are also the world's leading source for ship navigation equipment, marine electricity generators, and the superpowerful pumping equipment used in oil tankers.

Meanwhile, various European shipbuilders have withstood the Korean challenge by concentrating on especially sophisticated vessels. Finland has been a standout in this regard as a leading maker of both luxury liners and ice-breakers. European shipbuilders have also become big suppliers of offshore oil-drilling equipment. This has proven to be a lifesaver in particular for Belfast-based Harland and Wolff. After suffering a near-death experience in oil tankers in the 1970s, Harland and Wolff has now gone over completely to building oil rigs and FPSOs (floating production, storage, and offloading vessels). Although the company is a mere shadow of its former self (in its glory days as the world's most advanced shipyard, it built the *Titanic*), it boasts important expertise in various technologies that have enabled the oil industry to drill in ever deeper water. As recently as the 1970s, offshore rigs were rarely capable of operating in water more than two hundred meters deep, but these days FPSOs can operate in fifteen times that depth.

In Japan too, product innovation has been a key strategy in responding successfully to the Korean challenge. Japanese shipyards have led the industry, for instance, in developing liquid natural gas carriers. These are highly sophisticated vessels that require, among other things, advanced refrigeration equipment and super-reliable safety systems. The Japanese have also pioneered the introduction of double-hulled oil tankers, which are designed to minimize the risk of disastrous leaks of oil following collisions and other mishaps.

In common with other Japanese manufacturing industries, the Japanese shipbuilding industry is constantly scanning the horizon for opportunities to create innovative products. Here are some key areas where Japanese shipbuilders have recently been concentrating their research and development spending.

Wave power electricity-generating plants: Under the guidance of the Japanese government, Japanese shipbuilders are developing special vessels that will harness wave power as a new environmentally friendly source of energy. They have already built a working prototype, the *Mighty Whale,* which has demonstrated the idea's viability in certain specialized uses such as powering coastal fish farms and water purification facilities.

Faster ships: Japanese shipbuilding engineers are developing dramatically faster ships that not only offer greater speed for passengers but enable operators to get more work out of their fleets. An early example of Japan's new generation of fast ships is a high-speed car ferry launched by Mitsubishi Heavy Industries in 1997. Built according to a relatively conventional steel-based design, it achieves a top speed of nearly fifty miles an hour and cruises at forty miles an hour. It can thus cut journey times by as much as one-half compared to earlier car ferries. Now Japan's naval architects are leveraging aerodynamic techniques learned from the airplane industry to develop new catamaran-style and hydrofoil vessels that will achieve even greater speeds. A team led by Kawasaki Heavy Industries, for instance, is well advanced with a high-speed cargo ship that will cruise at fifty-eight miles an hour — nearly three times as fast as the most modern conventional cargo vessels. Perhaps the ultimate dream in the high-speed genre is superconductivity-driven ships, which are now being developed as part of a national research project. The aim is to build ships with cruising speeds of one hundred miles an hour or more.

Floating airports: These are being mooted by Japanese shipbuilders as an elegant way to relieve chronic congestion at many of the world's airports. The idea is to create new airports that float in the sea near major coastal cities. These airports would rest on thousands of huge, shallow-bottomed pontoons made from a special new corrosion-resistant type of steel. The pontoons would be locked together to create so-called mega-floats. One key advantage of floating airports is that they can minimize noise pollution by ensuring that takeoffs and landings are routed over water. These airports could be towed to other locations if necessary, and they would save, of course, on land acquisition costs — a crucial consideration for many major East Asian cities that are chronically short of space. They would be invulnerable to earthquakes and, so long as they were not sited in shallow inshore water, to tsunamis. Moreover, variants on the mega-float idea are being promoted as environmentally desirable solutions for siting many other infrastructure facilities such as container berths, oil storage facilities, power-generation plants, and waste disposal facilities.

The message of all this innovation is clear: for all the postindustrialists' gloom, the shipbuilding industry is not only alive and well but likely to remain a key provider of high-wage manufacturing jobs for many years to come. Certainly its record so far has been impressive. Moreover, not only has the shipbuilding industry survived as a First World activity, but it remains particularly strong in precisely those First World nations where wages are highest. Take Denmark. With a per capita income at last count about 19 percent higher than that of the

United States, Denmark boasts one of Europe's largest shipbuilding industries.

Or take Singapore, where per capita income at market exchange rates was recently about 5 percent higher than that in the United States. Singapore's shipbuilding launches as of 1996 totaled 192,000 deadweight tons, an increase of 68 percent in five years and more than *seven times* the American shipbuilding industry's total output. In many ways, Singapore's performance is even more striking compared with that of the United Kingdom, a nation that for historical and geographic reasons has always been a bigger player in shipbuilding than the United States. As of 1996, the British shipbuilding industry's launches trailed those of tiny Singapore by 5,000 deadweight tons. Rubbing salt in the wounds for the British is the fact that wages in Singapore now run nearly 45 percent higher than in the United Kingdom. What a turnaround compared to the early 1950s, when the United Kingdom, then a notably high-wage economy, dominated the world shipbuilding industry and Singapore, then a low-wage British colony, was known mainly for doing repair work for the Royal Navy.

Of course, the real eye-opener for those who maintain that shipbuilding can no longer support First World jobs is Japan. As should be abundantly apparent by now, Japan has doggedly maintained its lead as the world's largest and most successful shipbuilding nation despite paying some of the world's highest wages. The result is that as of 1996 Japanese shipbuilders and their suppliers employed fully 115,000 workers, many of them in such affluent places as Yokohama, Kobe, and Nagasaki.

Few postindustrialists can be more surprised by all this than the noted postindustrialist John Naisbitt, who in his book *Megatrends* predicted that Japan would soon be toppled as the world's dominant shipbuilder by Brazil. That was in 1982. As of the late 1990s Naisbitt has been confounded twice over. First, of course, by the Japanese, who boosted their output by fully 20 percent in the interim and held a global market share of 37 percent at last count. Perhaps even more embarrassing for Naisbitt was Brazil's performance. At last count, Brazil's global market share languished at a mere 0.6 percent.

Evidently the idea that shipbuilding was destined to become a Third World activity was less a megatrend than a megablooper.

A stitch in time: the world's oldest industry invests for tomorrow

The textile industry is probably the world's oldest manufacturing industry. Certainly it can claim to be one of the first industries in which full-scale machines, as opposed to simple tools such as axes and knives, were put to use in boosting human productivity. Both the spinning wheel and the cotton gin, for instance, go back to ancient India. Silk was produced on an industrial scale in China five thousand years ago. And weaving machines were used by the Egyptians even earlier.

As of the late twentieth century, therefore, the textile industry is undeniably mature. But does this mean that the postindustrialists are right to suggest that its glory days as a mainstay of First World employment are over? Hardly. In truth, the postindustrialists' dim view of the textile industry is based on an entirely superficial view of what the industry does. When they think of the textile industry, they consider mainly just one sector — apparel making. Apparel making is, of course, a highly labor-intensive activity that requires little or no proprietary production know-how. Thus, it is now, for understandable reasons, migrating rapidly to lower-wage nations.

What the postindustrialists forget is that apparel making is only the final stage in a series of production processes and as such accounts for a relatively small proportion of the textile industry's total value added. Many of the industry's earlier stages, such as spinning and weaving, are much more economically sophisticated. And before these stages, there is an even more sophisticated stage — the production of the many advanced machines used these days to make the world's fabrics and apparel. Thus, when we take a broader view of the textile industry, we find plenty of activities that require large amounts of both capital and proprietary know-how and as such provide numerous secure and well-paid First World jobs.

Of course, it has to be admitted that the textile industry is not a fast-growing one. But even in this respect, it has more to offer than the postindustrialists give it credit for. As the top Japanese textile executive Hidetane Iijima has pointed out, viewed in global terms, textile making remains a growth industry. After all, most people wear clothes most of the time, and with rising populations, there are more people to clothe every year. This helps explain, for instance, why many subsectors of the industry have shown strong growth in recent years. In the synthetics industry, for instance, output has more than tripled since 1970. Nor is the synthetics story merely one of rising volumes: many of the world's textile makers have boosted their revenues by moving into the production of higher-quality fibers and fabrics as consumers become more affluent. The industry's growth has been further spurred by constant product innovation, which has taken textile makers way beyond clothes and even household furnishings into highly innovative new product categories.

All this helps explain why the big players in the world synthetics industry are such advanced companies as Hoechst of Germany and Toray of Japan, not to mention Milliken & Company and Du Pont of the United States. Admittedly, some developing nations have also entered the business lately. Taiwan in particular has done so successfully, but that is hardly an indication that the entire synthetics business is migrating to the Third World. Quite the reverse: as with the rise of South Korea in shipbuilding, the real significance of Taiwan's emergence in synthetics is that Taiwan is rapidly converging on First World standards of industrial sophistication. Certainly Taiwan can no longer be considered a low-wage economy. Thanks to three decades of breakneck growth in which its per capita income increased thirty-three-fold, its wage levels have now drawn level with those of several member nations of the European Union.

One thing is clear: the synthetics business generally requires First World levels of investment. Billions of dollars of capital have been invested in polyester alone in recent years, and the result is that manufacturers have reaped an abundant harvest in booming sales of advanced new forms of polyester fiber. Using the latest production technologies, leading manufacturers can now make polyester in weights as low as 0.7 dpf (deniers per foot — the standard measure of fineness in the textile business), which is finer than silk. By contrast, as recently as the 1970s even the best manufacturers failed to achieve a fineness much better than 5 dpf, which resulted in a thick, unsupple fiber that became notorious for its uncomfortable texture and dowdy appearance.

According to Martha M. Hamilton, writing in the *Washington Post,* textile mills and yarn spinners in the United States alone have been investing more than $2 billion a year in upgrading equipment as demand for polyester has increased. But the really big capital spending programs have been in Japan, where major textile companies like Toray now derive as much as one-fifth of their sales revenues from new forms of polyester. The Japanese have been highly successful in developing *shingosen* versions of polyester endowed with special properties that have suddenly made them favorites with the world's fashion designers. The result is a proliferation of amazing new fabrics. As reported by Gale Eisenstodt of *Forbes*, some *shingosen* fabrics have a feel similar to wool gabardine, others have a surface like peach skin, and still others resemble a blend of silk and linen.

Moreover, polyester boasts practical advantages for the textile industry in that its enormous strength has paved the way for the use of advanced production equipment such as new, ultra-fast looms of the sort pioneered in the United States by Milliken & Company. And though polyester's ability to keep its shape is not to everyone's taste, it is a boon for many consumers. Polyester is, for instance, the key ingredient in many of the most modern versions of no-iron shirts.

The higher grades of polyester are increasingly seen not as a substitute for, or supplement to, natural fibers, but as fibers that can stand on their own merits and are in many ways superior to natural fibers. In fact, some of the new fibers are so stylish that women's jackets made from 100 percent polyester can be sold for more than $1,000.

As the Du Pont marketing executive Jeff McGuire points out, polyester's great advantage is the same feature for which it has been reviled in the past: it is plastic. "With a man-made fiber, you can custom-make the fiber to get a different aesthetic," he says. "You can't reengineer cotton or wool."

If the synthetics industry's success were confined to apparel, it would be significant enough. But the industry has also been developing many markets far removed from apparel. Take, for instance, the rapidly growing use of new types of high-strength nylon in car airbags and tires. This market has been successfully targeted by, among others, Solutia Corporation, a new company formed in 1997 as a spin-off of Monsanto Corporation's textile interests. Using the latest production technology licensed from Japan, Solutia operates a notably advanced nylon facility in South Carolina serving the automobile industry.

In their search for new markets, some textile companies have ventured even further afield. The Dutch giant Akzo Nobel, for instance, has developed a lucrative business making membranes for such high-tech medical applications as blood oxygenation and hemodialysis.

Interestingly, Akzo Nobel makes its membranes at Wuppertal, in Germany's high-wage Ruhr Valley. Moreover, its factory there is the successor to a textile-dyeing business founded in the eighteenth century. There could hardly be a more persuasive illustration of the fact that an old industry *can* keep reinventing itself — and in the process continue to support a wide range of well-paid First World jobs.

Nor is Akzo Nobel alone in choosing to locate its membrane business in an advanced First World nation. Its Paris-based rival, Rhône-Poulenc, makes membranes in Switzerland. Given that Rhône-Poulenc operates in more than 160 countries, it could easily have located its membrane operation somewhere with lower wages. So why Switzerland? Part of the answer undoubtedly is that because membrane-making is a high-tech business requiring both large amounts of know-how and capital, factory wages represent only a small proportion of total costs. By locating its production in Switzerland, Rhône-Poulenc suffers only a relatively small disadvantage in higher wage costs — a disadvantage that is more than offset by such key Swiss advantages as high-quality labor and a generally superb industrial infrastructure.

Among the many advanced products into which the textile industry has diversified in recent years, probably none has been more technologically challenging than carbon fiber. The manufacturing process starts with polyacrylonitrile fibers, which are similar to the synthetic fibers widely used in the knitwear industry. These are first carbonized and then wound into filaments. Simple though this series of steps may seem, high-quality carbon fiber has proven extremely difficult to produce in volume — so much so that, as the industry has moved to ever higher levels of production technology in recent decades, many weaker players have fallen by the wayside. The manufacture of this key material has thus become more and more concentrated in the hands of a few ultra-advanced Japanese textile manufacturers that have invested billions of dollars in constantly improving their production technologies. As of the late 1990s, it was clear that this investment had paid off. With vital applications in everything from sports goods to aircraft components, carbon fiber is one of the world's fastest-growing high-tech materials. Even Boeing must buy its carbon fiber from high-wage Japan because no other nation can make the material to the appropriate specifications.

So much for fibers. Now let's look at the machinery side of the textiles business, which, as already mentioned, is particularly sophisticated and therefore a superb source of First World jobs in countries like Japan, Germany, and Switzerland.

The story of the rise of the Swiss textile equipment industry is particularly instructive. Boasting a reputed global market share of 31 percent in 1997, the Swiss claim to be the world's largest suppliers of textile equipment. As reported by Peter Marsh of the *Financial Times*, this means that Swiss companies more than doubled their share of the textile equipment market in just ten years. Admittedly, much of their expansion has come not through internal growth but rather through takeovers of foreign rivals. But far from undermining jobs at home, this expansion has probably strengthened them. For one thing, the newly acquired foreign operations provide the home factories in Switzerland with new markets for advanced components and subassemblies. And in any case, the Swiss have little incentive to move domestic jobs to foreign subsidiaries because most of these subsidiaries are located in other notably high-wage countries. Take the big Swiss weaving equipment maker Sulzer Ruti. Besides Switzerland, it manufactures in only two other countries — Japan and Germany. Meanwhile, the leading Swiss-based maker of spinning machinery, Rieter, does most of its foreign production in places like the United States and Germany.

Why has the Swiss industry been so successful? For a start, it boasts a long tradition of technical expertise. Rieter, for instance, has been making spinning equipment since the early 1800s. Admittedly, as the precipitate decline of both the British and American textile equipment industries has demonstrated, long experience alone is hardly sufficient in an industry as sophisticated as this one. Thus, we have to look elsewhere for the decisive factors in Switzerland's success.

Investment has clearly been one such factor. Where investment is concerned, the Swiss tend to reserve the lion's share for the home factories. At Rieter, for instance, although only 35 percent of the workers are employed in Switzerland, its home textile equipment operations consume nearly half of all its capital spending.

High levels of spending on research and development have also been a crucial factor in Switzerland's success. As of the late 1990s, Saurer Gruppe, a Swiss-based maker of spinning and twisting equipment, was investing fully 6 percent of its sales in R&D. Spending on this scale helps explain why Saurer is constantly launching new products — to the point where as of 1999 about 80 percent of its sales revenues were coming from machines launched in the previous two years. One key objective has been to redesign its machines to minimize the number of parts. In some of its ring-spinning machines, for instance, it has reduced the part count by as much as 45 percent. This has not only helped streamline Saurer's manufacturing processes but rendered its machines both more reliable and easier to maintain. Thus, Saurer's Germany-based Zinser division is now the market leader in ring-spinning equipment, ahead of Swiss rival Rieter and Japan's Toyoda. Meanwhile, in winding machines, the company's Schlafhorst division boasts a market share of 30 percent, putting it second only to Japan's Murata, with 40 percent of the market. Perhaps the sweetest news of all is that Schlafhorst's open-end spinning machines boast a world market share of 60 percent. At Sulzer Ruti, too, research and development has been a major factor in the company's success. Particularly owing to the introduction of air-jet technology in the 1970s, Sulzer Ruti claims to have boosted the operational efficiency of its machines by 300 percent.

The bottom line for our purposes is that the Swiss textile equipment industry employed about 10,000 workers as of 1998 in Switzerland alone, not to mention another 15,000 overseas. In view of the fact that not only are Swiss wages among the world's highest but virtually all of Switzerland's textile equipment is exported, there could hardly be a clearer demonstration of the enduring strengths of manufacturing.

Moreover, for its customers in the wider textile industry, Switzerland's success in building ever more reliable and more productive textile equipment has been a key reason why many of the world's most advanced spinning and weaving companies continue to employ thousands of well-paid workers throughout the First World.

Clearly the textile industry has come a long way in the last several thou- sand years. But one thing has not changed: it is still a business in which the leading nations of the day can compete to win.

Steel: a "sunset" industry on which the sun never sets

Steel, our third golden oldie, is the classic of the genre. Almost universally scorned by the postindustrialists, steel is widely considered to represent the very antithesis of all the promise of the information economy. In particular, steel is regarded as facing notably poor growth prospects in the developed world. On the face of it, this view seems to be well grounded in the facts. After all, steel output has been stagnant in most developed nations in the 1990s. Thus, despite strong growth in certain developing countries — notably China — the world's total output of steel fell by 4 percent in the first seven years of the 1990s.

But there is less to the steel industry's stagnation than meets the eye — much less. For a start, the global output figures have been distorted by the collapse of the old Soviet Union, which has resulted in widespread industrial disruption in many Eastern European countries. If Eastern European production cuts are excluded, we find that global output actually increased by about 10 percent in the period. Even in the First World, the picture of apparent stagnation is far less serious than it appears. For one thing, much of the sluggishness has resulted from a unique factor that now seems to have largely run its course — a regulation-driven effort to reduce car weights. This spurred a secular move by carmakers to use plastics and aluminum instead of steel in many applications, but the steel industry is now fighting back vigorously by investing in new ways to improve steel's strength-to-weight ratio. In particular, thirty-five of the world's top steelmakers are cooperating in the ULSAB (ultra light steel auto body) research program, which is being undertaken jointly with the world automobile industry. The program's aim is to come up with ways of increasing steel's strength-to-weight ratio to improve its competitiveness vis-à-vis plastics and aluminum.

The effort to develop better steel for the car industry is an example of a general trend among the world's most advanced steelmakers to compensate for stagnant *volume* by raising the *quality* of their output — a strategy that has helped keep unit prices rising buoyantly. Thus, even in the most developed nations the picture of stagnating volume conceals a much less disturbing underlying trend in sales revenues.

At the end of the day, therefore, we find that the steel industry supports thousands of notably well-paid jobs in some of the world's richest nations. Take the United States. Even after years of closing outdated steel mills, the United States remains one of the world's biggest steel producers and produces more steel per capita than, for instance, lower-wage Britain. A significant correlation between high steel output and high wages is also observable in other rich nations, such as Germany, Switzerland, Sweden, Austria, and Belgium.

Nowhere is this correlation exemplified more spectacularly than in tiny Luxembourg, whose ARBED steel company now produces more steel than USX-U.S. Steel. In fact, steel accounts for nearly one-quarter of the principality's total exports. Given that Luxembourg recently boasted the world's second-highest per capita income after Switzerland, this would certainly seem to give the lie to the idea that steel is a low-wage industry.

If further proof is needed that the steel industry has a future in the developed world, it lies in the high levels of investment apparent at many of the world's leading steelmakers. In Japan, for instance, in the first six years of the 1990s alone, steelmakers invested ¥5.4 trillion — or about $48 billion. They were thus investing at about three times the rate of their American counterparts, a fact that helps explain why, even though wages are now much higher in Japan than in the United States, the United States has continued even in the 1990s to import huge amounts of steel from Japan. (Japanese dumping, of course, helps explain some of the U.S. imports — but this is significant only in the case of a few kinds of steel.)

All this is not to suggest that everything in the garden is rosy. Certainly steel is hardly the most persuasive example of the strengths of manufacturing. It is, of course, notorious for cutting jobs. In the United States alone, the industry has cut its workforce by close to one-half since 1980. And the cuts have been even more severe in the United Kingdom and France. Given the industry's job-cutting record, it would be natural to conclude that the industry is a loser. Natural — but wrong.

The truth is that the industry's tendency to cut jobs is the flip side of its greatest success — the enormous progress it has made in raising labor productivity in the last fifty years. The key to this progress has been heavy investment in new production technologies. As the economic commentator Robert Kuttner has pointed out, steel is a classic example of a supposed "sunset" industry that in reality boasts some highly advanced technologies.

The industry's progress has been driven in large part by innovations in the blast-furnace method of producing steel, which is used almost universally in the world's largest steel mills. Blast-furnace productivity has been dramatically boosted in the last fifty years by the adoption of the basic-oxygen process. This process, invented by a state-owned Austrian steel mill, involves pumping vast amounts of oxygen at supersonic speed into the furnace to boost heat levels, thereby drastically speeding production. The basic-oxygen process in turn was made possible by earlier breakthroughs in the chemical industry that dramatically reduced the price of industrial oxygen.

Steel industry productivity has also received a strong boost from the introduction of continuous casting, an energy-saving process in which steel billets are produced in a single step. This replaced a wasteful two-step process in which the metal had to be heated twice over.

The Japanese have been among the earliest to exploit both basic-oxygen furnaces and continuous casting, and as a result they have not only cut their unit labor costs by 90 percent in the last five decades but achieved reductions of up to 50 percent in their energy consumption. All this helps explain why Japan has multiplied its steel output twentyfold in the last five decades — and in the process has gone from an obscure also-ran to the world's largest steel exporter.

A very different production process figures in another part of the steel industry's spectacular story of rising productivity — the electric-arc process. In contrast to the blast-furnace method, scrap iron rather than iron ore is generally the major input in this process. One key benefit of the electric-arc process is that it uses much less energy. It also provides a convenient way to recycle vast amounts of scrap metal that would otherwise represent a major environmental problem. Moreover, since it uses electricity rather than coke as the heating agent, it cuts down on the notorious levels of noxious emissions entailed in steelmaking.

Beyond these advantages, electric-arc furnaces offer a chance to achieve ultra-high levels of labor productivity, as the rise of the North Carolina–based Nucor Corporation has spectacularly demonstrated. Nucor's proudest boast is that it pays some of the world's highest blue-collar wages while achieving unit labor costs that are among the world's lowest. Powered by leading-edge electric-arc furnace production technology, it has multiplied sales revenues 180 times in thirty years. Boasting an annual output of 1,273 tons per worker — or about double the steel output per worker at a blast-furnace operator like USX-U.S. Steel — Nucor has never laid off a single employee, let alone shut a plant.

Since scrap is expensive to transport, electric-arc furnaces are at their best operating on a small scale and using whatever scrap can be sourced locally. Their small scale is an advantage in that they can be operated more flexibly than blast furnaces and in particular their output can be fine-tuned to take advantage of short-term changes in demand for different kinds of steel.

All in all, the electric-arc method has been tremendously successful. As of the early 1990s, the electricity required to produce a ton of steel by this method had been cut to just 400 kilowatt-hours — down from as much as 635 kilowatt-hours in 1965.

So successful has the electric-arc method been that by the mid-1990s demand from mini-mills had pushed scrap prices to record levels in many nations. In fact, a growing shortage of scrap is now powering a leap to a new variant on the technology using specially preprocessed iron ore known as DRI (direct reduced iron).

Even with the blast-furnace method under pressure from environmentalists and the mini-mill business increasingly constrained by scrap shortages, the industry expects to continue to increase output quite substantially in the years ahead with the help of DRI-fed electric-arc furnaces and other innovations. According to one European expert, the global industry's output in 2010 will exceed 980 million tons — an increase of more than 30 percent over 1996's 750 million tons.

Besides improving productivity, steelmakers in the world's most advanced nations have also been making dramatic improvements in the quality of their products in recent years. In particular, they have been developing stronger steels for a variety of applications from car engine parts and radial tires to machine tools and precision equipment. They have also developed new varieties of steel with special properties that, for instance, improve the efficiency of electric motors, generators, and other electrical devices. Other new steels are designed to damp down vibration and, by extension, noise. They have important applications in everything from motorcycles and washing machines to fan heaters and photocopiers.

Beyond improving their products, some of the world's most aggressive steelmakers are also developing new markets for steel. The Japanese, for instance, have been leading the development of lightweight forms of galvanized steel to replace traditional two-by-four lumber in house-building. Steel's advantages include not only low cost but resistance to fires and earthquakes. And given that a typical wood-framed house consumes nearly forty trees, steel-frame housing is also being promoted as an environmentally friendly alternative that saves the world's forests. Japanese steelmakers are also finding new markets for especially strong, weldable steel for skyscrapers. Nippon Steel has suggested that such steel may soon enable the construction industry to build buildings as high as three hundred floors — or nearly three times the height of Chicago's Sears Tower.

Another key growth strategy for many of the world's top steel companies has been to supply steelmaking equipment to other steelmakers around the world. Austria's Voest-Alpine, for instance, is a big maker of continuous casting equipment. The Demag subsidiary of the big German steelmaker Mannesmann makes both rolling mills and continuous casting equipment. In Japan, Kobe Steel leads in DRI equipment, Nippon Steel makes mini-mill equipment, and NKK makes both mini-mill equipment and advanced, environmentally friendly coke-making equipment.

One thing is clear: the equipment business is one of the steel industry's brightest areas of growth. All postindustrial talk to the contrary, the world desperately needs more steelmaking capacity if residents of the developing world are ever to approach Western-style living standards. China alone represents a huge market for equipment — a point that is obvious when we remember that China will need to boost its steel output to a colossal 800 million tons a year if it is ever to match Japanese output levels on a per capita basis. At that point, China's output would be more than that of the entire global industry as of the late 1990s.

All this growth is driven by a fundamental factor too often overlooked by the postindustrialists: steel is a great material. It is notably easy to work and shape. And in its various forms, its hardness and tensile strength are highly useful to the human race. It also boasts valuable electrical and thermal properties. Best of all, it is extremely inexpensive thanks to the abundance of iron ore in many parts of the world. (Constituting 5.1 percent of the earth's crust, iron ore is the fourth most abundant element after oxygen, silicon, and aluminum.)

No wonder the president of Nippon Steel, Akira Chihaya, recently commented: "Steel has been and will remain a basic material in our lives. The steel industry is not only alive and well in the information society but can be expected to continue expanding."

Let's now take a look at a specific example of a leading-edge First World steel mill and see how it illustrates this chapter's main message — that an old and apparently terminally troubled industry still has plenty of potential to create superb First World jobs.

Sumitomo: pipe maker to the world

For visitors to Sumitomo Metal Industries' new pipe-making works three hundred miles west of Tokyo, the first impression is of a typical rust-belt operation. The pipe works is one unit buried deep within a huge fifty-year-old steelmaking complex that positively fills the landscape on the outskirts of Wakayama City.

From the main gate, you are taken by chauffeur-driven limousine on a meandering one-and-a-half-mile journey through a maze of machine-age towers, vents, and cranes. But on arrival at the new pipe works, you are suddenly fast-forwarded into the robot age. Viewing the production process from a gangway high above the works floor, you immediately notice that the plant is fully automated. So much so in fact that the works floor is normally completely devoid of labor. And what a works floor it is: measuring 850 yards long, 110 yards wide, and 30 yards high, it is equal to the area of about ten soccer fields.

The day this writer visited happened to be exceptional in that a single tiny human figure was just visible amid the plant's vast sea of clattering and hissing machines — a maintenance engineer who, clipboard in hand, was checking on one of the vast machines.

The only other humans to be seen anywhere were five blue-collar workers watching computer monitors in a quiet, glass-enclosed aerie perched well above the works floor. The glass shields these workers from one of the noisiest environments imaginable. The main production process involves taking solid cylinders of orange-red steel and then hollowing them out in a single swift and deafening ramming action. The cylinders, measuring about one foot in diameter and as much as ten feet in length, are tossed around like so many drum majorettes' batons as they are prepared and positioned for the ramming process. Even on a cold November day, the glow from each cylinder as it passed at a distance of fifty feet away recalled the reflected heat from a city sidewalk in August.

The only disappointment is that the end-products of all this twenty-first-century industrial magic seem pretty unremarkable: to the nontechnical eye, after all, pipes are merely pipes. But in the eyes of pipe users, Sumitomo pipes are to other pipes what Rolls-Royces are to other cars — the best. Measuring as much as sixteen inches in diameter in finished form, they are destined to be used in applications where extreme strength and reliability are critically important. A key market is in the world oil industry, where their unrivaled ability to withstand high pressures and corrosive chemicals is now enabling oil producers to develop wells in ever more hostile and remote environments.

One key to the reliability of Sumitomo's pipes is their extreme smoothness. They are almost entirely free of the surface blemishes that can greatly weaken other pipes after prolonged exposure to hostile conditions. Sumitomo's pipes, moreover, are made in lengths of up to forty-four feet, about 20 percent longer than those of most of its rivals. Again, to a nontechnical observer this feature seems unremarkable, but as the Sumitomo general manager, Takeshi Kirimoto, points out, pipelines made from longer pipes require less welding — a key saving given how expensive it can be to deploy expert welders in remotely situated oil fields.

It is not surprising, therefore, that Sumitomo's pipes fetch notably high prices. Whereas ordinary steel pipes sell for about $800 per metric ton, Sumitomo's products typically sell for about $1,350 — and some, such as ultra-high-performance pipes containing 13 percent chromium, fetch much more. One thing is clear: Sumitomo is having no difficulty getting its prices. In fact, demand has been so strong that the plant has been working around the clock since it opened.

All this adds up to a superb business that makes a strong contribution to the health of the Japanese economy. For a start, the plant exports about half of its total output. Surprisingly perhaps, given its high degree of automation, the plant has also created a plethora of excellent jobs. In addition to the five men in the control room, about 1,500 employees work four shifts a day behind the scenes in maintenance, inventory management, and other support functions. Best of all, with about 60 percent of its workers being high-school graduates, the plant has clearly created a well-balanced range of jobs.

Moreover, these jobs look highly secure for as far ahead as anyone can see. The point is that the plant cost $700 million; thus, each job is backed by nearly $470,000 of capital on average. The plant is also very knowledge-intensive. Its production is based on a new process that has been in development since the 1960s. Sumitomo reckons that the new process achieves about 30 percent more output per worker than the well-known Mannesmann process, which hitherto has been the world steel industry's standard method of making high-quality pipes.

The bottom line on Wakayama is this: with bonuses, an ordinary forty-five-year-old blue-collar worker earns about $65,000 a year. This is three times what some of India's most brilliant minds earn writing world-class software in Bangalore.

Having satisfied ourselves that even old and troubled industries can play a surprisingly strong role in the world economy as we enter the twenty-first century, let's now move to the other end of the manufacturing industry spectrum and look at the exciting prospects that await us in new manufacturing industries now just ready to take off.

7

The Future:
An Expanding Universe

What of the future of manufacturing? Almost without exception, economic commentators are gloomy about the prospects. Somehow it has become conventional wisdom that most of the world's manufacturing industries are fated at best to grow only slowly in coming decades. To the commentators, it seems that the world's manufacturing industries are so glutted with overcapacity that there is simply not enough purchasing power to buy all the goods that could be made. One such commentator is William Greider, whose gloomy articulation of this view in his book *One World, Ready or Not* was widely discussed in the American media in 1997.

But the truth is that the gloomsters could hardly be more wrong. As we will see in this chapter, it is absurd to suggest that the world's manufacturing industries are suffering from a general glut of capacity. In the twenty-first century, as in the past, the world's consumers will be more than happy to increase their consumption as fast as their budgets allow, and thus they will provide a ready market for all the merchandisable goods that can be made. Moreover, they will increasingly insist that these goods be made in the most environmentally friendly ways possible. All of this adds up to a historic challenge for the world's leading manufacturers — and a historic opportunity.

Unlimited horizons: the challenge of the developing world

One key growth opportunity for great manufacturers lies in the developing world. This point has been memorably made by the leading Japanese industrialist Akio Morita in *Made in Japan,* a book he wrote with Edwin M. Reingold and Mitsuko Shimomura. Morita believes that as manufacturers continue to boost their production efficiency they can hope to bring prosperity to more and more of the world's poorer regions. This view has been a factor in his thinking ever since the early 1960s, when his Sony Corporation first broke through in a big way in world markets.

> It seemed to me at the time that with two-thirds of the world's population living at a very low economic level, the developed world had a responsibility and opportunity to help them into a higher economic sphere, which would be a benefit to everyone. . . . I am reminded of the story of two shoe salesmen who visited an underdeveloped country. One cabled his office, "NO PROSPECT OF SALES BECAUSE NOBODY HERE WEARS SHOES." The other salesman cabled, "SEND STOCK IMMEDIATELY — INHABITANTS BAREFOOTED — DESPERATELY NEED SHOES."

Morita's point is that developing economies can be viewed two ways — optimistically or pessimistically. And Morita himself is a convinced optimist. His ebullient message is that manufacturers will never lack for exciting new challenges while so many of the developing world's people have yet to attain the basics of a Western consumer lifestyle.

This message should not come as a surprise to us. In fact, the whole history of the world's progress toward ever increasing prosperity bears out Morita's optimistic view. Remember that every market started with barefooted customers. Little more than two centuries ago, even today's most advanced nations were probably no richer than most of the present-day Third World. The fact that these nations have in the interim achieved steadily increasing incomes is a tribute to the enormous progress manufacturers have made over the years in boosting their efficiency and thereby both increasing their output and making their products affordable to an ever expanding range of consumers.

Even in recent decades the speed with which manufacturers have spread prosperity further into previously poor parts of the world has been spectacular. According to Care International, the proportion of the world's people who live in absolute poverty has fallen from 70 percent to 30 percent in just the last three decades.

Of course, Morita's story is intended as a parable, and as such it somewhat oversimplifies the process by which the First World can benefit from growth in the developing world. In reality, the First World sells few shoes to emerging nations. Instead, it sells such nations *the means to make shoes for themselves.* Specifically, it sells them shoe manufacturing equipment. And the First World's increasing efficiency in making shoe manufacturing equipment has enabled local shoe manufacturers in the developing world to achieve big increases in output, thus making their products affordable to more and more people. Hence, people in formerly barefoot nations such as South Korea and Taiwan are now as well shod as people in the West.

The point is that the First World's role in fostering the prosperity of poorer nations is to provide producers' goods, not consumer goods. The First World also enjoys fine opportunities to sell the emerging economies all sorts of sophisticated infrastructural equipment, such as power-generation plant, telecommunications systems, earth-moving equipment, oil refineries, railroad locomotives, ships, and aircraft.

Clearly, for the First World suppliers of such goods, the potential for future sales growth is almost limitless. That being so, why do so many Western commentators imagine that the future world economy will be dogged by an increasingly severe glut of manufacturing capacity? These commentators fail to realize that an economy is a highly dynamic instrument that adjusts constantly to the changing balance between supply and demand. This dynamism is apparent in the way that demand increases rapidly in newly industrializing nations. The gloomsters forget that when the workers of any particular nation approach First World standards in their manufacturing efficiency, they almost automatically acquire the purchasing power to make a commensurate increase in their consumption. This increased purchasing power enables them either to buy the products they make or to buy imported goods paid for by exporting such products. Either way, for the world's consumption to increase in step with rising production capacity, all that is needed is for governments to maintain reasonably intelligent demand-management policies.

One factor that powerfully contributes to the false impression that the future global economy will be permanently paralyzed by a dearth of purchasing power is that many emerging economies save much of their income. Thus, in the short run, consumer demand in these nations consistently seems to Westerners to be lower than it "should" be. But the gloomsters overlook the fact that to forgo consumption today is not necessarily to forgo it forever. To the extent that these nations save more today, they will assuredly consume more later — because their high savings rates can be counted on to accelerate the speed at which they will become rich. In any case — and this is the crucial point — the high savings rates of these nations today in no way diminish the First World's immediate export prospects. Quite the reverse: because these nations are saving so much, they represent major markets for *investment goods* such as factory machinery, construction equipment, electricity-generating plant, telecommunications equipment, and a host of other sophisticated machinery — precisely the sort of manufactured products that do the most to sustain the prosperity of the world's most sophisticated economies.

One thing is certain: many emerging nations will become rich much sooner than almost anyone in the West anticipates. Even more important than capital, education is a key driver of growth in such nations. With literacy now spreading rapidly in many parts of the Second and Third Worlds, previously poor nations have suddenly acquired an unprecedented capacity to absorb efficient new production technologies from richer nations. As the noted Hong Kong–based investment manager J. Mark Mobius has pointed out, Indonesia is a prime example. Sixty years ago, only one in ten Indonesians could read; now well over 60 percent can do so. Moreover, better communications are accelerating the speed with which emerging economies absorb new production technologies. Thus, in common with most other seasoned observers in the East Asian region, Mobius believes that the East Asian financial crisis of 1997–98 will prove to have been little more than an isolated air pocket with negligible consequences for the region's long-term prosperity. In that sense, the crisis closely resembles the financial panics that periodically afflicted the United States in the latter half of the nineteenth century. This was a period when fast-expanding industries like steel often suffered devastating bouts of overcapacity as entrepreneurs like Andrew Carnegie got ahead of themselves in their soaring optimism about the future. Yet this optimism was vindicated by later recoveries that carried the United States to successively higher levels of prosperity.

Thus, although the East Asian crisis undoubtedly uncovered examples of large-scale temporary overcapacity in various industries, the likely postscript is that the recovery of such industries will be even more exuberant than the recoveries enjoyed by the United States in its era of fastest growth.

The key point here is that the process of industrialization is becoming easier all the time as the technologies available to each successive emerging economy become more efficient and easier to use. Hence, each newly industrializing nation achieves developed-country status faster than its predecessors. As the first nation to industrialize, the United Kingdom took fully fifty-eight years to double its output; the United States took forty-seven years, and Japan just thirty-four years. These days, as China's recent growth has demonstrated, this feat can be performed in as little as ten years. And, on Mobius's predictions, other emerging nations may soon beat even China's record.

All in all, the developing world is clearly set to grow at a fast pace in the years ahead — and for the First World's most advanced manufacturers, this growth will bring an embarrassment of export opportunities.

Opportunities nearer home

Even in the world's richest nations, the idea that there is any general glut of manufacturing capacity is clearly absurd. The reality is that most citizens of the advanced world still have plenty of obvious unsatisfied needs — needs that they would be delighted to satisfy if only they could afford to. Thus, the only thing that stands in the way of even greater consumption in the advanced world is the ability of manufacturers to achieve further reductions in their production costs — reductions that would make their products affordable to a wider range of First World consumers.

The potential for further increases in consumption in the First World is particularly obvious in the case of the 10 to 20 percent of the First World's population who live below the poverty line. But few even among the First World's better-off residents feel as affluent as they would like. Certainly in an era of keeping up with the Joneses, they can think of a long list of material goods that are still beyond their means — a better car, a new living room suite, a second home, a remodeled kitchen, a sailboat. . . . The list is almost endless, and it will keep the world's manufacturers busy for many years to come.

As if this were not enough, the world's manufacturers will also be called on to manufacture many new kinds of goods that have not yet even been invented. Leadership in such innovative products has long represented one of the main sources of high-quality manufacturing jobs for advanced economies, and there is no reason to expect this to change in the twenty-first century. That said, innovation is constantly underestimated as a source of economic growth and employment. By definition, it is difficult to predict the exact nature of future inventions. But the point, for our purposes, is that history is on our side in suggesting that the future contributions of new inventions will prove of far greater economic importance than anyone currently expects. Certainly all past evidence indicates that the market potential for revolutionary new products and technologies has consistently been underestimated even by the supposedly best-informed experts.

Take the telephone. It seems amazing now, but when Alexander Graham Bell unveiled this epoch-making invention to the world, few even in the telecommunications industry understood its enormous market potential. Executives of Western Union, for instance, were so unimpressed that they turned down Bell's offer to sell his patents for a mere $100,000 — an amount that within a few years seemed like a pittance in comparison to the device's explosive growth. Western Union's attitude reflected a general view in the American telegraph industry that the new talking device was merely a "toy." In the British telegraph industry too, the experts were notably skeptical. Speaking in the British House of Commons in 1879, Sir William Preece, a top British telegraph executive, said of the telephone: "I fancy the descriptions we get of its use in America are a little exaggerated, though there are conditions in America which necessitate the use of such instruments more than here. Here we have a superabundance of messengers."

Here are instances of other inventions whose epochal economic significance at first went unrecognized:

Computers: When computers were first used in World War II, most experts viewed computing as a military technology that would have few peacetime uses. Even top executives of IBM were reputedly highly skeptical about the prospects for computers.

Transistors: Experts initially believed that applications for transistors would be confined largely to a narrow range of special devices, such as hearing aids, where the advantages of miniaturization were particularly obvious. The general lack of excitement was reflected in the *New York Times*'s decision to give the first report of the invention just four column-inches at the bottom of page 46 (below an item about *Waltz Time,* an NBC radio show that enjoyed some modest prominence at the time).

Copiers: After a tiny company called Haloid invented a plain-paper copier in 1959, it invited several major manufacturing corporations to help it develop the idea — but met with a wall of yawning ennui. Studying the idea on behalf of a major corporate client, the consulting firm Arthur D. Little dismissed plain-paper copying as a narrow niche unworthy of the attention of a large corporation. In the end, after running out of other options, tiny Haloid went it alone and quickly proved the skeptics wrong. So much so that, under its new name of the Xerox Corporation, Haloid went on to become one of the fastest-growing manufacturers of the mid-twentieth century.

Lasers: The laser was originally so underappreciated that even patent lawyers at Bell Laboratories, where the device was invented in the 1950s, wondered whether it was worth patenting. In truth, of course, lasers were soon to become one of the key enabling technologies in a host of advanced industries, not least in Ma Bell's own heartland of telecommunications.

Microprocessors: When the microprocessor was invented in 1970, its potential to revolutionize the computer industry was widely overlooked. Industry experts imagined that the computer industry would buy no more than 2,000 microprocessors annually. Even Intel, which invented the device and went on to make huge profits from it, was slow to recognize the potential and initially concentrated on selling microprocessors to makers of such minor products as pocket calculators, vending machines, and cash registers.

Countless other similar instances could be cited of great new manufacturing opportunities that were unrecognized at first — but the point is already clear. Even industry experts rarely have the vision to see more than a few years ahead in anticipating the often huge economic consequences of new products and manufacturing technologies. We should not be too hard on them: caution is generally prudent at the outset because there are usually enormous production engineering challenges to be overcome before an invention can be turned into a low-cost mass-market product. Of course, time and again, engineers subsequently succeed in achieving huge reductions in production costs, but these reductions are by no means guaranteed and cannot be taken for granted at the outset.

Moreover, it is precisely the most innovative products — in particular those that cater to hitherto unmet human needs — that are the most difficult for early observers to evaluate accurately. As the science writer Robert Pool has pointed out in his book *Beyond Engineering,* it takes more imagination than most people possess to recognize an unmet human need and to realize that a particular invention will satisfy it.

How far ahead into the future can we assume that innovation will continue to deliver exciting new manufacturing opportunities? Actually, the potential for innovation to power future growth in manufacturing is almost unlimited. In the future, as in the past, the font of manufacturing progress will be science, a font that humans are only beginning to exploit. As the iconoclastic young Stanford University economist Paul Romer has pointed out, the world has as yet hardly even scratched the surface in exploring science's secrets. Writing in *Time* magazine in 1998, he points out that only a tiny fraction of all the materials that will play an important economic role in the future have so far been discovered.

He poses the question: "Suppose you gave a child a chemistry set containing sixty different chemicals from the Periodic Table. How many distinct mixtures could she make?"

The amazing answer: 100 billion billion mixtures.

As Romer acknowledges, many of these mixtures would prove to be "boring." But others would be highly exciting. He adds:

Humans are adept at converting low-value raw materials into high-value mixtures. This is in fact the essence of economic growth. First we find new recipes for mixtures that are more valuable than their ingredients. Then once we have a good recipe, we do a lot of cooking. . . . Counting the number of random mixtures possible with different elements from the Periodic Table only begins to suggest the scope for future discovery. The realm of possible things is incomprehensibly larger than the realm of existing things. We will never run out of things to discover — a reassuring fact since the process of discovery is the mainspring of economic growth. . . . The opportunities symbolized by the child's chemistry set mean that growth in income per person can persist into the indefinite future.

In short, the future of manufacturing is an expanding universe, and any nation that wants to continue to play a prominent role in world affairs in the new century should bear this uppermost in mind.

Prospects for innovative products: an endless list

Having satisfied ourselves that in principle the future for innovative new manufactured products is almost limitless, let's now attempt to sketch out a few specific examples of how technology may soon create important new opportunities for First World manufacturers.

Robots and automation

Heralded for generations, robots are taking a long time coming — but they *are* coming. In fact, unseen by consumers, they are already an increasingly important factor in industrial production. In particular, as we noted in chapter 5, they have helped both shipbuilders and steelmakers achieve dramatic gains in labor productivity in recent years. Robots also play a key role in the electronics industry. They are invaluable, for instance, in assembling devices, such as laptop computers, whose components are too small for human hands to manipulate accurately. That said, the world has nowhere near exploited the full potential of automation to reduce labor costs in both manufacturing and service industries. In the future we are going to see many radical new uses for automation. One idea: automated door-to-door distribution systems that would deliver goods to urban stores and homes by robots operating in vast new underground transportation networks. The Japanese are already considering building such a system under Tokyo; it would dramatically reduce the number of goods vehicles on the city's crowded roads, leading to a general speeding up of traffic.

Voice recognition systems

Scientists have been working for years to develop electronic devices that can understand the human voice. Although such devices have hardly been developed beyond the primitive stage, they are expected by the early decades of the new century to reach a level of sophistication at which they will enable humans to operate a broad range of electronic equipment entirely by voice command. Although voice recognition seems at first sight to be mainly an opportunity for software makers (Bill Gates in particular is reportedly eyeing it excitedly), its implications for hardware manufacturers are probably even larger than for software makers. Certainly the world's semiconductor manufacturers have long viewed voice recognition as a potentially prodigious user of semiconductors. In addition, the rise of voice recognition will greatly expand the usefulness of — and market for — various types of established electronic gadgets, such as the personal computer. Now confined mainly to offices and homes, the personal computer could soon acquire a new lease on life as standard equipment in cars. With voice recognition cutting out the need for a keyboard, drivers would for the first time be able to operate a personal computer safely while they commuted.

Environmental protection

If rising world consumption is not to lead to environmental disaster, manufacturers right across the board will have to develop more environmentally friendly products. Perhaps even more important, manufacturers will have to develop more environmentally friendly *methods of production*. As the environmentalist Ross Gelbspan has pointed out, the widely held view that environmental protection laws hurt a nation's economy is simply false. The truth is the opposite: good environmental policies create rather than destroy jobs.

The most urgent priority is to install so-called end-of-pipe pollution mitigation devices in every factory and power plant that currently pollutes the environment. The classic example of such a device is the "scrubber" — a machine that cleans the emissions from industrial smokestacks. Scrubbers have been in general use in the West's major economies for many years, and it is now urgent that they also be deployed in the nations of the former East Bloc and in the developing world. These devices must also be made more effective and less expensive. Longer-term, entirely new and cleaner methods of production will have to be developed to minimize environmental damage.

Another key goal will be to develop ways to conserve energy and materials. As the environmentalists Amory and Hunter Lovins have documented, many household gadgets, such as refrigerators and air conditioning systems, could be made much more energy-efficient at little cost if only manufacturers focused on energy efficiency as a key goal. Spurred partly by greater consumer awareness and partly by international regulation, advanced manufacturing nations will focus on making the world a cleaner place — and will reap great economic advantages from that endeavor.

Health care
The population of people aged sixty-five and over is set to double in many of the world's most advanced nations in the next thirty years. Besides generating rapidly rising sales for manufacturers of everything from hair restorers to heart pacemakers, this boom in the number of seniors will require innovative solutions to the problem of long-term nursing care. As we have seen, household robots are coming, and they undoubtedly will provide part of the solution. More generally, mechanized devices like stairlifts will become much more prevalent. Other new technologies, such as superconductivity and biotechnology, will open up opportunities for advanced manufacturers to develop lucrative new approaches to health care.

Hydrology
The world's water resources are signally failing to keep up with expanding populations. The result is that, according to World Bank figures, per capita water supplies have fallen by one-third in the last twenty-five years. The water shortage in many nations not only is a drastic problem in itself but is beginning to constrain the growth in world food supplies. Yet, if the World Bank's forecasts are to believed, demand for water will increase by 650 percent by 2025. Clearly the world is facing a major crisis — but one that advanced manufacturers can play a key role in overcoming.

Manufacturers can, for instance, help the world use existing water supplies more intensively. To take just one example, large amounts of water could be saved in agriculture alone if new drip systems were widely adopted to channel water directly to where it is needed — at the crops' roots. Already drip systems are being manufactured on a limited scale; as reported by Sandra Postel in *Technology Review,* they have in some cases cut farm water usage by as much as 60 percent. So far, however, drip systems have been too expensive to be widely adopted by the world's farmers. The race is on to find ways of manufacturing them more economically.

Another approach to the looming crisis is to build more efficient and effective systems for recycling waste water. Already this challenge is providing useful opportunities for various manufacturers in the First World, notably in Germany and Japan. Moreover, in the longer term, breakthroughs in desalination may come to the rescue. President John F. Kennedy once suggested that inventing an inexpensive way to produce freshwater from the sea would dwarf all other scientific achievements. He may have overstated the case, but desalination has already grown to be a significant industry. Its growth prospects, however, are constrained by the fact that existing desalination technologies require enormous amounts of energy; hence the fact that desalination so far has been little used outside a few oil-rich nations. (As of the mid-1990s, just three such nations — Saudi Arabia, the United Arab Emirates, and Kuwait — accounted for 46 percent of the world's entire desalination capacity.) Now engineers are racing to develop more energy-efficient approaches. One promising system, announced by Desalinadoras AVF of Spain, would use the natural pressure of gravity in a seven-hundred-meter shaft to force seawater through a fine membrane that filters out the salt. As reported by David White of the *Financial Times* of London, this system promises to cut energy costs by 72 percent and would also be considerably less expensive in capital expenditures.

Nanotechnology
The nanometer — one-billionth of a meter — has given its name to a promising new industry devoted to hyper-miniaturized manufacturing techniques that aim to manipulate matter on an atom-by-atom basis. The most famous example so far of nanotechnology in action has been a successful effort by researchers at IBM to arrange thirty-five atoms of xenon to form their employer's name. While this feat may in itself seem to be of only trivial significance, it represents a spectacular demonstration of the principle that atoms can indeed be manipulated individually. It therefore presages the possibility of producing a vast array of consumer goods by new atom-by-atom production methods. In an example cited by *The Economist,* we may one day be able literally to assemble beefsteaks in a highly efficient, entirely artificial process that dispenses with the clumsy and land-intensive business of raising cattle

— a business that has, of course, changed little since the Stone Age. In *The Economist*'s vision, billions of tiny assembly-robots housed in a new kind of kitchen gadget would start with a supply of atoms of carbon, nitrogen, hydrogen, and oxygen. By pushing these atoms around in appropriate ways, the robots would in a matter of minutes create a confection of proteins and carbohydrates that in all respects would not only look and taste like steak but contain the same nutritional elements. After their meal, consumers could disassemble the leftovers back into the original atoms, thus obviating the need for any cleaning up. All this is still, of course, little more than science fiction. But in the fullness of time, nanotechnology promises huge increases in efficiency over traditional production methods.

Let's now take an extended look at a few areas in which future manufacturing opportunities appear to be particularly obvious. We will begin by looking at the prospects in various energy-related fields and then move on to transportation.

A noble quest: energy for all

All late-1990s conventional wisdom to the contrary, the world is *not* awash in surplus energy. True, measured in real terms, energy prices have dropped to levels not seen since the halcyon days of the early 1970s. But to imagine, as many Western commentators do, that energy today is "ultra-cheap" is a classic example of the Western tendency to view the world too narrowly. The fact is that, for most of the world's population, energy remains as scarce today as ever.

So scarce in fact that, on a per capita basis, energy consumption levels in many Third World nations run less than one-fiftieth that of the United States. Even many better-off citizens in such nations still use kerosene for heat and light; poorer people make do with burning cow dung and other agricultural wastes. Either way, such energy sources are a serious health hazard. Breathing kerosene fumes, for instance, can do as much damage as smoking two packs of cigarettes a day. Moreover, kerosene is a notorious cause of household fires. Meanwhile, in addition to being a health hazard, the burning of agricultural wastes deprives the land of important soil nutrients, thereby contributing to a general cycle of increasing rural destitution.

Clearly, therefore, even in the midst of the energy "glut" of the

1990s, many — perhaps a majority — of the world's people remain pitifully short of energy for such basic needs as light and heat. Moreover, their output of all sorts of basic consumer products remains cruelly stunted because of a lack of energy. Remember that energy is the largest single cost in the production of many crucial industrial materials and components. It accounts for about one-fifth of the cost of steel, for instance, and nearly one-third of the cost of aluminum. And of course, large amounts of energy are needed to run factory machines and to power the trucks that distribute the factories' output to consumers.

Plentiful supplies of energy are needed even in the efficient production of food, which is, of course, the most basic consumer product of all. If the world only had more energy, it could dramatically increase its output of many key farm products. Just a few kilowatt-hours of electricity expended on stirring the water in Third World fish ponds, for instance, could boost production of shrimps by 100 percent. Similarly modest amounts of electricity to power Third World chicken coops could greatly increase the output of eggs. If the Third World had enough energy to operate advanced mechanized agricultural methods, it could multiply its output of such important crops as wheat and rice severalfold.

All in all, therefore, if the rest of the world is ever to match First World living standards, the pressure on world energy supplies is inevitably going to increase. In fact, the enrichment of China alone makes this almost a foregone conclusion. If China's growth continues at a fast pace, the Chinese by 2020 may need as much energy as the entire world consumed in 1990. Thus, even if by dint of rigorous conservation measures the West were to cut its energy consumption by one-third (a big if), world energy supplies will have to increase by more than 70 percent simply to accommodate China's rise.

Where is all this energy going to come from? This is a crucial question for the security of the world in the twenty-first century. And it is one that must be urgently addressed if we are not to return to the periodic energy crises that twice sent the world economy into a tailspin in the 1970s.

Unfortunately, the supposed energy "glut" of recent years has bred a dangerous sense of complacency among the world's policy makers and opinion leaders. Nowhere has this complacency been less justified than in the case of oil. The truth is that in believing that the world enjoys a permanent glut of oil, the energy optimists are living in a fool's paradise. As Franco Bernabé, chief executive of Italy's national oil company, ENI, has pointed out, recent optimism has been driven by inflated estimates of the world's reserves of oil. In particular, the officially stated estimates of proven oil reserves for many member nations of both the OPEC oil cartel and the former Soviet bloc have, for various reasons, been greatly exaggerated.

Thus, although the official figures seem to suggest that the world has been finding more oil than it consumes, in reality the reverse is the case. Speaking to *Forbes* magazine's Howard Banks in the summer of 1998, Bernabé pointed out that a mere half a dozen major new oil fields have been discovered in the last thirty years. The rate of discovery of new oil has fallen by more than 85 percent since the early 1960s.

In any case, even in the unlikely event that the world's pace of oil discovery speeds up in the years ahead, concerns about global warming clearly place an upper limit on the extent to which the world can rely on oil for its future energy needs. After all, the consensus among the world's scientists is that consumption of oil and other fossil fuels must be sharply reduced if we are to avoid a disastrous warming of the earth's atmosphere in the next century. Meanwhile, the other major established source of energy, nuclear power, seems unlikely to fill the gap, given growing concerns about the possibility of such negative side effects as Chernobyl-style meltdowns.

In the circumstances, therefore, it is reasonable to expect that renewable energy will play an increasingly important part in boosting the world's energy supplies in the years ahead. The problem so far has been the high cost of the equipment needed to turn renewable energy into electricity. But several of the world's leading manufacturers are now making rapid progress in developing more efficient production technologies that will greatly expand the prospects for renewable energy in the new century. Certainly developing such technologies will prove to be one of the most important manufacturing challenges in coming decades. To this exciting challenge we now turn.

Nature's inexhaustible bounty: water, wind, and sunshine

Of the main sources of renewable energy, only water power has been widely exploited. Wind power is still greatly underexploited, and solar power has hardly even begun to make a contribution.

Clearly the potential for renewable energy is huge. Even water power, which in some estimates already generates fully one-fifth of the world's total electricity supplies, has tremendous potential for further growth. Particularly in the Second and Third Worlds, there remain numerous opportunities for further development of water power. The point is illustrated by China's development of the spectacular Three Gorges Dam. This giant fifteen-year project will raise the water level of the Yangtze River by as much as 590 feet and promises to supply an astounding one-tenth of all China's expected electricity needs by the time of completion in 2009. This will represent about twice the electricity output of Egypt's Aswan Dam, the famously large hydroelectric project of the midtwentieth century.

Its displacement of 1.3 million people is just one of the reasons the Three Gorges project is highly controversial, but the important point for our purposes is that, with a budgeted cost of $24 billion, it offers huge opportunities to top First World manufacturers to supply everything from pile drivers to bulldozers. The pickings will be particularly rich for a few key Japanese, German, and Swiss electrical companies that will supply a total of twenty-six sets of power-generation equipment. Making such equipment is a classic example of the sort of advanced manufacturing business that postindustrialists overlook in belittling manufacturing's contribution to the prosperity of the world's richest nations. Virtually invisible to the public, this industry nonetheless already boasts annual revenues of nearly $80 billion. For generations it has been dominated by a cozy club of top engineering companies like Westinghouse and General Electric of the United States, Hitachi and Toshiba of Japan, Brown Boveri of Switzerland, and Siemens of Germany. Given that would-be challengers face huge entry barriers, the industry's incumbents are likely to remain safely protected from competition from low-wage nations for many years to come. It is a formula not only for large profits and high wages but for strong exports.

Another traditional form of renewable energy that has been creating many new manufacturing jobs in the First World is wind power. Wind power's prospects have been transformed in recent years by technical breakthroughs that have dramatically increased its electrical efficiency. One major improvement has been better design for wind turbines. Wind turbine blades used to be based inappropriately on aircraft propeller designs. Manufacturers have now redesigned the blades to capture wind energy efficiently over a broader range of wind speeds and directions. In addition, certain undesirable side effects of the earlier turbines, particularly noise emission and interference with television reception, have been eliminated or suppressed.

Already wind power has become fully economical in many parts of the Third World, particularly in remote villages far from national electricity grids. Such villages have typically had to rely on diesel generators, but wind power is now a more competitive option. Diesel generators are being replaced by wind turbines in nations like Indonesia, South Africa, Chile, and Argentina, and the electricity needs of one million households in India and nearly one hundred thousand in Mongolia are now powered by wind.

All this helps explain why, with an annual growth rate of 25 percent, wind power is the fastest-growing energy source of the 1990s. As of the late 1990s, its contribution to the world's electricity supply was running about eight times higher than in 1985. Yet the growth in wind energy has nowhere near run its course. According to the leading environmentalist Christopher Flavin, China alone boasts enough untapped wind power to double its existing electricity supplies. The United States boasts even more spectacular wind power opportunities. The untapped wind power in just its three windiest states — North Dakota, South Dakota, and Texas — is enough to supply all U.S. electricity needs.

Of course, there are major technical problems in making full use of available wind power. For a start, the world's windiest places are typically so remote that the power they might generate would be largely lost in transmission before it reached significant population centers. Nonetheless, as the technology improves, even moderately windy sites that are much nearer to big cities may soon become fully competitive sources of power. Certainly the pace of progress in the technology has been impressive: the cost of wind-generated electricity has declined steadily by about 10 percent a year since the early 1980s. No wonder that Roger Taylor of the Colorado-based U.S. National Renewable Energy Laboratory has predicted that wind may soon be a more economical source of power than coal. If optimists such as Joseph J. Romm and Charles B. Curtis are to believed, by 2020 annual sales of wind-generated electricity could reach as high as $50 billion — a scale that would presage immense opportunities for many First World manufacturers.

Who will reap the richest prizes? Judging by the early running, German manufacturers seem particularly well placed. Germany's wind turbine makers have benefited from state subsidies that have dramatically increased wind power use in recent years — so much so that Germany has now passed the United States to become the world's largest producer of wind-generated electricity. Among German suppliers, the Thyssen steel group seems particularly strong, given its edge in corrosion-resistant steels that promise to transform the wind turbine industry's lackluster reliability record. Denmark, like Germany, boasts an extensive subsidy program and now derives 6 percent of its electricity from wind; the result is that it too is strong in the manufacture of wind turbines. Meanwhile, Japan seems to have targeted wind turbines as a key export business of the future. The Osaka-based trading company Tomen, for instance, has already launched a $1.2 billion program to install one thousand wind turbines in various parts of Europe.

Another traditional source of renewable energy that promises many exciting opportunities for the world's advanced manufacturers is so-called biomass. The term refers to a host of biological materials that can be burned to create heat, the most familiar form of which is firewood. Until recently biomass was little used in generating electricity because much of the heat created from burning it went to waste. Biomass was thus a viable source of electricity only in a few areas where it could be harvested particularly cheaply. Now, however, technological breakthroughs in gas turbines have dramatically increased biomass's yield of electricity. This development, of course, opens the way for power stations to pay much higher prices for biomass — a possibility that could powerfully stimulate supply by making it economical for farmers to produce biomass as a main crop rather than an incidental one. That would be good news for the world's environmental future given that biomass boasts a low sulfur content that contrasts particularly with that of coal. Biomass also emits much less carbon dioxide.

Of course, for true believers in renewable energy, even biomass is a secondary player compared to solar energy. The challenge of harnessing the sun's power has been a cause célèbre for visionaries and utopians since 1839, when the French scientist Edmond Becquerel discovered that sunshine can generate electricity in photovoltaic materials. And there is good reason to pursue this challenge: as calculated by the Deutsches Museum in Munich, the amount of solar energy hitting the earth totals about 1.4 billion kilowatt-hours a year — equal to about 15,000 times the earth's entire energy consumption in the mid-1990s. It will never be possible to harness more than a tiny fraction of this energy, but even so, the potential is huge.

Unfortunately, solar energy has an image problem because of a long record of failing to live up to the promises of its most ardent supporters. "Solar power is one of those things that's always just around the corner," commented Jonathan Weber, writing in the *Los Angeles Times* in 1997. "Just a few more technical advances over here, and a little government help over there, and we'll have solved all our energy and pollution problems once and for all — it seems like we've been hearing that for thirty years now."

Nonetheless, as Weber went on to point out, the public's waning interest in solar energy is unwarranted. The truth is that in the last two decades solar has made great strides toward establishing its right to be taken seriously. In particular, the solar energy industry has greatly improved its production efficiency, to the point where its costs as of the mid-1990s had fallen by 90 percent compared to 1975.

And this is evidently just the beginning. The solar energy industry has high hopes of making further cost cuts thanks to, for instance, lower prices for photovoltaic silicon, the key enabling material used in most solar panels. Like semiconductor-grade silicon, which it closely resembles, photovoltaic silicon is an extremely expensive material in itself, and it is also expensive to process. Several solar panel makers, most notably Munich-based Siemens Solar, a subsidiary of Germany's giant Siemens electrical corporation, are now racing to develop thin-film photovoltaic materials. These are typically less than one-fiftieth the thickness of the 300- to 400-micron layers of photovoltaic silicon used in conventional solar panels. Of course, such thin-film versions of silicon are generally less efficient in converting sunshine into power. On balance, however, because they are so much less expensive, they offer clear advantages in many applications. These advantages seem to be increasing all the time as ways are found to boost thin-film's energy conversion ratio.

The early leader in the race to develop thin-film seems to be Siemens Solar, which is already the world's largest maker of solar panels with a world market share of almost one-fifth. Siemens is betting on a variety of thin-film known as copper indium diselenide (CIS). In combination with a subsidiary in California, Siemens in 1997 achieved a world record with CIS-based panels: an energy conversion ratio of 11.1 percent. This was a significant improvement on the previous world record, also set by Siemens, of 10.1 percent. It is even more impressive compared with the rates of around 5 percent that thin-film materials were typically achieving as recently as the early 1990s.

Now experts like Princeton's Robert Williams are predicting that both CIS and another version of thin-film known as cadmium-telluride could achieve energy conversion rates as high as 15 percent by 2010. Thus, assuming the industry simultaneously reduces production costs, solar panels could come close to matching the competitiveness of ordinary coal-generated grid electricity within a decade.

The industry's prospects of achieving further cuts in its manufacturing costs look good. As John Driver, head of manufacturing at London-based BP Solar, points out, experience in other manufacturing industries suggests that with every doubling of cumulative volume, unit costs fall by around 20 percent. He adds: "We see no reason why our experience with solar panels should be any different."

Even in the absence of dramatic improvements in production efficiency, it is clear that solar energy is here to stay. Solar is already a fully competitive source of energy in remote areas that do not have grid electricity. Such areas are mainly in the Third World but are by no means confined to it — even some remote parts of the United States do not have grid electricity. To the extent that such areas have had any electricity at all, they have generally drawn it from diesel generators. So how does solar energy compare with diesel? In the first few years, not very well. Even given the recent significant reductions in the cost of solar panels, solar energy systems are typically at least twice as expensive to install as diesel generators. But as the years go by their low running costs — just one-tenth those of diesel — add up to a huge advantage: thus measured over a period of ten years, a solar energy system is only about half as expensive as a diesel generator.

Solar's edge is not only that it requires no fuel but that, with no moving parts, it requires virtually no maintenance. Thus, it is particularly competitive in remote regions where deliveries of fuel and parts are often hampered by bad roads. Moreover, solar enjoys an important additional advantage: it is much more environmentally friendly than diesel. It does not emit noxious gases into the atmosphere, and it is silent — a big bonus for anyone who has ever had to put up with the constant din of a diesel generator. Moreover, solar dispenses with the risk of fuel spillages, which are a serious problem with diesel generators. Such spillages are particularly unfortunate when they occur in remote mountainous areas because they can pollute the drinking water of thousands of residents lower down.

With all these advantages, solar is already fully viable in a rapidly growing number of special applications. A good example is remote communications facilities. Everywhere from Sulfur Mountain in California to Antikythira in Greece, repeater stations, which relay telephone and broadcast signals, are now powered by the sun. Radio listeners in Cyprus can thank twenty-eight solar-powered stations installed in 1989 for their radio reception. The world's intercontinental aircraft now rely on signals from solar-powered terrestrial beacons on certain routes. Solar energy also comes into its own in powering remote lighthouses.

Of course, applications of this sort are extremely specialized, and even in the aggregate they do not add up to very much. But they provide good profits that go a long way toward funding the industry's heavy ongoing program of research and development. The hope is, of course, that in the long run research and development will bring costs down to the point where the industry can develop a potentially vast market in the Third World. Just how vast the prospects are is apparent from the fact that fully 40 percent of the world's entire population still does not have grid electricity. Solar promises to be particularly efficacious in certain regions of India, China, South America, and Africa, where the proportion of residents without grid electricity rises to as much as 90 percent. Moreover, most such people are unlikely to be connected to the grid anytime soon given that the cost of building transmission lines — at as much as $10,000 per mile — is vast in relation to local income levels.

Already the solar energy industry has made a start on tapping the potential of the Third World. These are some showcase examples of how dramatically just a little solar energy can transform the lives of thousands of Third World residents.

Water supply: Solar-powered pumps are providing 300 tons of drinking water daily in the arid Sahel region of Senegal. The water is sufficient for the needs of 6,000 villagers and their livestock.

Health care: Vaccines stored in more than 250 solar-powered refrigerators in Kenya have enabled the World Health Organization to vaccinate 70 percent of the nation's children against polio.

Communications: Ten remote islands off Fiji now have a modern telephone service thanks to solar panels supplied by BP Solar. Meanwhile, Siemens has supplied solar-powered equipment that has connected 8,500 new telephone users in rural Mexico to the country's central telephone system.

Contemplating the opportunities in the Third World, Siemens Solar chief executive Gernot J. Oswald waxes ecstatic. "It is very exciting," he says. "A typical Third World system may generate enough power for only three 50-watt lamps and a black-and-white television, but for consumers who would otherwise have no electricity, this is very high-quality power."

According to Siemens's calculations, if the total installed capacity of solar energy panels were to grow by just 15 percent a year, enough electricity would be created by around 2020 to meet the household needs of 1.2 billion Third World citizens and to power water-pumping and medical facilities.

Unfortunately, however, residents of the Third World are generally too poor to finance even the modest $300–500 up-front investment required from each household for a basic solar energy system. Most of the Third World installations showcased in the industry's brochures have been funded by First World aid organizations. Still, there is hope. As John Driver of BP Solar points out, in most parts of the Third World there is *some* disposable income, as is evidenced by, for instance, the number of scooters on the roads. Moreover, solar is cheaper in the long run than the candles, kerosene, diesel fuel, and batteries that currently provide energy to 2 billion Third World residents.

Oswald suggests that the solution is the development of so-called microbanking services to collect payments of as little as a few dollars from householders, who thus purchase their energy systems in regular installments. The idea has been pioneered by Bangladesh's Grameen Bank, with famously successful results, and Oswald is hopeful that it can be widely adopted elsewhere in the poorer parts of Asia. He is less hopeful, however, about some parts of Africa, where, he declares gloomily, "there is no money."

Assuming that solar costs continue to come down and that micro-banking systems are successfully developed in Third World markets, Oswald foresees that solar energy will prove a powerful catalyst for change. Solar's role merely in lighting homes at night will transform millions of lives, particularly in equatorial regions where the sun sets early all through the year. Children can continue their education into the evening and adults will watch television, a pastime that Oswald suggests will do much to curb Third World birth rates.

We have already cited solar's role in pumping water in Senegal. Pumping water is in fact regarded as one of the most productive and cost-effective early applications for solar. Without energy to power pumps, Third World villagers often have to draw their water by hand. Typically this task falls to women, who in some parts of the Third World must walk as many as three miles a day fetching water for their families. Thus, just a little energy could transform the lives of millions of women, who would then be free to apply their time to such potentially enriching pursuits as intensive gardening.

Solar can also contribute directly to boosting the output of Third World craft workers, who often work in places too dimly lit for efficient production. Oswald cites a project in India in which textile workers doubled their production and achieved a tenfold increase in quality after electric lights were installed.

In the long term, cheap solar-powered telecommunications could help Third World residents participate in the global economy. It is not inconceivable, for instance, that within a few decades educated young citizens of previously remote parts of the Third World could start producing computer software under contract for the wealthy corporations of the developed world. This would boost the local income structure, enabling more residents to finance their own solar energy installations without the need for First World subsidies. In fact, solar could improve lifestyles in remote areas so much that the flight of young people to the Third World's already grossly overcrowded mega-cities could be significantly reduced.

Thus, as solar helps many parts of the Third World bootstrap themselves out of abject poverty, it will simultaneously become a major First World manufacturing industry. A virtuous circle of effects will appear as rising sales volumes help the industry cut its prices, lower prices stimulate demand, and sales are thereby further increased. At some point, solar's costs could become widely competitive with fossil fuels, presaging explosive growth even in advanced nations.

Not surprisingly, despite much professional caution among photovoltaic engineers, several well-informed optimists continue to talk up the industry's prospects. Take John Browne, chairman of British Petroleum, which owns BP Solar. In a highly optimistic speech in 1997, he predicted that the entire renewable energy industry could account for more than 5 percent of the world's total energy by 2020, and perhaps as much as 50 percent by 2047. Although he did not specify what solar's share in the total would be, it was clear that he believed it would play a leading role.

Browne's expectations are modest, however, compared to the analysis of the Boulder-based energy expert William Hoagland. Writing in *Scientific American* in 1995, Hoagland predicted that solar energy alone could provide as much as 60 percent of the world's electricity by 2025. The full significance of this prediction is apparent only when you realize that Hoagland's figures project a 265 percent increase in global demand for electricity by then.

One thing is undeniable: from an admittedly tiny base, the manufacturing opportunities in solar energy are now growing very rapidly. In conservative estimates, sales revenues are growing by between 15 and 20 percent a year. And some key players seem to be quietly doing considerably better than the average. Take Siemens Solar. Notwithstanding its public concern about the difficulties that lie ahead, Siemens Solar is planning to sell five times more photovoltaic capacity in the five years to 2001 than it had sold in its entire thirty-year history. Meanwhile, as reported by Leyla Boulton in the *Financial Times* in 1997, BP Solar is planning to increase its output tenfold in the ten years to 2007 — in the hope that by then solar will be competitive with expensive peak-load grid electricity.

Perhaps the most encouraging news from the solar energy industry is that it has made considerable progress on a crucial — if little known — measure of fundamental efficiency: the industry's energy input-output ratio. This ratio compares the total amount of energy produced by solar panels with the amount expended in manufacturing them. Whereas in the early days the input of energy required was typically three times the eventual total output, the position has now been exactly reversed: as of the late 1990s, solar panels generated at least three times as much energy as the energy required to make them. In other words, in energy terms, if not in terms of total costs, solar is already showing a large net "profit" for planet earth.

If solar fulfills its promise, it will be a massive source not only of excellent jobs but of lucrative export opportunities for many First World nations. Already a host of First World companies are participating in the industry. The most visible players are, of course, the solar panel makers, a category that includes not only British Petroleum, Solarex, and Siemens but Tokyo-based Showa Shell Sekiyu and Kyoto-based Kyocera. These players depend in turn on a host of suppliers for key inputs such as photovoltaic materials. The making of such materials is a highly sophisticated First World business that has so far been dominated by German and Japanese chemical companies.

How much will the solar energy business add to the world's manufacturing job base? For optimists, the prospects are almost limitless. According to Hermann Scheer, a member of the German parliament who is also president of an association called Eurosolar, the solar energy industry could eventually employ an astonishing 2 million workers worldwide. Meanwhile, Romm and Curtis contend that, taken in aggregate, the entire range of renewables may prove to be a larger source of new jobs than the much-vaunted information industry. Their conclusion:

> The world is on the verge of a revolution in energy and environmental technologies. . . . This revolution can be expected to create a number of industries that collectively will provide one of the largest international markets and one of the largest sources of new high-wage jobs in the next century, with annual sales in excess of $800 billion.

So much for energy. Now let's look at future manufacturing opportunities in one of the industries that stands to gain the most from more abundant energy — transportation.

Going places: new frontiers in transportation

The American transportation expert Martin Wachs has perhaps put it best: "Mobility is an underrated human right. You can never have enough of it."

Certainly experience in the United States suggests that a nation's desire to travel grows with each passing year. As of the early 1990s, the total distance traveled annually by a typical American — including commuting, business travel, and pleasure trips — was about 15,000 miles. This represented a rise of about 100 percent in 30 years — a period in which real incomes in the United States rose by about the same proportion. According to the American transportation experts Andreas Schafer and David Victor, this correlation is not a coincidence. Writing in *Scientific American,* they have posited a fundamental relationship: for each increase of one percentage point in living standards, Americans tend to increase their travel mileage by one percentage point as well. In the developing world, the propensity for people to travel more as they get richer is even more pronounced: in the thirty years to 1990, the Chinese, for instance, increased their travel mileage by three percentage points for every one-percentage-point increase in living standards.

Schafer and Victor predict that people everywhere will continue to increase their mileage in the twenty-first century. And because people tend to allocate a relatively fixed amount of time to travel, they will use ever faster vehicles.

All this presages vast business opportunities for manufacturers of everything from bicycles and buses to helicopters and supersonic jets. Adding spice to the challenge is the likelihood that makers of the transportation equipment of the future will have to contend with increasingly tough environmental regulation and considerably higher fossil-fuel costs. These considerations demand the utmost manufacturing creativity, and it is already apparent that many of the world's great manufacturers are enlisting their best production engineers and designers in the effort to meet the challenge.

One key area of opportunity is cars. All late 1990s conventional wisdom to the contrary, the global car industry is suffering no permanent glut of capacity. As Alex Taylor III of *Fortune* has argued, demand for cars in emerging economies in particular is likely to soar in the years ahead. The reason is that for every person who owns a car in the developing world today there are probably at least twenty others who aspire to own a car one day. With rising productivity, the car industry will successfully cater to more and more of this potential market as the years go by.

The real challenge for the global car industry is not to find markets to absorb its ever increasing production capacity but rather to meet progressively tighter environmental regulations. Thus, there is little doubt that those carmakers that lead in developing more environmentally friendly products will be well placed to dominate the industry in the next century.

In the long term perhaps the most exciting source of environmentally friendly power for cars is so-called fuel cells. But for the immediate future, many leading companies are focusing on electric cars. These cars generate virtually no noxious gases, provided, of course, they are run on a nonpolluting source of electricity such as hydropower; they are nearly silent and, in part because they dissipate little energy when braking, highly energy-efficient. When the driver needs to slow down, excess momentum is removed by using the motor as a dynamo: the slowing effect created simultaneously generates electricity that recharges the battery. Electric cars also enjoy the advantage that, in contrast to gasoline-driven cars, they consume no energy while idling.

Unfortunately, however, until battery capacity can be dramatically increased, it looks like electric cars will play only a minor role on the world's roads in the twenty-first century. In the meantime, leading automakers are well advanced in developing a compromise solution, so-called hybrid cars, which use an electric motor in tandem with a conventional gasoline engine. The concept relies heavily on highly sophisticated electronic controls that enable the car to switch smoothly from one power source to the other as speed and road conditions dictate. In common with electric cars, hybrids achieve excellent energy efficiency because their electric motors function as generators that recharge the battery while braking. Hybrids also offer a considerable reduction in noise levels and in emissions of noxious gases.

Another exciting challenge for advanced manufacturing nations is to develop so-called intelligent cars that will eventually drive themselves. A stepping stone toward this goal will be to build electronic safety systems into both cars and roads to reduce the risk of accidents. One noted prophet of such systems is Masakazu Iguchi, director of the Japan Automobile Research Center. Pointing out that human error is responsible for nearly 90 percent of car accidents, he has called on the car industry to develop safety precautions that would prevent drivers from falling asleep, delaying necessary maneuvers, or failing to watch the road. He suggests that sensors be installed in roads to measure driving conditions and set limits on each car's speed. At the approach to a bend in the road, for instance, a device in the road might alert the car's on-board control system to apply the brakes automatically. Similarly, an optical system might detect a pedestrian in a car's path and take appropriate avoiding action.

As for the goal of driverless cars, European engineers have already built an experimental car equipped with eighteen video cameras that has driven itself at speeds of up to nearly one hundred miles an hour on German highways. Of course, manufacturers will have to overcome many problems before a vehicle like this is feasible for ordinary driving conditions, but Iguchi expects automated driving to become a reality on expressways by the mid-twenty-first century. In the meantime, the first driverless vehicles are likely to be used in routine service in limited environments such as large factories and airports. But in the fullness of time, automatic control systems may become so effective that the elderly, the sick, and even the very young may eventually be able to venture out unaccompanied in driverless cars and be assured that they will arrive safely.

Of course, no matter how much progress the world's leading manufacturers make in developing intelligent road systems and better, more economical cars, such breakthroughs alone will be far from sufficient to provide all the mobility the world will need in the twenty-first century. If experts like Schafer and Victor are right, the share of world traffic volume accounted for by high-speed transport — a category to which they assign both planes and ultra-fast trains — will soar from just 9 percent in 1990 to 25 percent by 2020. Given that the whole transportation pie will also increase dramatically, this means that, in absolute numbers, passenger miles traveled by high-speed transport will multiply more than six times.

Not surprisingly, therefore, the world's passenger jet makers foresee a bonanza in the twenty-first century. China's growth alone could presage an "astounding" increase in demand, according to Boeing's chief executive, Philip Condit. Already various plans are being floated for faster passenger jets. The Japanese, for instance, have unveiled a plan to build a supersonic passenger plane that would fly about twice as fast as today's conventional jets — in fact, 20 percent faster than the Concorde, the aging Anglo-French supersonic plane. With 300 seats, the proposed Japanese plane would boast three times the Concorde's carrying capacity, and at 7,000 miles, its range would be 70 percent longer than Concorde's.

Other leading manufacturers see the key opportunity as making larger rather than faster planes. The European Airbus consortium, for instance, is planning to build a giant new plane with as many as 656 seats. A key advantage of the new plane would be lower operating costs: according to Airbus's figures, the cost per seat-mile would be 23 percent less than for the Boeing 747–400.

Of course, given the limits on the world's energy and other resources, much more dramatic cost reductions than this will be necessary if long-distance travel is ever to become a routine prerogative of residents of today's Third World. As it happens, such cost reductions are already in sight in the form of high-speed trains. As the economist Wallace C. Peterson has pointed out, these trains can be as much as ten times more fuel-efficient than planes. And unlike planes, they do virtually no damage to the earth's threatened ozone layer.

Of course, even the fastest trains are not as fast as planes. Running at up to 190 miles an hour, both Japan's famous bullet train and France's TGV are less than half as fast as a typical passenger jet. But this is less of a disadvantage than it appears given that train stations are usually more accessible than airports. In reality, total door-to-door journey times for fast trains often compare remarkably well with air travel time.

Not surprisingly, the fast-train business is a highly promising one for many leading manufacturers. In China alone the opportunities are immense. Officials are investing $12 billion in a new 800-mile high-speed track between Beijing and Shanghai. The investment is the centerpiece of a major overhaul of the country's decrepit rail network, and it will enable trains to achieve speeds of more than 150 miles an hour — a dramatic improvement in a country where until the mid-1990s train speeds of less than 40 miles an hour were the norm. Meanwhile, South Korea and Taiwan are also developing ultra-fast train networks. In Europe too, major rail investments are planned that will link Eastern Europe with the fast-train networks of France and Germany.

In the worldwide race to develop faster train systems, one nation is conspicuously on the sidelines — the United States. In truth, passenger rail service has advanced little in the United States since the 1930s (when, as Glenn Miller's "Chattanooga Choo Choo" reminds us, American trains set the pace for the rest of the world). The United States was passed in rail technology by leading Japanese and French rolling stock manufacturers in the 1960s, and it has continued to fall further behind ever since. In fact, even in the late 1990s few American trains run faster than about eighty miles an hour — little more than half the speed that the Chinese are now aiming for. Yet there is no inherent lack of potentially profitable routes for fast trains in the United States. In fact, given that American cities are dispersed widely over a huge land mass, the United States could probably make better use of fast trains than almost any other nation.

American manufacturers will have to work hard, however, to catch up with the Europeans and the Japanese in the key manufacturing technologies on which the fast-train idea is based. The French in particular are leaders in the field. They claim, for instance, a considerable edge in various technologies designed to reduce the weight of trains. Lower weight is, of course, a key objective in that the damage caused to tracks by fast-moving trains is otherwise prohibitively expensive to repair. The French have, for instance, designed cars with just one bogie instead of two. (Bogies, the sets of wheels on which the train is carried, account for a considerable proportion of a train's total weight.) The French have also taken large amounts of weight out of the trains' enormous electrical transformers as well as the car bodies. These innovations have encouraged the French to talk about manufacturing a new generation of trains that will cruise at up to 225 miles an hour and could eventually achieve speeds as high as 250 miles an hour.

As if this were not enough, German and Japanese manufacturers are now close to success in developing a completely new type of train propulsion system that could eventually achieve still higher speeds. In this new system, known as magnetic levitation (or "maglev" for short), the train is supported not by wheels but by high-strength magnets, which enable it to hover about an inch or so above the track. With mechanical friction thus greatly reduced, the train can deliver a notably smooth ride even at extremely high speeds.

One problem for the maglev concept, however, is the vast investment required, not only in new trains but in the construction of a completely new type of track. Moreover, the success with which engineers have been able to speed up conventional trains in recent decades has dramatically narrowed the once commanding lead in speed and comfort that maglev promised when research began on the concept more than three decades ago.

Nonetheless, the prospects are good that maglev will generate major manufacturing opportunities in the end. Certainly the huge up-front costs entailed in laying down maglev tracks are not necessarily a barrier for capital-rich nations like Japan and Germany. Such nations can afford to take an ultra-long-term view, given that the maglev concept's heavy up-front costs can be readily recovered over literally centuries of subsequent service. In fact, maglev promises to be an excellent long-term investment in that its plane-style advantages in speed and comfort will allow maglev operators to price their seats at close to airline levels. Operators' outlays on energy and other ongoing costs will be only a fraction of airlines' costs.

Beyond maglev, the transportation industry bristles with a host of other opportunities for innovative manufacturers. Private planes and helicopters, for instance, are likely to enjoy enormous growth in the twenty-first century as their cost falls rapidly thanks to more efficient manufacturing methods. Opportunities will also abound in road freight transportation. Trainlike trucks may be developed to pull several trailers, each equipped with automatic guidance equipment and independent brakes to ensure that it remains safely on the road. The result would be large savings not only in drivers' wages but in general overheads.

Clearly, therefore, the manufacturing opportunities in transportation are, if anything, even larger than in the energy industry. Already the contenders in the field read like a *Who's Who* of the world's great manufacturing companies. In the race to develop better cars, for instance, key players include Japan's Toyota Motor and Mitsubishi Motors, which are both world leaders in hybrids. In Europe the race to build hybrids is being led by Germany's Volkswagen, with France's Peugeot and Renault in hot pursuit. Meanwhile, in Japan, Matsushita Electric, Japan Storage Battery, and Sony are well advanced in developing batteries for electric cars. In the United States, General Motors' Ovonic subsidiary is a leader in battery technology. All three of the big Detroit carmakers are participating in the Partnership for a New Generation of Vehicles, a public-private program launched by the Clinton administration in 1993 to develop radically more fuel-efficient cars.

The coming of intelligent roads will also prove a bonanza for manufacturers. The major beneficiaries will probably be makers of semiconductors, sensors, and other electronic devices. Future developments in planes will benefit not only obvious players like Boeing and Airbus but a host of makers of advanced materials and components located in the United States, Japan, and Europe. Meanwhile, France's Alsthom, Canada's Bombardier, and Japan's Mitsubishi group are among several major engineering companies poised for big gains as fast trains catch on around the world. If the maglev train is built, winners will include Daimler-Benz of Germany and the Hitachi group of Japan.

How big the transportation equipment industry will eventually become is anyone's guess. But think of it this way: if the transportation experts Andreas Schafer and David Victor are to believed, the world's population will be traveling a total of 64 trillion passenger-miles a year by 2050. This would represent more than four times the 1990 total of 14 trillion. Clearly all this moving around will keep many millions of manufacturing workers in gainful employment for as far ahead as anyone can see. Given future growth on this scale in just one limited sector of the manufacturing economy, it seems unbelievable that many respected commentators in the 1990s could have been suggesting that manufacturing had by then already reached an upper limit.

IV

Toward a Manufacturing Renaissance

8

Time to Take
the Blinders Off

If America's drift into postindustrialism continues unchecked, we can safely predict a drastic deterioration in the American economy's performance in the decades ahead. In particular, the outlook is for continuing subpar growth in personal incomes. And the worst affected are likely to be poorer Americans. Given that, on the author John E. Schwarz's figures, the proportion of Americans who are poor has risen from 17 percent to 25 percent since 1972, postindustrialism clearly presages a further worsening of the single most conspicuous economic problem the United States has suffered in recent decades. Even for middle-class Americans the income outlook is for, at best, lackluster growth — certainly much lower growth than what middle-class Americans had become used to up to the mid-1970s.

Postindustrialism also bodes ill for America's foreign trade position and, by extension, for its continued ability to project economic power abroad. Although many feel-good commentators try to gloss over the significance of trade (America's imports, they say, don't matter very much because they account for "just" 12 percent of gross domestic product), trade is actually crucially important. Trade, after all, is a nation's fundamental economic connection with the outside world, and among other things, this means that in the long run it is the most important determinant of a nation's ranking in the world income league. Thus, nations that fail to produce enough of the right sort of exports inexorably sink down the league table.

Anyone who is unconvinced on this point need merely look at other nations that in the past have failed to rectify persistent trade deficits. The fate of Argentina is perhaps the ultimate warning of what could be in store. Like the United States today, Argentina in the early part of this century ranked among the world's richest nations in per capita income. But thanks in large part to persistent neglect of its chronic trade deficits, it dropped steadily in the world income league table over the years to the point where it recently ranked lower than such developing countries as Thailand, Syria, and Lithuania. If the United States continues to neglect its own trade problems, the moment of truth is likely to come in the form of a major dollar crisis. In the event of another dollar crisis similar in scale to the crisis it suffered in the early 1990s, the American economy could be displaced almost overnight by Japan as the world's largest economy. At this stage, about the only thing left that is supporting the dollar is a dogged determination by top Washington officials to maintain a high exchange rate through the end of President Bill Clinton's term of office. For now, America's main foreign trade partners seem to be cooperating in this objective, but this does not alter the fundamental position that continued current account deficits will sooner or later precipitate a major dollar devaluation. And the longer the devaluation is postponed, the more devastating it will be.

Clearly, therefore, the need for drastic policy changes is now urgent. But before the United States can implement realistic measures to recover its lost manufacturing leadership, it must first understand the full extent of its problems. Unfortunately, a whole host of factors have hitherto hidden from Americans the full seriousness of their predicament. We have mentioned one of these factors already — free-market ideology, which, as we noted in chapter 1, powerfully but spuriously supports the postindustrialists' confidence in the information economy as a superior source of future wealth. Many other factors are also at work, and we will consider them in this chapter.

"A frenzy of religious intensity": the press and postindustrialism

One of the key reasons the American people are so complacent about America's drift into deindustrialization is that they have been badly blindsided by the American press. Although the American press can generally claim a proud record of objectivity and reliability in its coverage of most types of news, it is far from a neutral observer in the postindustrial debate. Not only are press commentators among the most extreme enthusiasts of postindustrialism but, to the extent that they canvass other opinions and insights on how the world economy works, they tend to gravitate to like-minded sources in think tanks and academic life.

Perhaps we shouldn't be too surprised by the press's partisanship. After all, given that the press is a founder member of the information society, its own vested interests are clearly at stake in the postindustrial debate. Even though reporters rarely if ever consciously take this into account in their coverage, the fact remains that they display a marked unconscious bias in favor of postindustrialism.

In any case, at a personal level press reporters have their own reasons to feel good about the information revolution. They have, for instance, benefited disproportionately from the emergence of ubiquitous and user-friendly word-processing in recent years. Certainly few reporters who remember the multiple retypings and messy handwritten changes of predigital journalism would want to turn the clock back.

Another factor that favorably influences journalists' attitudes to the information economy is the Internet. Although, as we have seen, the Internet is generally still too shallow to be of much value for serious business research, it is a godsend for reporters and editors in, for instance, checking routine facts. At the click of a mouse, a reporter can turn up anything from a government official's middle initial to a screen actor's marital record. For reporters who remember the old days when they had to pore over faded clippings in a dusty news library, conjuring up such information effortlessly out of the ether seems like magic. We need hardly be surprised, therefore, that, as the syndicated columnist Richard Harwood has noted, the press's hyping of the Internet has been indefatigable.

Essentially, as Kurt Andersen pointed out recently in the *New Yorker*, journalists, in common with financial professionals, have become profoundly computer-dependent. He adds: "What journalists and financial professionals haven't understood . . . is that almost no one else finds computers and the Internet quite so essential. As a result of this improbable accident of history, . . . [information] technology now sits at the center of a speculative frenzy of religious intensity."

Even some of the world's most influential media organizations have clearly succumbed to this frenzy. The *Wall Street Journal* and *The Economist* magazine are notable cases in point. Each betrays a consistently uncritical enthusiasm for postindustrialism that clearly owes much to a doctrinally driven tendency to endorse almost any new trend that emerges in America's free-market economy. Unfortunately, where doctrinal issues are at stake, neither *The Economist* nor the *Wall Street Journal* (at least in its editorial pages) can be relied on to report contrary evidence accurately, let alone fairly. *The Economist*'s attempts to understand the issues are further distorted by the disadvantage of its British base. Although the British economy has been in relative decline since the midnineteenth century, this does not stop *The Economist* from presenting the United Kingdom as still the world economy's ultimate trend-setter. Thus, just as the United Kingdom long ago began exiting manufacturing for such postindustrial services as finance, *The Economist* argues that the United States should be following the Mother Country's "lead."

If the postindustrial mania were limited to doctrinally driven publications like *The Economist* and the *Wall Street Journal*, it would be bad enough. But unfortunately, the mania has now also gripped other publications less noted for their doctrinal biases. Take *Fortune* magazine. Here is an institution that up to 1993 was so convinced of the pivotal importance of manufacturing that it refused to include anything but manufacturing companies in its famous Fortune 500 roll call of America's ultimate corporate greats. In recent years, however, *Fortune* has swung so violently to the opposite extreme that it often seems to be an uncritical booster of all things postindustrial. *Fortune*'s enthusiasm for postindustrialism is notably apparent, for instance, in a portentous list of "cool companies" it has been publishing annually since 1993. "Cool" in this case is intended to mean technologically exciting, and the unmistakable subtext of *Fortune*'s cool company list is that manufacturing is no longer cool. The 1997 list was typical of the genre in that not a single manufacturer was considered worthy of inclusion. All fifteen companies that did make the list not only were postindustrial operations but were almost laughably insignificant. One of them, a sort of electronic clippings service called ideaMarket, employed just eighteen people, and most of the others were not much larger. In aggregate, all fifteen companies employed a total of a mere 2,781 — in other words, little more than the number of people IBM hired in a good month in its days of manufacturing leadership (when its contribution to America's job base made it a truly cool company).

If the press's role were limited merely to lionizing obscure, untried cyberspace start-ups, things would be bad enough. But the press has done its readers' understanding of the issues an even greater disservice in its constant hyping of the American economy's performance in the deindustrializing 1990s. By the latter half of the decade, many press commentators had become so convinced that the United States had undergone a full-scale economic renaissance that they were talking as if American corporations had "the world at their feet."

At first sight, the euphoria might seem to have been well justified given corporate America's healthy profits and Wall Street's soaring stock prices. But there was another side to the story that clearly raised large questions about whether the United States really had "the world at its feet." The point was, of course, that the U.S. current account deficits were more or less spiraling out of control. And to the extent that America's manufactured imports were coming largely from such ultra-high-wage nations as Germany and Japan, it was hard to see how "healthy and competitive" the American economy truly was. After all, the sense of American economic decline that had been so much discussed in previous decades was driven more than anything by the perennially deteriorating trade position. But to press commentators, the trade problems were merely a "quibble." Some quibble. In the first seven years of the 1990s, America's current account deficits totaled $726 billion, up 79 percent on the first seven years of the 1980s — and this despite a massive devaluation of the dollar that supposedly had wrought a dramatic turnaround in American competitiveness that would soon dispose of the deficits for good.

To the extent that commentators have focused at all on the U.S. trade problem, they have tended to see it somehow as evidence of America's fundamental economic superiority. Their argument is that the deficits stem from the fact that a booming United States has been sucking in imports from the "stagnant" economies of Europe and East Asia.

Just one of the many obvious problems with this argument, however, is that more than one-quarter of America's imports are coming from nations where wages are actually higher than those of the United States. This begs a historic question: Why isn't the United States capable of making such goods for itself? Few press commentators have asked the question. Even fewer have answered it. The sad reality is that after the rundown of so many once great American manufacturing industries in the previous two decades, the United States simply does not have the capacity anymore to meet its consumers' needs from its own manufacturing resources.

The press's role in obscuring the extent to which American manufacturers are failing to hack it in world markets is compounded by its portrayal of manufacturing as a consistently dull activity worthy only of self-evident second-raters. This explains why, as noted in *Made in America,* a study published by the Massachusetts Institute of Technology in 1989, manufacturing departments in corporate America have come to be regarded as dead ends — places "where you go and stay until you die." This contrasts sharply with the position of manufacturing in Japan, where, as the MIT study reported, "production hasfar greater stature [than in the United States] and attracts some of the most qualified and competent technical and management professionals."

The American press's tendency to belittle manufacturing naturally colors its attitude to the world's great manufacturing economies. This is notably apparent in the case of Germany, whose economic arrangements are constantly being slighted by ill-informed American press commentators. An article in *Fortune* in 1997 illustrates the pattern. The magazine reported that manufacturing accounts for 30 percent of jobs in Germany versus just 16 percent in the United States. *Fortune* commented that this was "a sure sign" that German manufacturers were "seriously overstaffed." But were they? For anyone who had eyes to see, the real reason for Germany's large manufacturing workforce was obvious: trade. Given that Germany exports nearly two-thirds of its manufactured output, it clearly has a good excuse for employing a large manufacturing labor force. Moreover, trade also helps explain why the United States has such a small manufacturing labor force — because, of course, the United States these days relies on imports for nearly one-third of all its consumption of manufactured goods. One thing is certain: with German wages running well above American levels as of the late 1990s, Germany's manufacturers did not become dominant players in export markets by being "overstaffed."

Press commentators also tend to be absurdly disparaging about the manufacturing economies of East Asia. In particular, they tend to be patronizing about Japan's key high-tech industries. A notable case in point is computers, a field in which Japan is consistently portrayed as an also-ran. The only evidence adduced for this assertion is that the Japanese do little exporting of desktop computers. But this hardly means the Japanese are absent from the world computer market: far from it. The fact is that, as we have seen, the Japanese are absolutely dominant in other areas of the computer industry — areas that are invariably much more sophisticated than the desktop business. The most important such area is components, particularly the most miniaturized components. A classic example of such components is the tiny laser diodes that, as we pointed out in chapter 5, play such an important enabling role in the Information Age. Japan's leadership in miniaturization is easy to overlook, but the point is that, since the industry's earliest days, the key technological challenge in computers has always been to get ever greater performance out of ever smaller components. This is by no means an insignificant challenge. To make things smaller requires not only ever higher standards of purity in materials and accuracy in machining but constant innovation in addressing problems like overheating (which is a key concern in, for instance, tiny friction-bearing parts of the sort used in CD-ROMs). In essence, the superpowerful notebook computers made by such Japanese giants as Toshiba, Fujitsu, and Hitachi are the pinnacle of the computer industry's fifty-year quest to pack ever more performance into ever smaller packages.

The press's uncomprehending attitude to Japan's extraordinary success in computer miniaturization is part of a fashion for the business press to dismiss many highly sophisticated manufactured products as "commodities." The term is much used in reference to, for instance, advanced electronic components that are made to industry-standard designs. Typical of such components are liquid-crystal displays. The key to success in such a product is supreme manufacturing efficiency and consistently high quality. Companies that fail to meet these tests have nowhere to hide. The result is that the field of contenders in such undifferentiated, "commodity" products has thinned rapidly to a highly exclusive group of massively capitalized, relentlessly hard-driven Japanese companies like Toshiba, Hitachi, NEC, Sony, and Sharp. These are the Wimbledon finalists of manufacturing — companies whose production technology is so far advanced that, even though they pay higher wages than their American counterparts, they are little troubled by American competition. In other words, they are a charmed circle. Yet when the press refers to such companies' products as "commodities," the implication is the diametric opposite — that the fields concerned are wide open to competition from low-wage countries. Thus, *commodities* is a weasel word that hides from the American reading public how far ahead Japanese manufacturing companies truly are.

Of course, if Japanese manufacturers are doing so much better than their American counterparts, this prompts an obvious question: why has the Japanese economy been doing so badly in recent years? Why indeed. It is time to find out what really happened to the Japanese economy in the 1990s.

The enigma of Japanese economics: it's the surpluses, stupid!

One of the biggest factors encouraging Americans to view postindustrialism complacently in recent years has been the conviction that the United States now stands gloriously unchallenged as the world's sole economic superpower. It is all such a contrast with the 1980s, when the United States was widely perceived as losing ground inexorably to an ever burgeoning Japan. To the postindustrialists, therefore, the logic would appear to be watertight: because in the 1990s a postindustrial United States has "turned the tables" on Japan's "machine age" economy, there could hardly be a clearer demonstration of the superiority of postindustrialism.

There is only one problem with this: the United States has not turned the tables on Japan. Far from it. In the ways that matter most to policy makers on both sides of the Pacific, Japan has continued to gain on the United States in the 1990s and has done so precisely because it has stayed the course in manufacturing.

But how can all this be reconciled with the American press's picture of Japan as the worst-performing major economy of the 1990s? It cannot, of course. In reality, Western observers suffer major comprehension problems in covering Japan's highly counterintuitive economy — problems that in recent years have consistently concealed the Japanese economy's enormous underlying strengths.

We'll look at these comprehension problems in a moment, but first let's be clear: not everything has been coming up roses for the Japanese economy recently. No economy fires on all cylinders all the time, and certainly the Japanese economy has had its share of problems in the 1990s. The most obvious of these has, of course, been the Tokyo stock market crash. This began early in 1990 and was accompanied by an even bigger — if less publicized — slump in the Tokyo real estate market. The resulting knock-on effects have included the impoverishment of much of Japan's erstwhile free-spending speculator class, not to mention the traumatic weakening of Japan's big banks and securities companies.

All this has led respected American economic commentators to portray Japan as suffering one of the worst slumps in world economic history. Thus, by early 1999 Floyd Norris of the *New York Times,* for instance, was writing: "The histories of Japan in the 1990s and the United States in the 1930s argue that bursting bubbles devastate economies."

In reality, however, the idea that Japan has been suffering a slump, let alone a 1930s-style Great Depression, is absurd. Of course, in some ways Japan's performance in the 1990s bears a passing resemblance to that of the United States in the 1930s. But this resemblance is strictly limited to the financial sector, which is just one relatively small part of a huge economy. And even in the financial sector, the resemblance is hardly total: for one thing, whereas about half of all American banks collapsed in the 1930s, in Japan in the 1990s just one significant bank, Hokkaido Takushoku, has gone out of business. The truth is that, thanks to exceptionally robust firewalls built into the Japanese economy, the problems have been tightly contained within the financial sector and most of the rest of the economy has come out of the 1990s largely or totally unscathed. Thus, whether judged by employment levels, exports, savings rates, or a host of other crucial measures of economic health, the contrast with Depression-era America could hardly be more startling.

Perhaps the most surprising case in point is living standards. With the exception of a tiny minority of bankrupt speculators, most Japanese citizens have been enjoying unprecedented affluence in recent years. Nearly 2.2 million more Japanese households now own a car, for instance, than in the 1980s. And in the case of those who already owned a car a decade ago, most now own a much more powerful and comfortable model. Japan's executive class, for instance, has migrated en masse to such toney limousines as the Toyota Celsior (or Lexus, as it is known in the West) that are a world away from the antiquated Toyota Century that was standard issue for the corporate elite just a decade ago. Meanwhile, countless major road construction projects have improved driving conditions throughout Japan. Examples include such latter-day civil engineering miracles as the Tokyo Bay undersea road tunnel and the Akashi suspension bridge, both of which have set new world records for length.

The Japanese people's increasing affluence in the 1990s is also apparent in the range and quality of their household electronic gadgetry. Fully 33 percent of Japanese households now boast at least one video camera, for instance, up from just 16 percent in 1990. And household ownership of personal computers has grown even faster. There have been big increases also in the ownership of everything from home fax machines and mobile telephones to rooftop satellite dishes and digital versatile disk players.

On vacation, too, the Japanese people have never had it so good. Fully 13,773,000 Japanese citizens vacationed abroad in 1996 (the last year for which figures were available at press time). That represented an increase of a phenomenal 69.9 percent on 1989. In a notably backhanded compliment to their spending power, the Japanese have in many cases now displaced Americans as the prime targets of the world tourist industry's various tricks for fleecing affluent foreigners. Hotels in favorite Japanese vacationing spots everywhere from Cairns in Australia to Mount Whistler in Canada, for instance, now routinely charge special "Japan rates" that are as much as 50 percent higher than rates quoted to other tourists, including Americans.

Even in housing, a category in which as recently as the 1980s Japan notoriously lagged behind other advanced nations, Japanese citizens have been catching up fast: whether they are buying or renting, they now receive as much as 50 percent more space for their money as a decade ago. As a result, although jerry-built homes from the postwar reconstruction era continue to mar Japan's inner-city vistas, Japan has drawn broadly level with nations like France and the United Kingdom in overall housing standards.

Of course, none of this is to suggest that the Japanese have achieved any kind of consumer nirvana. Japan's highly regulated economy continues to suppress consumption in various ways that clearly diminish the potential for the good life. But the point is that Japanese consumers saw probably as big a lifestyle improvement in the 1980s as any other major nation — and the ultimate symbol of that improvement, as we have already noted, is that Japan has now climbed to the top of the world life expectancy league table.

Underlying the improvement in living standards has been another crucial strength that belies Japan's image as the "sick man" of the global economy — its remarkably robust labor market. In the face of unprecedented financial turmoil, unemployment averaged less than 4 percent in the first eight years of the 1990s; up to early 1999, the highest it had gone at any stage in the decade was 4.4 percent. Although this was certainly high by previous Japanese standards, it was the ultimate rebuke to those who would suggest that Japan has been suffering Great Depression–level problems. Remember that the unemployment rate in the United States reached as high as 25 percent for a time in the early 1930s.

All this helps explain what is perhaps Japan's most remarkable strength in the late 1990s — its world-beating export industries. Maintaining consistently high levels of employment through thick and thin (and despite paying some of the world's highest wages), Japanese exporters have been achieving muscular increases in output almost every year. The result is that, as measured in dollars, Japan's total exports rose by a cumulative 53 percent in the first eight years of the decade. Adjusted for dollar inflation, this represents real growth of more than 18 percent. And all this was the more impressive for the fact that already a decade ago Japan's exports were so large that they were considered to have unbalanced the world trading system.

Of course, it has to be admitted that compared to earlier decades economic growth in Japan has been relatively slow in the 1990s. Things could hardly be otherwise given that most Japanese industries long ago completed their catch-up phase and therefore no longer enjoy the benefit of piggybacking on new production technologies pioneered elsewhere. But even in the matter of economic growth, the news has not been remotely as bad as most press commentators have implied. Certainly the Japanese economy has had some poor years lately, but it has also had some excellent ones, and the overall trend has been amazingly better than readers of the American press have been led to believe. In fact, as the Economic Policy Institute economists John Schmitt and Lawrence Mishel have pointed out, per capita gross domestic product actually grew faster in Japan than in the supposedly booming

United States in the first eight years of the 1990s. Moreover, Japan's growth — at an average 2.1 percent a year — looks even more impressive compared to that of most European nations. It exceeded by nearly 50 percent the performance of the United Kingdom, for instance — and we need hardly add that no one has been suggesting that the United Kingdom has been suffering a Great Depression in the 1990s.

That said, Japan's performance has been even better than these comparisons suggest. For a start the foregoing figures measure gross domestic product (GDP), whereas the most appropriate yardstick for a comparison of this sort is gross national product (GNP): the distinction is that GNP is a more comprehensive measure that, unlike GDP, takes account of debits and credits relating to cross-border investments. As the United States has become an increasingly large net importer of capital in recent years, its GNP is actually now considerably less than its GDP. By contrast, because Japan has long been a major net exporter of capital, its GNP is considerably larger than its GDP. How much of a difference does this make? Unfortunately, we can't be sure, because both the United States and Japan switched to a GDP reporting basis a decade ago. But at a guess, the distorting effect of GDP numbers makes the American economy appear at least three percentage points larger relative to that of Japan than it really is.

Various other adjustments are also necessary to conduct a fully fair comparison, and most of these also favor the Japanese side. For one thing, as the economist Dean Baker has pointed out, U.S. national income figures have been inflated in recent years by a significant element of double counting. This arises from an explosion in the use of stock options to remunerate both executives and rank-and-file employees. Properly accounted for, such options are a cost that should be deducted in calculating profits, but few corporations actually do this. The result is that American national income figures are bloated by an increasingly large element of "funny money" in corporate profit statements.

All this helps explain an otherwise inexplicable aspect of the 1990s — a persistent tendency for the yen to gain relative to the dollar. A particularly notable illustration of this pattern was in 1998, when the yen gained a net 13 percent at a time when the newspapers were outspokenly gloomy about the state of the Japanese economy. Of course, not too much should be read into any one year's currency trend (and 1998 was indeed, in most other respects, a bad year for Japan).

But with the yen gaining a net 24 percent between 1989 and 1998, the long-term trend is clear — and highly troubling for the United States. In this regard, it is worth remembering that, if other things are equal, the strength of a nation's currency is the ultimate determinant of the size of its economy — and the ultimate symbol of its economic health. In the 1960s, President John F. Kennedy felt so strongly about this that he ranked dollar devaluation alongside nuclear war as the two things he feared most!

Given the strength of all the evidence to the contrary, we must wonder why the press has so consistently and outspokenly portrayed the Japanese economy as a basket case in recent years.

In attempting to interpret Japanese economic affairs, the main mistake the American press makes is to see everything through the simplistic logic of American-style laissez-faire. The truth is that the Japanese economic system is not based on laissez-faire but rather is a much more complicated animal whose inner workings require special knowledge to interpret. In struggling to make sense of the Japanese economy's bewildering divergences from American economic logic, the American press is rather like someone whose knowledge of board games is limited to checkers but who nonetheless has been called upon to provide a running commentary on a Grand Master chess match!

To be fair, it has to be noted that the press's comprehension problems have been greatly exacerbated by the highly counterintuitive nature of Japan's international public relations strategy in recent years. Basically the Japanese economic system's leaders and spokesmen speak and behave as if Japan's economic situation were much worse than it really is. They evidently believe that it is in Japan's national interest not to appear too strong — and certainly not to seem like a "threat" to American influence in the world economy. Their rationale is obvious: so long as Japan is regarded abroad as somehow an especially "dysfunctional" nation whose economic victories are invariably Pyrrhic ones, Western policy makers will continue to take a patient and indulgent view of Japan's controversial trade policies. In this regard, the Japanese learned an important lesson in the late 1980s when, with the Tokyo stock market hitting new highs almost every day, Western policy makers swung to the opposite extreme and became momentarily highly alarmed at what they saw as an all-conquering juggernaut. This helped galvanize Western governments to demand major reforms of Japan's perennially controversial trade policies.

That said, the idea that a nation would go out of its way to play down its economic strengths seems so counterintuitive that it is hard for Westerners to credit. Remember, though, that a strong modesty ethic pervades Japanese culture. This makes it almost second nature for the Japanese to cast themselves and their institutions in a ritually negative light. Another factor that helps sustain the Japanese establishment's downbeat slant on the news is that Japanese economic leaders and institutions have little or no need to court the admiration of anyone outside the closed circle of their immediate peers.

Perhaps the clearest evidence of the lengths to which Japanese leaders are prepared to go to understate their economy's true strengths is in the way they talk about the Japanese government's budget. All through the 1990s they have suggested that the government has been running huge deficits — deficits ostensibly intended to stimulate consumption, particularly consumption of imported goods. So successful have they been in this regard that America's most respected media organizations — organizations of the caliber of the *New York Times,* the *Washington Post,* and the *Wall Street Journal* — have fallen for the story. Thus, year after year Americans have been treated to a deluge of reports that Japan was supposedly running huge government deficits. In reality, as authoritative figures from the OECD demonstrate, Japan was running huge government surpluses! In 1995, for instance, a year when the *Wall Street Journal* reported that Japan was running a budgetary deficit of 2 percent, the OECD found that the government achieved a budgetary surplus of 3.5 percent. In fact, according to the OECD's figures, which were published each year in the widely circulated yearbook *OECD in Figures,* not only was Japan's surplus one of the strongest of any OECD nation, but Japan was the only major nation that had a budget surplus at all that year. By comparison, the United Kingdom, for instance, ran a deficit of 5.0 percent, and America's deficit was 2.2 percent. Any full analysis of the Japanese economy's performance in the 1990s can produce dozens of other similar discrepancies between an image of an apparently weak economy and an underlying reality of enormous strength.

Another factor that contributes powerfully to the American press's comprehension problems in Japan is the role played by securities analysts. Many of them are, to say the least, not wholly reliable. As the *International Herald Tribune*'s Hong Kong correspondent Philip Bowring has pointed out, many analysts quoted in the press are clearly intent on winning business for their firms or on gaining personal publicity for themselves rather than enlightening the public. This point has been echoed scathingly by the *U.S. News* writer and longtime Japan watcher William Holstein, who has pointed out that many of the securities analysts the press has relied on for its understanding of various problems in the Japanese financial system actually had little or no knowledge of that system. Referring to such analysts, he said: "They build their careers by getting quoted. Since inflammatory remarks get quoted, they say inflammatory things. It doesn't matter whether they're right or wrong. They don't care. Other rent-a-quote specialists aren't even on the ground in Asia, yet they also get quoted making the most sweeping Armageddon-like statements."

One thing is certain: had the press checked, it would have discovered that most of the analysts it had been quoting so liberally over the years have egregiously bad records in interpreting the Japanese economy. Many of them were influential in creating the impression in the West that the Japanese government was running large budget deficits in the 1990s when in fact it was the only major nation that was running surpluses. Moreover, virtually none of the many prominent analysts who lived in Tokyo in the bubble era predicted the coming crash that began in January 1990 — or at least, they did not do so publicly. Even in the last wild weeks of the bull market, most analysts remained outspokenly bullish. Strange as it now seems, even the great American credit rating agencies continued to accord the Japanese banks ultra-high credit ratings even as those banks' wild lending was driving up Tokyo real estate prices to stratospheric levels. (This was the time when, at prevailing land values, the Imperial Park in central Tokyo was supposed to be worth more than the entire state of California!) In justifying their bullishness, American and British analysts in Tokyo repeated as a mantra that "Japanese real estate prices never fall." With guides like this, no wonder the press so often grasps the wrong end of the stick.

(To those who might accuse this present writer of Monday morning quarterbacking, he has a ready reply. As a Tokyo-based banking writer in 1989, he argued that the "sky-high stock market" was headed for "a disastrous accident" that would lead to a "prolonged bear market." Earlier, in a seven-page article "Why the Japanese Banks Are Shaky," he had argued that the Tokyo real estate market had been pumped up to "giddy heights of folly" by hugely inflated bank lending and predicted an inexorable implosion that would badly damage the banks' balance sheets. The article was one of the first that forthrightly labeled Japan's financial excesses of the late 1980s a "bubble.")

Essentially, with their wildly bullish pronouncements to the press in the late 1980s, the analysts played a crucial part in inflating the bubble. Yet these same analysts had no compunction in turning around in the 1990s and painting the state of the wider Japanese economy in outlandishly dire terms. All this helps explain some otherwise unbelievable aspects of American reporting of Japan in the 1990s. Even in years when the Japanese economy performed outstandingly well, for instance, the American press consistently presented it as troubled. This was notably apparent in 1996, when everyone from the *Wall Street Journal* to the *Christian Science Monitor* was dismissing the Japanese economy as "sluggish" or "stagnant" or even "mired in a deep slump." In fact, Japan's growth rate that year, at 3.9 percent, was the best of any major economy and was significantly superior to the rate of 2.8 percent recorded in the booming United States.

The press's tendency to underestimate Japan reached something of an all-time record in 1997, the year of the East Asian financial crisis. For many Americans, the most memorable moment of the crisis was not the spectacular currency collapses in Thailand, Malaysia, and Korea, but a piece of comparative trivia: the demise of Japan's Yamaichi Securities. This made the main television news bulletins around the world after a hysterical Yamaichi executive tearfully appealed to other Japanese employers to hire the firm's laid-off employees. Rarely has such a minor event had so much attention. The distinctly limited significance of Yamaichi's demise can be gauged from the fact that the firm employed fewer than eight thousand workers in Japan — a drop in the ocean in an economy of more than sixty-six million workers. Moreover, the financial consequences of the collapse were minimal given that both Yamaichi's customers and its bankers came out entirely whole. In any case, the demise of even a big securities firm is hardly a devastating blow for a Japanese financial system in which the securities industry has never been more than a fringe player.

One of the few commentators who saw through the absurdity of it all at the time was William Holstein of *U.S. News*. He commented: "Here is the world's second largest economy, which commands $12 trillion or so in wealth, and the media have created the impression that the country is on the edge of breakdown."

So how strong is the Japanese economy really? This present writer has addressed this question before in a book in 1995 entitled *Blindside: Why Japan Is Still on Track to Overtake the United States by the Year 2000*. From his vantage point in Tokyo, he has seen little since then to undermine his confidence in his analysis. Certainly he has been vindicated in his central point, which was that Japan's current account surpluses would continue to soar in the latter half of the 1990s, thus giving the lie to much talk in the American press in the mid-1990s that Japan's export industries would be disastrously hollowed out by South Korea and other low-wage East Asian nations. The soaring surpluses, which have stemmed in part from a major rise in real terms in the dollar value of Japan's exports in the last decade and in part from dramatic falls in the prices of most of the commodities that Japan imports, represent the culmination of a century-long commitment by Japan to scientific mercantilism as the key to national economic power. While the jury is still out on whether, on conventional measures of economic size, Japan will pass the United States by 2000 (this prediction is based on the belief that the yawning trade imbalances with the United States will trigger another major dollar collapse), the soaring surpluses mean that Japan has now clearly surpassed the United States in its external economic clout. In this regard, Japan's savings performance is a crucial factor that conventional commentators have overlooked. Although experts like *The Economist*'s editor in chief, Bill Emmott, predicted a decade ago that Japan's savings rate would plunge in the 1990s, the truth is that at last count Japan was producing $708 billion of new savings a year — or nearly 60 percent more than America's total of $443 billion. Not only has this enabled Japanese industry to invest nearly twice as much per worker as the United States in the 1990s, but it has meant that Japan has now decisively surpassed the United States as the world's main source of capital. In short, Japan is now exporting more capital in real terms than any nation since America's greatest days of global economic leadership in the 1950s. Overlooked by the American press, the results are starkly apparent in IMF financial statistics, which show that Japan's net external assets jumped from $294 billion to $891 billion in the first seven years of the 1990s. By contrast, America's net external *liabilities* ballooned from $71 billion to $831 billion.

In the long run, this changing balance of financial power will be just about the only thing that historians will remember about U.S.-Japan economic rivalry in the 1990s — but it was the one thing that Western observers utterly overlooked at the time.

America's manufacturing comeback: a myth is born

Policy makers who might otherwise be concerned about America's industrial decline have been reassured by talk that many key American manufacturing industries have staged an impressive comeback in recent years. Unfortunately, this reported comeback is wishful thinking.

One of the most elaborate versions of the comeback myth has been propagated by Jerry Jasinowski, president of the National Association of Manufacturers. As he is clearly someone who should know what he is talking about, his views are worth examining in detail.

In his book *Making It in America,* written with the consultant Robert Hamrin, Jasinowski talks about a "historic" new dynamism in American industry and asserts:

> American industry has not just caught up to the competition; it has gone beyond the competition. American manufacturing is again becoming the industrial powerhouse of the world, making enormous contributions to the quality of American life. . . . In the mid-1990s there are unmistakable signs that America's manufacturers have made a comeback — a comeback so strong that it has once again firmly put them in a global leadership position. . . . Major industries in the U.S. have come back smartly to achieve world preeminence, led by autos, steel, and semiconductors. The overall result is a highly competitive economy. . . . It is fascinating that American manufacturing has led the American economy's competitive resurgence in recent years. This should finally put to rest all the talk about a postindustrial society and "deindustrialization."

Stirring words — and words that a lot of Americans evidently want to believe. Certainly Jasinowski's book has collected impressive endorsements from, among others, Chrysler Chairman Lee Iacocca and the management guru Tom Peters. But where are the facts to back up Jasinowski's sweeping assertions? Actually, most of his "facts" turn out to be mere assertions. He argues, for instance, that manufacturing's share of America's total economic output increased in the 1980s, and he produces an assertion by a Washington economic analyst to this effect. He omits to mention, however, that this analyst is an outlier whose estimate of a one-and-a-half percentage point increase in manufacturing's share is contradicted by many other sources, not least the U.S. government. In fact, official U.S. figures suggest that manufacturing's share of GDP fell by about three and a half percentage points in the period. Not only does Jasinowski fail to tell us why the numbers he cites should be trusted over the government's numbers, but he fails even to mention the contradictory evidence of the government's numbers. Quite clearly, if Jasinowski were confident of his case, he would meet the government's contradictory evidence head on. That he has not done so speaks volumes.

Elsewhere Jasinowski reports that there has been "a tremendous resurgence of American exports" since 1985. This is true — but it is hardly the clincher he would have us believe. In reality, much of the increase in American exports has been driven by an entirely predictable adjustment to currency movements: for the fact is that the dollar has lost more than half its value against major foreign currencies since 1985. In such an environment, it is not necessary for exporters to achieve any volume growth to show a strong rise in export revenues as denominated in dollars. The point is that merely by maintaining their prices unchanged in foreign currencies, American exporters' dollar revenues soar even without any volume growth. While the currency benefit is obviously a welcome one for many erstwhile hard-pressed American manufacturers, the larger issue here is that it has been achieved at the expense of one of the most precipitate depreciations of a major currency in economic history. A country whose currency loses more than half its value in a decade can hardly be said to be going from strength to strength.

While making much of America's export growth, Jasinowski has nothing to say about a less convenient fact: American imports have also risen. In fact, the import rise goes a long way to explain the export rise. There is a clear causal relationship here, because the final products American manufacturers export these days are assembled with the use of an ever rising proportion of imported components and materials. In large part, therefore, in boosting their exports American manufacturers have merely been piggybacking on the tremendous productivity increases that other nations have achieved in advanced manufacturing industries in recent years. The result is that, as we have noted earlier, America's current account deficits have consistently soared in the 1990s.

In view of the dollar's depreciation since the mid-1980s, the huge rise in America's imports is an especially telling indication of its waning manufacturing prowess. Remember that the dollar's fall created a historic opportunity for American companies to win back market share lost to foreign suppliers in the American home market in the early 1980s. And in fact, hopes that American manufacturers would do just that were a major reason why then Treasury Secretary James Baker agreed in 1985 to lower the dollar's value. Certainly, by any normal logic, America's imports should have fallen after the dollar crashed. In the event, as measured from 1984, the last full year before the dollar's depreciation began, America's imports rose at a compound rate of more than 7 percent — which, after allowing for inflation, represents a real growth of a disturbing 4 percent a year. Clearly there is little here to bolster Jasinowski's contention that "American manufacturing is again becoming the industrial powerhouse of the world."

Perhaps the most surprising thing about Jasinowski's analysis is the claims he makes for individual American industries. He maintains in particular that the American automobile industry has reestablished "world preeminence." But as with so many of his assertions, he offers no substantiation. Clearly the state of the international competitiveness of the American auto industry can be readily checked by reference to international trade figures. These are conspicuously absent from Jasinowski's analysis — perhaps understandably because they flatly contradict him. The truth is that the American auto industry continues to do virtually no exporting outside Canada and Mexico. Moreover, succumbing to periodic downsizings, the Detroit Big Three have continued to lose share even in the American domestic market — not least to Japanese competitors. Admittedly, this latter point has been somewhat obscured by a change in the composition of Japan's automotive exports. Whereas in earlier years Japanese exports consisted mainly of fully built cars, these days the Japanese automobile industry is moving more and more to exporting components and materials — and big increases in exports of such products are a key reason America's trade deficits with Japan have soared in the 1990s. Given that the business of making components and materials is generally a much more economically sophisticated one than assembling cars, the Japanese have benefited twice over — and the American automotive industry has suffered a double whammy.

Steel is another industry in which, on Jasinowski's analysis, the United States has won back "preeminence." He bases this assessment on various productivity surveys that purportedly show that the United States is the world's most efficient steel producer. What he does not mention is that such surveys are not only notoriously unreliable but, by dint of a judicious choice of assumptions, can be made to "prove" almost anything. Certainly the surveys he cites do not stand up to even cursory reality checking. The point is that, if the United States were truly the world's most efficient producer, we would expect it to be a major exporter. Instead, thanks to a doubling in the volume of its steel imports since 1983, the United States remains by far the world's largest importer! Of course, none of this is to disparage the efforts of many capable people who have tried to turn the American steel industry's fortunes around in the last two decades. The truth is that their efforts have been stymied by events beyond their control, specifically dumping by many foreign steel producers in the American market. This dumping has continued so long at such a high level that it has constantly deprived the American industry of the level of retained profits necessary to pursue vitally needed investments in efficient new production technologies. At the end of the day, the fact remains that the American steel industry is now so weak that it cannot compete with foreign producers even in third-country markets (that is, markets where there are no significant local producers and where typically, therefore, all the world's producers can compete against one another on a relatively level playing field). As in the case of autos, therefore, the story of an American comeback in steel is largely a myth.

So much for America's position in traditional manufacturing industries. But what of more glamorous industries? It is time to look at how America's high-tech manufacturers are doing.

American high-tech: back at the leading edge?

For many Washington policy makers, disappointments in steel and autos ultimately don't matter very much so long as the United States retains a decisive lead in more advanced manufacturing industries. So how is the United States doing in such industries? On the face of it, very well — and its apparent success has been crucial in quelling concerns about the precipitate decline in the overall size of America's manufacturing workforce in the last two decades. Unfortunately, however, this success is largely illusory. The reality is that, though American high-tech brand names are more visible than ever in the world's stores, the companies that stand behind these brand names are, in manufacturing terms, a mere shadow of their former selves. As America's high-tech manufacturers have "restructured" in recent years, they have come to depend more and more on outsourcing from East Asian rivals for their most sophisticated manufacturing processes.

A particularly significant point about corporate America's outsourcing is that much of it is done in ultra-high-wage Japan. Other things equal, when a lower-wage nation imports a product from a higher-wage one, we can reasonably assume that the manufacturing technology concerned is one in which the importing country is lacking.

Americans got used to the idea of such outsourcing in the 1970s and early 1980s when Japanese wages were still low by American standards. Thus, American corporations could justify outsourcing from Japan on the basis that they were relying on the Japanese merely for low-level, labor-intensive workmanship, thereby, in theory at least, freeing American workers to specialize in higher-level work. These days, however, with Japanese wages so much higher than American levels, American corporations that import from Japan are effectively admitting they lag behind in the technology race.

The outsourcing trend has become something of an embarrassment at many major American manufacturing companies these days. So much so that journalists who ask questions about such issues either are unceremoniously rebuffed or at best are fed a diet of highly misleading half-truths.

Of course, when a company outsources its production, this does not necessarily imply that it is outsourcing from abroad. But as a practical matter, when American manufacturers outsource, they do so largely from East Asia. Such supposedly strong American manufacturers as Hewlett-Packard and Compaq depend on East Asian rivals not only for crucial components but for entire manufacturing functions.

For a more complete view of the extent to which major American high-tech corporations have become dependent on outsourcing in recent years, it is useful to check American corporate disclosure documents filed with the Securities and Exchange Commission. In making these filings, corporations are under some pressure to acknowledge their dependence on foreign suppliers. Among other things, failure to do so may later expose them to expensive class-action lawsuits from disgruntled shareholders complaining of being blindsided by, for instance, currency-driven cost increases.

These SEC filings often contain surprising admissions of dependence on foreign suppliers — albeit admissions that have consistently been overlooked by American media commentators toasting corporate America's high-tech "supremacy." Take, for instance, this disclosure from Hewlett-Packard in 1997: "Portions of the company's manufacturing operations are dependent on the ability of significant suppliers to deliver completed products, integral subassemblies, and components in time to meet critical distribution and manufacturing schedules. The failure of suppliers to deliver these products, subassemblies, and components in a timely manner may adversely affect the company's operating results until alternate sourcing could be developed." Elsewhere Hewlett-Packard disclosed: "For many of its products, the company has existing alternate sources of supply, or such sources are readily available." This statement sounds reassuring, but in fact it is a lawyer's way of putting shareholders on notice that in the case of many other products, the company does not have any alternate sources of supply — and thus, Hewlett-Packard is effectively dependent on single suppliers for what are crucial enabling components without which it would be out of business.

Another major American high-tech manufacturer that is surprisingly dependent on foreign suppliers is the leading maker of semiconductor manufacturing equipment, Applied Materials. In SEC filings in 1996, Applied Materials disclosed:

> The company's manufacturing activities consist primarily of assembling various commercial and proprietary components into finished systems, principally in the United States, with additional operations in England, Japan, Korea, and Taiwan. Production requires some raw materials and a wide variety of mechanical and electrical components, which are manufactured to the company's specifications. Multiple commercial sources are available for most components. . . . There have been no significant delays in receiving components from sole source suppliers; however, the unavailability of any of these components could disrupt scheduled deliveries to customers.

Many other examples could be cited of how other key American high-tech manufacturers depend on foreign suppliers for their most sophisticated components.

But surely the United States has scored some real successes in high-tech manufacturing in the 1990s? Yes — but far fewer than even most experts realize. Perhaps the strongest remaining American high-tech manufacturer is Boeing. But even Boeing is doing less well than it used to. Quite apart from facing increasing competition from the European Airbus consortium, Boeing has been under considerable pressure from foreign governments to transfer jobs abroad, and it has duly done so. As William Greider has pointed out in his book *One World, Ready or Not,* 30 percent of the components used in Boeing's 777 jet are made abroad. By comparison in the 1960s, Boeing imported only 2 percent of its components. Thus, Boeing, like other erstwhile world-beating American manufacturers, is rapidly becoming a "virtual corporation" ever more dependent on suppliers in Japan and elsewhere abroad for its most advanced manufacturing needs.

Meanwhile, despite all the talk of a renaissance in the American semiconductor industry, there is actually only one truly strong American semiconductor manufacturer left: Intel. Moreover, Intel's success says little if anything about its manufacturing prowess. In fact, the company's twenty-four-fold growth in the fifteen years to 1997 has been driven not by any fundamental efficiency edge in production engineering but rather by the company's near-monopolistic franchise in producing microprocessors for the dominant "Wintel" standard in personal computers.

In any case, Intel is just one company — and judged by the all-important criterion of jobs, not a particularly large one. At last count it employed sixty-seven thousand people worldwide — little more than one-sixth of IBM's peak workforce in the mid-1980s before its domination of the computer industry collapsed under pressure from the rising Wintel standard. Moreover, Intel is not as advanced as it appears. In fact, its Wintel chips are based on an aging technology known as CISC (complex instruction set computing). In the last decade, CISC has been superseded by a technology called RISC (reduced instruction set computing). RISC chips, which are noted for their use in such high-performance computers as Sun Microsystems' network servers, are made mainly in Japan.

Intel apart, there are few other semiconductor manufacturers left in the United States. This may seem surprising in view of the fact that, according to such prophets of America's purported industrial renaissance as Jerry Jasinowski, the United States has now recovered strong leadership in semiconductors. He has reported that American semiconductor makers boosted their global market share from 40 percent in 1988 to 44 percent in 1993, and this supposedly has put the United States back in the "top spot" in the industry. After the big decline in America's share in the first half of the 1980s, all this seems like convincing evidence of a comeback. But the truth is that his 44 percent figure is bogus. It is based on highly misleading statistical procedures that categorize most chips outsourced by American companies from factories in East Asia and elsewhere as "American"! The only justification for this bizarre statistical treatment is that most such chips are made to American designs and bear American brand names. But that hardly means they are made in America. Even Dataquest, an information-industry consulting firm that is the ultimate source of data on world semiconductor production, compiles its statistics on this basis.

Given the prevalence of such misleading statistics, how do we gauge the true state of American competitiveness? Again, there is no substitute for international trade figures. These indicate that the United States ran a deficit of more than $3 billion with Japan alone in semiconductors in 1997. Given Japan's higher wage levels, therefore, it is clear that the idea that the United States has recovered world leadership in semiconductors is just another myth.

It has to be noted that many American executives think that it no longer matters that the United States imports most of its semiconductors so long as American companies do their chip design work in the United States. From the point of view of corporations intent on boosting their short-term profits, this argument no doubt makes sense. But from the point of view of the overall American national interest, things look quite different. The basic problem is this: product development as practiced in the United States these days has become a postindustrial function. As such, it is burdened with all the usual drawbacks of postindustrialism.

For a start, it comes up short on jobs: product development creates jobs mainly for a narrow elite of university-educated workers — the same sort of workers who are favored by most other postindustrial businesses.

Moreover, in the long run outsourcing works to the disadvantage even of American semiconductor companies' shareholders. The point is that by abandoning its manufacturing activities the American semiconductor industry loses all hope of establishing a lasting lead over foreign competitors. After all, American designs can be easily reverse-engineered, and as a matter of fact, America's best chip designs are often imitated in East Asia within weeks of their launch. Certainly they prove a far less enduring asset for a nation than proprietary manufacturing know-how. Thus, companies that lead in product development must keep on innovating merely to stay in the game, and unlike great manufacturing companies, they never get a chance to build up a reservoir of deep proprietary production knowledge that can see them through bad times.

At the end of the day, when American high-tech companies are lauded in the press as world leaders, what is being extolled is not solid manufacturing know-how but rather much less enduring postindustrial strengths.

The last illusion: uniquely inventive American manufacturing

We have already had much to say about the myth of superior American creativity. One further point needs to be added. Even among those few American policy makers who understand how hollowed out American manufacturing has already become, the creativity myth has had a powerful tranquilizing effect. Such policy makers reassure themselves that a relative lack of creativity will ensure that other nations' manufacturers, and particularly those of Japan, cannot independently race very far ahead of their American counterparts. Such policy makers therefore take it for granted that by dint of superior American creativity, the United States can easily get back into advanced manufacturing anytime it chooses.

But just as it is a myth that other nations lack the necessary creativity to succeed in postindustrial services, equally it is a myth that they cannot innovate in manufacturing. The ability of the Japanese in particular to pioneer new areas of advanced manufacturing should not be underestimated. As the British management commentator Robert Heller has pointed out, anyone who looks closely at Japanese products immediately sees that they display a high degree of creativity in product design.

The idea that the Japanese lack the ability to make independent innovations in manufacturing is also strongly rejected by the Clinton administration adviser Ira Magaziner, who is a noted authority on Japanese manufacturing. Commenting on one American manufacturer's characterization of Japan as a nation of copyists, Magaziner has said:

> This was a common refrain in the early 1980s. Many U.S. businessmen, policy officials, and media analysts saw our entrepreneurial small companies as untouchable by the Japanese. There were many pseudopsychologists of Japan with themes about why Japan's collectivist culture did not allow for the creativity and freedom necessary for invention and entrepreneurship. These arguments have proven baseless as Japanese companies have shown themselves quite capable of pioneering new technologies and products.

The proof of this is already abundantly apparent in the marketplace. The world's electronics stores in particular are now full of products that were developed largely or totally in Japan. These notably include the Walkman, the Handycam, the liquid-crystal display, the digital camera, the home videotape recorder, the compact disk player, the laptop computer, and the cellular phone.

In truth, as the MIT Commission on Industrial Productivity pointed out some years ago, the argument about superior American creativity in advanced manufacturing is an ironic one given the historical record. For this is not the first time that a flagging industrial power has imagined that the allegedly superior creativity of its people can arrest its relative decline. In the early part of the twentieth century, the United Kingdom and other European nations consoled themselves with similar arguments in the face of rising American manufacturing might. Up to World War II, Europe regarded itself as the fountainhead of world creativity, and it talked about American manufacturers' efforts to commercialize European inventions in the same condescending tones that many Americans now reserve for the Japanese.

Amusingly, that ultimate authority on the human psyche, Sigmund Freud, seems to have concurred with the Europeans' assessment of Americans as copyists. In an interview in 1930, Freud said: "Americans are clever generalizers. They are rarely creative thinkers." Of course, Freud was wrong, and after World War II this became obvious as Americans, leveraging their new advantage in abundant funding, took the lead in many prestigious areas of science, technology, and medicine that had previously been dominated by the Europeans.

Creativity, like beauty, is in the eye of the beholder. While few today would accuse Americans of lacking creativity, the idea that there is something uniquely creative about American culture is not a bankable proposition. Rather, it is a dangerous illusion.

So much for the myth of superior American manufacturing creativity. Having disposed of this last excuse for procrastination, we emphasize that drastic action is now urgently necessary. Let's now proceed to a look at what realistic policy options are open to American leaders in their efforts decisively to reverse the deindustrialization trend of the last three decades.

9

An Action Plan

What should American policy makers do to reverse the postindustrial trend? Any effective strategy would have to be drastic. But in its basic principles, it would be quite simple:

- Boost the nation's savings.
- Channel a larger proportion of those savings into industrial investment, particularly productivity-enhancing production engineering.
- Ensure that manufacturers earn a reasonable return on their investment.
- Upgrade workers' skills.
- Stem the leakage of world-beating production technologies abroad.

Setting aside for a moment the task of raising the savings rate, many practical measures are available to facilitate most of the rest of this agenda. Tax incentives, for instance, can be readily devised to ensure that as much as possible of the nation's savings is channeled into manufacturing. The quality of management in manufacturing industries can be bolstered by ensuring that the nation's educational system places a stronger emphasis on technical subjects. Such a focus would help attract more of the nation's best brains into engineering, and particularly production engineering.

Concomitant measures would be needed to lessen the counterattractions of careers in finance and other postindustrial services whose compensation levels are now disproportionately high. The securities industry's size, for instance, could be drastically curtailed by imposing a transaction tax of, say, 0.5 percent on stock trades.

To deliver an adequate return on manufacturing investment, the United States would have to make sure — really sure — that its exporters competed in world trade on terms at least as favorable as those enjoyed by their foreign rivals. As a first step, the United States would have to dramatically beef up its notably half-hearted trade diplomacy. It might also be necessary to relax antitrust rules to ensure that the nation's manufacturers could agree on product standards and avoid wasteful duplication of effort by cooperating in research and development.

All this would undoubtedly boost the profitability of manufacturing industries. But higher profits are not enough. If U.S. competitiveness is to be boosted, profits must be plowed back into raising worker productivity, rather than siphoned off in large compensation packages for a wealthy elite. Among other things, executive stock options would have to be reengineered to force managers to focus on boosting their corporations' *long-term* prospects. Managers might be required as a general principle to be vested for a minimum of, say, seven years before they could cash in their stock-option gains. Moreover, they would forfeit their options completely in any vesting period in which they laid off American workers. This would powerfully focus management's attention on providing workers with *secure* jobs — a task that requires managers to think long-term in investing both in new production facilities and in research and development. In a regimen in which managers were punished personally for laying off workers, companies would be much more concerned with bolstering the quality of jobs at home; they would have a strong incentive, for instance, not to transfer their most advanced technologies and their most capital-intensive manufacturing processes overseas. The new corporate orientation toward the long term could be further bolstered by financial regulation giving long-term investors more say in corporate affairs, while frustrating the destabilizing activities of short term–minded takeover artists and stock market speculators.

So far so good. But we are left with the fundamental problem that the U.S. savings rate is far too low. How can the American people be induced to save more? Many remedies have been tried over the years, but almost invariably they have only seemed to make the problem worse. This is not to suggest that effective methods to raise a nation's savings rate do not exist. The whole history of the East Asian economic miracle demonstrates otherwise. Even in Singapore, one of the freest societies in the East, the savings rate was successfully boosted by a system of forced savings instituted by Lee Kuan Yew shortly after the city-state won independence.

The problem, of course, is that the United States is not Singapore. Any attempt to impose a Singapore-style savings program on Americans would undoubtedly spark a political firestorm.

Nonetheless, the task of reviving U.S. manufacturing prowess is of vital historic importance and clearly demands exceptional measures. By a process of elimination, only one policy option remains to be considered — an option that has so far been regarded as second only to nuclear war in unthinkability. That option is tariffs. Even the mere mention of the word generates a frisson of fear and loathing among today's generation of American policy makers. That is understandable. After all, many of them experienced at firsthand the unforgettable One World optimism of the Flower Power era, and like most decent people, they would like to believe that the world is ready for the close economic and political integration that global free trade implies. But after nearly fourteen years studying East-West relations from a vantage point in Tokyo, this writer has no illusions about the practical difficulties that face Western leaders who want to "teach the world to sing in perfect harmony." Certainly in the absence of major breakthroughs in trade diplomacy in the very near future, the tariff option must be included in any serious consideration of how U.S. manufacturing prowess can be revived. Otherwise, American manufacturers will be condemned to a perpetually unequal struggle in trying to compete with foreign manufacturers that enjoy the enormous advantage of a protected home market.

Let's be clear: As Patrick Buchanan has extensively documented in *The Great Betrayal,* the poor image that tariffs suffer in the current American economic debate is largely undeserved. Their image problem stems almost entirely from the allegedly major part they played in causing the Great Depression. In reality, however, they played a minor role in that disaster and were much less significant certainly than the general mismanagement of domestic demand in the United States and elsewhere in those years. In any case, to judge tariffs by referring to Depression-era experience with them is hardly more appropriate than to judge luxury liners by the unfortunate fate of the *Titanic.*

For any sane consideration of tariffs, the appropriate reference point is not the Hoover years but rather the Eisenhower years. Eisenhower's time, after all, was one of unprecedented prosperity, not only for the United States but for most of the rest of the world. Accompanied by supporting policies, such as careful demand management and fair regulation of financial markets, tariffs clearly played a major role in providing the economic stability needed for manufacturing industries to thrive.

The great advantage of tariffs is that they powerfully counter the effect of other nations' industrial policies in undermining the profitability of American manufacturing industries. Competing with one another behind a modest but adequate wall of tariffs, American companies would be provided with a generally appropriate level of profitability. They would reinvest those profits in the confident knowledge that, if they managed their businesses wisely, they would earn a fair return in the future. Tariffs could go a long way toward end-running the savings shortages and poor returns on investment that have discouraged so many American manufacturers from creating the world-beating production technologies that the American worker needs to stay at the leading edge in world productivity.

Of course, tariffs, like most economic tools, generate minuses as well as pluses. Certainly compared to a world of perfect free trade, they result in a less than optimum distribution of global industrial capacity. But for an economy as large as that of the United States (or for a large trading bloc, such as the European Union), the disadvantages involved in maintaining some firewalls against the vagaries of globalization are quite minor. In any case, absolute economic efficiency is by no means the only consideration here. It hardly ever is in real life. Remember that if economic efficiency were the only concern, most of our economic arrangements would be very different. Families would live in commune-style accommodation, for instance, rather than in self-contained one-family housing units. Just as people do not consider simply crude economic efficiency and are prepared to pay a bit extra for their own private bathrooms, kitchens, laundry facilities, and so on, it is reasonable for a major economy to waive the dictates of crude economic efficiency in ensuring that it is self-reliant in at least the most important of its fundamental manufacturing needs. Essentially the point here is that good fences make good neighbors.

The need to build firewalls against the worst excesses of globalization may not enter into economists' equations, but it is a real enough consideration nonetheless for anyone who has a wider concern for the human condition. Globalization might work if all the world's people shared substantially the same cultural values. In reality, however, as anyone who has actually lived for an extended period in, for instance, East Asia can testify, we are still an awfully long way from such a prospect. Those who think otherwise have been misled by the much publicized Westernization that has become apparent in many non-Western nations around the world in recent decades. But this Westernization is typically highly superficial. Certainly the fact that people eat McDonald's hamburgers and drink Coca-Cola is no guarantee that they share an American attitude to economics or politics. Absent carefully thought-through safeguards, therefore, any attempt to mesh diverse cultures together is likely to end in tears.

Of course, any talk of a pulling back from globalization is likely to appall the American financial elite. And here we come to the nub of the problem: so long as the current economic fashion for laissez-faire holds sway in elite circles, any serious attempt to map out a detailed program to revive American manufacturing would be a waste of words.

The fundamental question is not how to craft a workable program, therefore, but rather how to slay the prevailing zeitgeist.

Encouragingly, the zeitgeist has already been coming under increasing attack from many quarters around the world in recent years. In the United States the charge against the excesses of laissez-faire has been led by such notable thinkers as James Fallows, Lester Thurow, William Wolman, Clyde Prestowitz, Chalmers Johnson, Bennett Harrison, Patrick Buchanan, George Soros, John Judis, Robert Kuttner, and Barry Bluestone. Even in the United Kingdom, that ultimate font of postindustrial choplogic, laissez-faire is coming under increasing vigorous attack from such authors as Will Hutton and Paul Ormerod. That said, it has to be admitted that on both sides of the Atlantic the dogmatists still reign supreme. In fact, they have survived a well-deserved measure of opprobrium in the immediate aftermath of the Reagan-Thatcher era to come back in arguably even more potent form than ever in the late 1990s.

In any effort to beat back the dogmatists and vested interests, the media can and should play a pivotal role. After all, the media profoundly shape the intellectual climate in which politicians must compete for votes. The editors of the world's leading newspapers should be leading from the front in questioning the obvious contradictions in the prevailing dogma.

So far, however, they have generally shrunk from the task, no doubt in part because they are intimidated by the economics profession's pretensions to scientific certainty. But in truth they have no reason to be intimidated. Although academic economists delight in cloaking their work in abstruse mathematics, the truth is that real-world policy making rarely demands anything much more abstruse than simple arithmetic. The advanced mathematical tools used by the "experts" are useful merely in analyzing highly theoretical models that assume away the imperfection and complexity of the real world. By contrast, analyzing the real world generally requires little more than common sense. As John Kenneth Galbraith has pointed out, economists have yet to come up with any worthwhile practical insights that cannot be clearly and completely explained in plain English. Far from hiding important truths, the economics profession's cloak of mathematical abstruseness merely camouflages the worthlessness of its insights in guiding practical policy making.

Another reason the media shrink from challenging the zeitgeist is that laissez-faire's claims to be the one true faith have been consistently validated by the way the Nobel Prize for economics has been conferred over the years. Most of the prize's recipients have been dyed-in-the-wool advocates of laissez-faire. This naturally has given the impression that there is a general consensus among the world's intellectual leaders that laissez-faire is the only valid form of economics. The truth could hardly be more different. In reality, as *Business Week*'s economics editor, Michael Mandel, has pointed out, the world of academic economics is a seething mass of controversy in which there is virtually no consensus on anything anymore. Thus, the laissez-faire zealots who have won the Nobel Prize represent just one faction in a dysfunctional and demoralized profession, and their thinking is fiercely contested by others in the profession.

The great irony is that the laissez-faire bias in the awarding of the prize seems to reflect nothing more significant than the views of the Stockholm-based Sveriges Riksbank. Known in English as the Bank of Sweden, it administers the Nobel Prize in economics. The pattern it follows in conferring the prize faithfully reflects the tendency of the Stockholm financial elite to seek laissez-faire solutions to Sweden's economic problems in recent years.

One thing is certain: the world needs no lessons in economics from present-day Stockholm. In fact, Sweden's recent history has been an object lesson in how not to run an economy. Since the 1970s Swedish economic policy making has been increasingly shaped by laissez-faire thinking, and the result has been a consistently disappointing economic performance. Between 1970 and 1997, Sweden's per capita income in current dollars rose a mere sixfold — the poorest performance of any advanced economy with the exception of the United States and Canada. Its recent history contrasts starkly with the early years after World War II, when Sweden ran one of the most avowedly interventionist economies in the Western world. The formula included a powerful labor movement, a government-dominated savings system, high taxes, price controls, and a close partnership between big business and government. The result was one of the strongest and richest postwar economies: Sweden boosted its real output by two-thirds in just the first fifteen years after World War II.

Disastrous though the Swedish economy's encounter with laissez-faire economic dogma may have proved, the Bank of Sweden's baleful orthodoxy has profoundly influenced the world's universities, particularly those of the United States, which vie fiercely to win as many Nobel Prizes as possible. The result is that college administrators increasingly select for advancement those economics scholars whose views are most likely to please the Bank of Sweden and its right-leaning nominating committees.

That the Bank of Sweden's unfortunate influence on American economic thought has been almost completely overlooked in media discussions speaks volumes about the seriousness — or rather, lack of seriousness — with which the editors of the great American media organizations take their responsibility to cover economics. The task for the media is clear: they must move firmly to hold the economics profession as accountable as they would other key players in public life. Although American reporters delight in setting traps for politicians and disgracing them over essentially irrelevant aspects of their private lives, they have rarely done any reality checking on the economics profession's very public — and generally counterproductive — role in shaping the nation's destiny.

A first step on the road to more reliable and searching media coverage of economics would be for top editors to take direct responsibility for that coverage rather than delegating it to their business sections.

They should hire an entirely new cadre of top economic writers who are free from the institutional biases of the business sections. Chosen from the cream of the intellectual crop, such writers would be well versed in the principles of standard economics — and well versed also in deflating those ivory-tower theorists who present standard economics as a set of sacred truths.

By contrast, the current practice of delegating economic coverage to business reporters is a recipe for bias and misinformation. Business reporters are too close to their Wall Street sources, and they almost automatically identify with the Wall Street view, which happens to be an especially deadly formulation of the prevailing dogma. When reporters from the *New York Times,* the *Washington Post,* and other key media organizations call Wall Street analysts to put the latest economic developments "in context," the result is often pure spin.

Business reporters generally share the stock analysts' kneejerk tendency to identify exclusively with the interests of capital and are therefore implicitly or explicitly hostile to the much more economically significant interests of labor. Wall Street may be forgiven for focusing tightly on maximizing its own narrow interests, but the press is supposed to be bound by higher ideals. It is obligated to see the larger picture — and in particular to recognize the obvious truth that a nation cannot be rich if its workers are poor. This truth gets short shrift on Wall Street, which cares not at all if American workers lose their edge in the productivity league tables as America's most valuable production technologies are transferred abroad. The only criterion that matters to Wall Street is whether such transfers will pay off in boosting a corporation's short-term profits. But it is the press's job to keep an eye on the longer term and to stand up for the interests of the community as a whole.

The press's reliance on Wall Street for economic insights also introduces into its reportage an irrational bias against regulation. In any discussion of the need for regulatory action to correct the undesirable economic tendencies innate to extreme laissez-faire, Wall Street has a huge vested interest to protect: not to put too fine a point on it, but the more relaxed the regulatory backdrop in finance, the easier it is for financial professionals to feather their own nests at the expense of the nation's savers. Wall Street analysts thus naturally tend to be unsympathetic toward regulation in all its forms. But again, it is the press's job to see things in a wider focus, and in particular to look out for the national interest.

The truth is that, for all the glib talk of globalism in recent years, the peoples of the world still find group strength in their national identities. We pay our taxes to the nation, for instance, and it is, for the most part, from the nation that we draw our social security and other benefits. Moreover, when it comes to helping the sick and the old, it is entirely natural for us to think that charity begins at home. Even in this era of globalism, the nation assuredly still counts.

The irony of the global view of economics that underpins laissez-faire is its assumption that other nations are prepared to abandon all national concerns and behave as true globalists in managing their economies. It should be obvious that this is a utopian reading of human nature. In fact, in most parts of the world people are still very concerned about their own nation's relative position in the world economy. This is true even of the United States, where globalism has gone much further than almost anywhere else. There is probably hardly a single American who does not yearn for a return to the halcyon years of the Eisenhower and Kennedy presidencies, when American manufacturers paid the highest wages in the world yet nonetheless almost effortlessly dominated world markets. Such concern for one's nation's economic standing in the world is quite natural and, within reason, a good thing: it is really just community spirit writ large.

The final question is one of balance. On the one hand, one's nation should strive to cooperate to make this planet a better place; on the other hand, it should stand up for its own citizens' interests when these are at stake. Striking the correct balance is a matter of common sense, not dogma. It is time our media led the search for a better way to balance these interests.

NOTES

BIBLIOGRAPHY

ACKNOWLEDGMENTS

INDEX

Notes

1. Three Strikes Against the New Economy

page

  10 But given that this present writer: See in particular Eamonn Fingleton, "Why the Japanese Banks Are Shaky," *Euromoney* (September 1987), which was probably the first clear warning in print of the coming mayhem in Japanese finance. The article included this statement: "Two essential ingredients for financial disaster are present: the [Tokyo] real estate industry has clearly been pumped up to giddy heights of folly and the banks have a much greater exposure to risky real estate lending than appears from the crude statistics." As the article recorded, this gloomy view ran completely counter to the mood at the time among Western analysts, who were almost universally bullish about both the Japanese banks and the Tokyo real estate market. This mood was notably enshrined in the "Tiffany" credit ratings accorded the Japanese banks by the two main American credit rating agencies. Moody's, for instance, had triple A ratings on no less than eight of fourteen major Japanese banks in the summer of 1987. Tokyo real estate prices duly slumped soon after the article appeared, and a subsequent rally in 1991 stopped well short of exceeding the record prices set in the summer of 1987. That said, it was not until 1992 that the generality of Western analysts and reporters came to see the extent of the problems the mid-1980s real estate boom had created for the banks. As for Tokyo stock prices, see Eamonn Fingleton, "Making Hay," *Euromoney* (February 1989), which predicted "a prolonged bear market." The big bear market in stocks duly arrived in January 1990 and continued until October 1998.

  16 In fact, as William Wolman and Anne Colamosca have pointed out:

William Wolman and Anne Colamosca, *The Judas Economy: The Triumph of Capital and the Betrayal of Work* (Reading, Mass.: Addison-Wesley, 1997), p. 97.

17 First, it weakens the national's export strength: It should be noted that U.S. exports have grown rapidly in the 1990s. But there is less to this performance than appears at first sight. As soaring U.S. imports of high-tech parts and materials indicate, less and less of what the United States exports these days actually represents U.S. content. As the American economy has globalized, American manufacturers have become little more than mere assemblers, accounting for an ever dwindling proportion of the manufactured content in their products. In essence, in such activities American exporters are merely piggybacking on the manufacturing prowess of Japan and other major manufacturing economies.

18 As recounted by Larry Kahaner: Larry Kahaner, *Competitive Intelligence* (New York: Simon & Schuster, 1996), p. 177.

22 As recorded in the 1998 edition: The figures for Japan and Germany are converted at ruling market exchange rates in late 1998 (in Japan's case, ¥120 to the dollar).

It should be noted that these numbers offer only an approximate insight into how wages vary in the three nations. A true apples-to-apples comparison is virtually impossible because of many complicating factors such as bonuses and benefits. The exact value of benefits, for instance, is often open to dispute, particularly in the case of pensions and other deferred benefits. That said, though any figures one might quote are open to challenge from definitional purists, there is no question about the basic point: as any major American multinational corporation with Japanese and German operations will confirm, wages in both Japan and Germany have consistently been considerably higher than in the United States in recent years.

23 That there is no large hidden army of unemployed people: See, for instance, the annual publication *OECD in Figures,* where unemployment figures for the various member nations are stated on a standardized apples-to-apples basis.

23 This reflects the fact that manufactured goods: To suggest that manufactured goods are more universal in appeal than postindustrial products does not, of course, imply that they need no adjustments to sell in foreign markets. Significant adjustments are often necessary to comply with differing tastes and regulations around the world. In the case of Japan's car exports, for instance, cars destined for the United States must meet different regulatory standards from those of the European Union or of the Japanese home market. But the key point is that making such

adjustments generally adds only fractionally to unit costs. Moreover, a foreign workforce can manufacture the appropriate products — different car exhaust systems, for instance, for different markets — without the slightest need to understand the general culture of the ultimate customers. By contrast, the adjustments required in the case of exports of postindustrial goods not only are often extensive and costly but may be so culture-specific that they must be performed largely or totally on the spot in the foreign markets concerned.

25 These days, by contrast, it achieves far better results: See John Naisbitt and Patricia Aburdene, *Megatrends 2000* (London: Pan Books, 1990), p. 7.

30 Even David Ricardo, the ultimate: As quoted by Doug Henwood, *Wall Street* (New York: Verso, 1997), p. 113.

33 A similarly outspoken disregard for the interests of American labor: Robert E. Reich, *The Work of Nations: Preparing Ourselves for Twenty-first-Century Capitalism* (New York: Vintage Books, 1992), p. 119.

2. A Hard Look at Computer Software

41 According to a study by International Planning and Research: *Asian Wall Street Journal,* December 19, 1996.

42 A notable case in point is the Korean market: *International Herald Tribune,* July 21, 1998.

42 Another American company whose pioneering software work: Information in this paragraph is derived from James Wallace and Jim Erickson, *Hard Drive: Bill Gates and the Making of the Microsoft Empire* (Chichester: John Wiley, 1993), pp. 269, 278, 282, 308, 315, 382, 390, and 394.

46 He reportedly can recall: See Wallace and Erickson, *Hard Drive,* p. 264.

60 As for the total worldwide cost: Steven Levy and Katie Hafner, *Newsweek,* June 2, 1997.

63 In his book *The Trouble with Computers:* See Thomas K. Landauer, *The Trouble with Computers: Usefulness, Usability, and Productivity* (Cambridge, Mass.: MIT Press, 1996), pp. 1–45.

65 As Paul A. Strassmann has pointed out: Paul A. Strassmann, *The Squandered Computer: Evaluating the Business Alignment of Information Technologies* (New Canaan, Conn.: Information Economics Press, 1997), p. 284.

67 As the editor of *Challenge* magazine, Jeff Madrick: As quoted by Richard Harwood, *Washington Post,* May 11, 1998.

3. Finance: A Cuckoo in the Economy's Nest

71 As reported by Nicholas D. Kristof: *International Herald Tribune,* September 2, 1998.

72 The result was what Robert Kuttner has aptly described: Robert Kuttner, *Everything for Sale: The Virtues and Limits of Markets* (New York: Knopf, 1996), p. 164.

74 The ultimate indictment of the chartists: Henwood, *Wall Street,* p. 105.

75 According to a survey in 1992: As cited by Prem C. Jain and Hemang Desai, *Journal of Finance* (September 1995).

76 In recent years he has become a vociferous advocate: Interview with George Soros, *Nightline,* ABC Television, November 5, 1997.

76 Rather, in Buffett's view: This and other comments by Warren Buffett are taken from *Letters to Shareholders 1987–1995* (Omaha, Neb.: Berkshire Hathaway, n.d.).

77 The end result of all this excessive marketing: This figure is an estimate based on information in a speech in 1996 by John C. Bogle of the Vanguard mutual fund group and assumes that the majority of America's institutionally managed holdings of stocks were passively managed by low-cost index funds.

80 As John Tagliabue of the *New York Times* has pointed out: *International Herald Tribune,* July 20, 1998.

83 As Steven D. Kaye has documented: *U.S. News & World Report,* July 7, 1997.

4. From Cyberspace to Tinseltown

88 Or take Barry Howard Minkin, a futurologist: Barry Howard Minkin, *Future in Sight: Important Trends, Implications, and Predictions for the New Millennium* (New York: Macmillan, 1995), pp. 54–56.

91 A pioneer in this regard has been Steve Ward: Cited by Michael L. Dertouzos, *What Will Be* (New York: HarperEdge, 1997), p. 90.

91 The truth is that much of the information: How irrelevant Internet information can be was rather dramatically brought home to this present writer after *Blindside,* his book on the hidden strengths of the Japanese economic system, was published in 1995. Suddenly Internet search engines began prominently displaying a racist website in New Jersey in search listings for his name. Although he had never heard of the site's operators and utterly abhorred the racist tone of their criticisms of Japanese economic policies, this site typically came up as the number-one item for searches under his name — and often appeared in different

guises as many as three more times in the first ten listings for his name. Meanwhile, the search engines overlooked various sites containing major articles he had written and other clearly relevant material. To someone who did not know him (and did not know how deeply he abhorred the site's references to the Japanese as "Japs" and its use of Satanic graphics), the conclusion seemed unavoidable — that he was the moving spirit behind the site and, by promoting such vicious hatred, had ruled himself out of the reckoning as a decent and serious commentator on U.S.-Japan relations. His embarrassment was compounded by the fact that the site's use of his name seemed to give credence to earlier allegations emanating from the Japanese economic system's Washington lobby that he was a "Japan-basher" — a label the lobby routinely confers on any writer who writes realistically about Japan's mercantilist trade policies.

Why did the site come up so prominently for his name? As explained by the site's operators, the reason was that the site carried several references to articles he had written for prominent journals such as *Foreign Affairs* and the *Atlantic*. In each case, these references included his name; thus, for search engines programmed to list items in order of the frequency with which keywords are used, the site automatically showed up prominently. What remained unexplained was why the racist site came up as many as four times in the top ten listings.

Perhaps even more disturbing was the sequel. While he engaged in protracted negotiations with the site's operators to stop associating itself with his name, he also notified various search engine companies that he had nothing to do with the offending site. Amazingly, the search engine companies refused to drop the site from listings for his name. In answer to his complaint, David Seuss, chief executive of the Boston-based search engine Northern Light, wrote: "Northern Light's index is generated completely by computers based on the text on the site and the results listed are generated on the fly in a completely automated fashion. We simply cannot intervene manually in this process. And philosophically, I don't think Northern Light wants to become the arbiter of what is and what is not appropriate in terms of views to express." In May 1999, nearly six months after Seuss received the complaint, his engine still listed the racist site as the third and eighth items for searches for this writer's name.

94 In the words of Mark Landler: Mark Landler, *International Herald Tribune,* January 12, 1998.

94 Typical is Nathan Morton: As quoted by Saul Hansell, *International Herald Tribune,* December 2, 1997.

95 As the *Newsweek* economics commentator Robert Samuelson: Robert Samuelson, *International Herald Tribune,* July 10, 1998.

96 She cited the example of Millipore: As cited by Mary Cronin, *Fortune,* May 9, 1997.

97 In a 1998 *Fortune* account of cyberquackery: See David Stipp, *Fortune,* January 12, 1998.

98 According to Sue Schneider: *Mainichi Daily News,* July 25, 1997.

99 In his book *To Renew America:* Newt Gingrich, *To Renew America* (New York: HarperCollins, 1995), p. 165.

103 The truth is that, in relation to: Valid figures for the overall size of the American entertainment industry's exports do not exist. Such exports are virtually impossible to measure because they take many different forms. Typically, when the American entertainment industry sells CDs and videocassettes abroad, these are manufactured in the markets concerned. Thus, they cannot be considered "exports" for the United States, as most of the revenues stay abroad and are expended on wages and overheads in foreign subsidiaries. As far as the United States is concerned, the export content of such sales may be confined largely to the flow of royalties to American artists and other U.S.-based copyright holders. Of course, this does not stop spokesmen and lobbyists for the American entertainment industry from conflating overseas sales with exports and thus giving the impression that the industry is a much greater contributor to the U.S. balance of payments than it really is. The clearest insight into how small the industry's contribution to the balance-of-payments position is in the audited accounts of major American entertainment companies. Such accounts almost invariably show that these companies' receipts from abroad are quite marginal in terms of total revenues.

108 As Paul Fahri and Megan Rosenfeld have pointed out: See Paul Fahri and Megan Rosenfeld, *International Herald Tribune,* October 26, 1998.

109 Certainly, as Samuel P. Huntington has pointed out: Samuel P. Huntington, *The Clash of Civilizations and the Remaking of World Order* (New York: Touchstone, 1997), p. 63.

5. A Showcase of Manufacturing Strengths

122 The concept was pioneered by the David W. Mann division: Peter N. Dunn, *Microlithography World* (Summer 1994).

129 Their position was famously encapsulated: Kuttner, *Everything for Sale,* p. 222.

6. Golden Oldies: Ships, Textiles, Steel

144 And even in these days of such vaunted "paperless" media: As quoted in *Mainichi Daily News,* May 9, 1997.

150 Few postindustrialists can be more surprised: John Naisbitt, *Megatrends* (New York: Warner Books, 1982), p. 58.

150 Yet as of the late 1990s: The figures cited are from the 1997 edition of *Zosen Kankei Shiryo.*

152 According to Martha M. Hamilton: Martha M. Hamilton, *Washington Post,* March 29, 1996.

158 As the economic commentator Robert Kuttner: Kuttner, *Everything for Sale,* p. 222.

159 The Japanese have been among the earliest: The source of the figures cited in this sentence is the Japanese steel company NKK.

7. The Future: An Expanding Universe

166 "It seemed to me at the time": As recounted in Akio Morita with Edwin M. Reingold and Mitsuko Shimomura, *Made in Japan* (New York: Signet, 1988), pp. 305–6.

188 Meanwhile, as reported by Leyla Boulton: Leyla Boulton, *Financial Times,* November 28, 1997.

190 According to the American transportation experts: This and other comments attributed to Andreas Schafer and David G. Victor are taken from their article "Global Mobility: Past and Future," *Scientific American* (October 1997).

8. Time to Take the Blinders Off

200 In the event of another dollar crisis: Few who are familiar with the strength of Japan's balance of payments doubt that Japanese exporters would be fully competitive at much higher yen exchange rates than those that prevailed in 1998 and 1999. This reflects not only superior productivity in the goods in which they compete globally but the fact that by dint of enjoying crucial monopolies or near-monopolies in a host of high-tech components and materials, they enjoy pricing leadership in Western markets.

Moreover, judging by how violently exchange rates have changed in the past, a dramatic rise in the yen's dollar value is far from a negligible possibility. After all, Japan's current account surplus as of 1998 ran more than three times its level of $35 billion in 1984 — and just as soaring surpluses led to a doubling of the yen between 1985 and 1987, the conditions as of early 1999 seemed similarly set to drive the yen sharply higher. One thing is certain: a doubling of the yen's value from its level in early 1999 would immediately give Japan the world's largest gross national product. (On the less complete but much more widely used measure of gross domestic product, the United States might still retain a slight edge, but only because GDP highly misleadingly excludes from the reckoning the vital effects of America's huge foreign debts — and Japan's huge foreign assets.)

That said, the Japanese economic system is clearly capable of tolerating an artificially undervalued yen for many years to come. This is because most of Japan's overseas trade is now conducted as internal transactions within Japan's now highly globalized corporations. Thus, the exact exchange rate used by, for instance, Sony in exporting from its Japanese subsidiaries to its American ones is little more than an accounting decision on where to allocate profits. Equally because Japanese corporations typically own the foreign coal mines, farms, and iron ore deposits that produce much of its imports, the exchange rate at which such imports enter Japan is largely moot as far as Japan's top policy makers are concerned.

202 Unfortunately, where doctrinal issues are at stake: The extent to which *The Economist* in particular is prepared to go to mislead its readers where matters of dogma are concerned is hard to exaggerate. This point was nicely illustrated in the magazine's belated review (in February 1998) of *Blindside,* this writer's 1995 book in which he offers a broad challenge to *The Economist*'s dogma-driven account of the Japanese economy. In virtually every sentence, the review contrived to misrepresent the book. It implied, for instance, that the book's conclusion that Japan would overtake the United States as the world's biggest economy represented an extrapolation from the dollar's momentary fall to below ¥80 in April 1995. In fact, this fall took place a month after *Blindside* was published, and more than seven months after it was completed. Moreover, the book contained a specific caution (p. 353) that at ¥98 as of the book's completion date in September 1994, the dollar had fallen too far too fast and would soon stage a "significant rally." That rally, which few other Tokyo-based observers anticipated in 1994, duly began in the early summer of 1995 and continued until 1998. *The Economist* also implied that *Blindside* denied rumors that Japanese banks were in serious financial trouble. In reality, the only rumor the book denied was a quite unfounded one that had been circulated by *The Economist* con-

cerning the banks' involvement in one minor Tokyo real estate transaction. That this writer cannot be accused of being unaware of the Japanese banks' real estate problems is obvious from the fact that he was probably the first Tokyo-based observer to predict those problems — in a seven-page article, "Why the Japanese Banks Are Shaky" (*Euromoney,* September 1987).

209 Maintaining consistently high levels of employment: It should be noted that the volume of Japan's exports has in many cases increased dramatically faster than their value. This is particularly true of high-tech components, which have often fallen quite sharply in price in the last decade — yet typically have improved sharply in function and performance.

212 Another factor that helps sustain: Even Japanese bankers conspicuously talk self-deprecatingly in public in the knowledge that they do little or no damage to their business. After all, Japan is now such a huge net exporter of capital that the Japanese banks' overseas subsidiaries can fund themselves almost entirely from the ever burgeoning offshore deposits of the Japanese economic system. Meanwhile, at home, Japanese bankers don't have to worry about their image among the general public either. The reason is that the Japanese savings market is so highly cartelized that Japanese savers have no choice but to accept interest rates as low as 0.5 percent or less!

212 In reality, as authoritative figures from the OECD: For the Japanese government's budget surplus in 1995, see the 1998 edition of *OECD in Figures,* pp. 46–47 (under the heading "Net Government Saving Percentage of GDP").

212 As the *International Herald Tribune*'s Hong Kong correspondent: See Philip Bowring, *International Herald Tribune,* October 10–11, 1998.

213 (To those who might accuse this present writer: For this writer's prediction concerning the banks' real estate loans, see Eamonn Fingleton, "Why the Japanese Banks Are Shaky" (*Euromoney,* September 1987). For his prediction of the stock market crash, see Eamonn Fingleton, "Making Hay" (*Euromoney,* February 1989). This writer's only subsequent public comment on the Japanese stock prospects came in a speech to the American Chamber of Commerce in Japan on October 9, 1998, when he suggested that Japanese stocks had little further to fall and would soon stage a recovery. The Nikkei index closed at 12,879.97 that day, which, it now turns out, was its lowest daily close so far in the 1990s. While it would be foolhardy to say with certainty that the great bear market is over, as this book went to press in March 1999, the index had recovered close to the 16,000 level. Boasting a gain of 23 percent

since its October 1998 low, Tokyo was the world's best-performing major stock market in the first three months of 1999.

215 Certainly he has been vindicated in his central point: *Blindside* has also already been vindicated on virtually all its other major themes. Specifically it argued that Japan would survive its financial and economic strains of the 1990s without making any significant moves to Westernize its economic institutions. In so doing, it rebutted almost every major theme of the American press's coverage of Japan in the first half of the 1990s. Some of the more important themes rebutted in *Blindside* were:

1. Japan's export industries were supposedly being hollowed out by South Korea and other developing countries.
2. Japan's current account surpluses were on the brink of diminishing or even disappearing.
3. The lifetime employment system was breaking down.
4. Japan's unemployment rate was set to spiral disastrously out of control.
5. Japan's super-high savings rate was supposedly headed dramatically lower.
6. Japan's cartels and *keiretsu*s (groupings of affiliated companies that favor one another in sourcing of inputs and services) were breaking down.
7. The Liberal Democratic Party's long reign as the dominant organization of Japanese politics supposedly ended forever in 1993.

The truth is that, with one partial exception, the press has now been confounded on all these themes. The partial exception concerns unemployment. Japan's unemployment rate did indeed rise in the 1990s, as the press commentators predicted. But even here the press has been proved largely wrong, because the unemployment rate never remotely approached the disastrous levels predicted in the first half of the 1990s.

223 These indicate that the United States ran a deficit: This is a conservative estimate based on figures supplied by the Electronic Industries Association of Japan. On the EIAJ's figures, Japan ran a net surplus in electronic components with North America of $8.2 billion as of 1997. Of this, at least half probably consisted of semiconductors, and close to 90 percent of these can be assumed to have been destined for the United States.

9. An Action Plan

233 The result was one of the strongest and richest postwar economies: See Sweden entry, *Encyclopaedia Britannica,* 1970.

Bibliography

Anchordoguy, Marie. *Computers Inc.: Japan's Challenge to IBM*. Cambridge, Mass.: Harvard University Press, 1989.

Branscomb, Anne Wells. *Who Owns Information?: From Privacy to Public Access*. New York: Basic Books, 1994.

Brinkley, Joel. *Defining Vision: The Battle for the Future of Television*. New York: Harcourt Brace, 1997.

Buchanan, Patrick. *The Great Betrayal*. Boston: Little, Brown, 1998.

Choate, Pat. *Agents of Influence*. New York: Alfred A. Knopf, 1990.

Cohen, Stephen S., and John Zysman. *Manufacturing Matters: The Myth of the Post-Industrial Economy*. New York: Basic Books, 1987.

Cringely, Robert X. *Accidental Empires: How the Boys of Silicon Valley Make Their Millions, Battle Foreign Competition, and Still Can't Get a Date*. New York: HarperBusiness, 1993.

Cusumano, Michael A., and Richard Selby. *Microsoft Secrets*. London: HarperCollins, 1995.

Danaher, Kevin, ed. *Corporations Are Going to Get Your Mama: Globalization and the Downsizing of the American Dream*. Monroe: Common Courage Press, 1996.

Dertouzos, Michael L. *What Will Be*. New York: HarperEdge, 1997.

Dertouzos, Michael L., Richard K. Lester, and Robert M. Solow. *Made in America: Regaining the Productive Edge*. Cambridge, Mass.: MIT Press, 1989.

Doremus, Paul N., ed. *The Myth of the Global Corporation*. Princeton, N.J.: Princeton University Press, 1998.

Fallows, James. *Looking at the Sun: The Rise of the New East Asian Economic and Political System*. New York: Pantheon, 1994.

Fialka, John J. *War by Other Means: Economic Espionage in America*. New York: W. W. Norton, 1997.

Fingleton, Eamonn. *Blindside: Why Japan Is Still on Track to Overtake the U.S. by the Year 2000*. Boston: Houghton Mifflin, 1995.

Fransman, Martin. *Japan's Computer and Communications Industry: The Evolution of Industrial Giants and Global Competitiveness*. Oxford: Oxford University Press, 1995.

Galbraith, John Kenneth. *A History of Economics: The Past as the Present*. London: Penguin Books, 1989.

Gingrich, Newt. *To Renew America*. New York: HarperCollins, 1995.

Goldsmith, Sir James. *The Trap*. New York: Carroll & Graf, 1994.

Halberstam, David. *The Reckoning*. London: Bantam Books, 1987.

Harrison, Bennett. *Lean and Mean: Why Large Corporations Will Continue to Dominate the Global Economy*. New York: Guilford Press, 1997.

Heller, Robert. *The Fate of IBM*. Boston: Little, Brown, 1994.

Henwood, Doug. *Wall Street*. New York: Verso, 1997.

Huntington, Samuel P. *The Clash of Civilizations and the Remaking of World Order*. New York: Touchstone, 1997.

Hutton, Will. *The State We're In*. London: Vintage, 1996.

Kahaner, Larry. *Competitive Intelligence*. New York: Simon & Schuster, 1996.

Kuttner, Robert. *Everything for Sale: The Virtues and Limits of Markets*. New York: Knopf, 1996.

Landauer, Thomas K. *The Trouble with Computers: Usefulness, Usability, and Productivity*. Cambridge, Mass.: MIT Press, 1996.

Landes, David S. *The Wealth and Poverty of Nations: Why Some Are So Rich and Some So Poor*. New York: W. W. Norton, 1998.

Lewis, Michael. *Liar's Poker: Rising Through the Wreckage of Wall Street*. New York: W. W. Norton, 1989.

Lind, Michael. *The New American Nation: The New Nationalism & the Fourth American Revolution*. New York: Free Press, 1995.

Luttwak, Edward. *Turbo Capitalism: Winners and Losers in the Global Economy*. New York: HarperCollins, 1999.

Madrick, Jeffrey. *The End of Affluence*. New York: Random House, 1995.

Magaziner, Ira C., and Mark Patinkin. *The Silent War: Inside the Global Business Battles Shaping America's Future*. New York: Random House, 1989.

Mander, Jerry, and Edward Goldsmith, eds. *The Case Against the Global Economy — And for a Turn to the Local*. San Francisco: Sierra Club Books, 1996.

McRae, Hamish. *The World in 2020: Power, Culture, and Prosperity — A Vision of the Future*. London: HarperCollins, 1995.

Minkin, Barry Howard. *Future in Sight: Important Trends, Implications, and Predictions for the New Millennium.* New York: Macmillan, 1995.

Morita, Akio, with Edwin M. Reingold and Mitsuko Shimomura. *Made in Japan.* New York: Signet, 1988.

Nader, Ralph. *"Introduction," in The Case Against "Free Trade": GATT, NAFTA, and the Globalization of Corporate Power.* San Francisco: Earth Island Press, 1993.

Naisbitt, John. *Megatrends.* New York: Warner Books, 1982.

Nakamura, Shuji, and Gerhard Fasol. *The Blue Laser Diode: GaN Based Light Emitters and Lasers.* Berlin: Springer-Verlag, 1997.

Negroponte, Nicholas. *Being Digital.* London: Coronet Books, 1995.

Pool, Robert. *Beyond Engineering: How Society Shapes Technology.* New York: Oxford University Press, 1997.

Prestowitz, Clyde V., Jr. *Trading Places: How America Allowed Japan to Take the Lead.* Tokyo: Charles E. Tuttle, 1988.

Reich, Robert B. *The Work of Nations: Preparing Ourselves for Twenty-first-Century Capitalism.* New York: Vintage Books, 1992.

Schenk, David. *Data Smog: Surviving the Information Glut.* San Francisco: HarperEdge, 1997.

Soros, George, with Byron Wien and Krisztina Koenen. *Soros on Soros: Staying Ahead of the Curve.* New York: John Wiley, 1995.

Stoll, Clifford. *Silicon Snake Oil: Second Thoughts on the Information Highway.* New York: Doubleday, 1995.

Strassmann, Paul A. *The Squandered Computer: Evaluating the Business Alignment of Information Technologies.* New Canaan, Conn.: Information Economics Press, 1997.

Thurow, Lester C. *The Future of Capitalism: How Today's Economic Forces Shape Tomorrow's World.* New York: William Morrow, 1996.

Tolchin, Martin, and Susan J. Tolchin. *Selling Our Security.* New York: Knopf, 1992.

Von Weizsäcker, Ernst, Amory B. Lovins, and L. Hunter Lovins. *Factor Four: Doubling Wealth — Halving Resource Use.* London: Earthscan, 1997.

Wallace, James, and Jim Erickson. *Hard Drive: Bill Gates and the Making of the Microsoft Empire.* Chichester: John Wiley, 1993.

Wolman, William, and Anne Colamosca. *The Judas Economy: The Triumph of Capital and the Betrayal of Work.* Reading, Mass.: Addison-Wesley, 1997.

Wright, Richard W., and Gunter A. Pauli. *The Second Wave.* London: Waterlow, 1987.

Acknowledgments

Many of the people who cooperated with my inquiries or otherwise helped me in the research for this book are acknowledged in the text or the notes. Others to whom I am grateful include Dirk Heinecke of Wacker Siltronic, Michael Henne of Siemens Solar, Clare Bebbington of BP Solar, Masamichi Shiraishi and Aston Bridgman of NEC, Donald Forsythe of LTV, Takashi Ogawa and Tsunehisa Yamashita of Nikon, Daniel Lintz of Sony, Firdous Khergamvala of the *Hindu,* Ashok Syal of HCL, Sreenivasan Mohanagopal of Tata Infotech, Sekhar Chatterjee of Tata Consultancy Services, Klaus Turck of Kaltenbach & Voigt, David Lammers of *Electronic Engineering Times,* Yoshiro Sasaki of Godo Steel, Takashi Asamura of Nippon Steel, Hirofumi Yamana of Sumitomo Metal Industries, Annanya Sarin of Ispat International, Roger Schreffler of EIU, and the Tokyo-based journalist Sam Jameson.

I benefited from discussing my ideas with various intellectual allies, including the Chicago-based attorney Thomas Flannigan; *Cartels of the Mind* author Ivan Hall; the Tokyo-based scholar of Japanese power, Brian McVeigh; and the translator of the French edition of *Blindside,* Catherine Lemaitre. More generally, I acknowledge a deep debt of gratitude to James Fallows, author of *Looking at the Sun,* whose generous espousal of my work in Washington and New York set me on the path to full-time authorship. Others whose support has been particularly appreciated include the Overseas Press Club of America's former president, William J. Holstein; Ivan Schlager of the U.S. Senate Committee on Commerce, Science, and Transportation; the Japan scholar Chalmers Johnson; the *Judas Economy* author William Wolman; and the speaker's agent Margaret Baxter.

I am greatly in the debt of several editors at Houghton Mifflin, notably Steve Fraser, Chris Coffin, Anton Mueller, Rebecca Saikia-Wilson, and Liz Duvall. I am also grateful to Cindy Buck for editing the manuscript and to

Sean Lawler for help on many fronts. My gratitude goes also to Masaya Kokubun at Hayakawa Shobo and my Japanese translator, Hitomi Sugiura, as well as to the editor of the British edition, Martin Liu of Orion Business Books.

The initial concept of the book was shaped in consultation with F. Joseph Spieler of the Spieler Agency in New York. For me, Joe Spieler has been not only a consistently astute adviser but an inspiring role model in the fortitude he has displayed in standing up for his ideals. I am also grateful to William Miller and Abner Stein for selling the rights to the Japanese and British editions, respectively.

On a more personal note, I would like to express my gratitude to my parents, Marian Fingleton and the late Simon Fingleton, for whose quintessentially Western values my respect grows with each passing year.

Finally, my greatest debt is to Yasuko Amako, my staunchest ally in that ultimate adventure, the quest for truth.

Eamonn Fingleton
Mita, Tokyo 108
efingleton@hotmail.com
May 26, 1999

Index

A. C. Nielsen, 102
ABC Television network, 107
Adhesives, 21
Advanced Systems Development Company, 53
Advertising agencies, 13–14
Advertising on the Internet, 95, 96
Aerospace industry, 21, 29, 116. *See also* Aircraft industry
Africa. *See* specific countries
Agfa-Gevaert, 22
Agriculture, 175–76, 178
Airbus consortium, 29, 193, 195, 222
Aircraft industry, 39, 192–93, 195, 222. *See also* Aerospace industry
Airplanes, 192–93, 195
Akzo Nobel, 153–54
Allison, Iain, 55
Alsthom, 195–96
Aluminum production, 178
Amazon.com, 96–97, 99
America. *See* United States
America Online, 95, 98
American Airlines, 58
American Express, 79
American International Group, 61
Andersen, Kurt, 201
Andersen Consulting, 58, 60

Apple Computer, 43
Applied Materials, 221
ARBED steel company, 158
Argentina, 181, 200
Arthur D. Little, 171
ASM Lithography, 120
Aswan Dam, 180
AT&T, 55, 57, 117
Atlantic, 243
Attewell, Paul, 63
Australia, 81
Austria: income and income growth in, 7, 8; steel industry in, 157, 161; unemployment in, 22
Autodesk, 39
Automobile industry: driverless cars, 191–92; electric cars, 191; electronic components for cars, 117; environmental regulation of, 191; future of, 190–92, 195; in Germany, 60, 115, 195; hybrid cars, 191, 195; intelligent cars, 191–92; in Japan, 115–16, 195, 218–19, 240; just-in-time inventory control system in, 51; sales in, 39; in South Korea, 116; and textile industry, 153; and ULSAB (ultra light steel auto body), 157; in United States, 39, 115, 195, 218–19; wages in, 116, 120

Baker, Dean, 210
Baker, James, 218
Bangladesh, 186–87
Bank of Sweden, 232, 233
BankBoston, 60
Banking industry. *See* Financial services industry
Banks, Howard, 179
Barnet, Richard J., 31
Barra, 67
Barshefsky, Charlene, 95
Bartz, Carol, 39
Basic-oxygen process in steel industry, 158–59
Battery technology, 191, 195
Bay Systems, 50
Becquerel, Edmond, 183
Belarus, 53
Belgium, 157
Bell, Alexander Graham, 170
Bell, Daniel, 12
Bell Laboratories, 171
Benhamou, Eric, 49
Bernabé, Franco, 179
Bertelsmann group, 103
Beyond Engineering (Pool), 172
Biomass, 182
Biotechnology, 153–54, 175
Blast-furnace method of steel production, 158–59, 160
Blindside (Fingleton), 215, 242–43, 246–47, 248
Blockbuster stores, 106
Blue lasers, 135–36
Blue light-emitting diodes, 135–36
Bluestone, Barry, 231
"Blur-mercials," 88–89
BMG, 103
Body-shopping, 61
Boeing, 29, 57, 154, 192, 193, 195, 222
Bogle, John C., 75, 242
Bombardier, 195–96
Bookstores on the Internet, 96–97, 99
Boskin, Michael, 129
Boulton, Leyla, 188

Bowring, Philip, 212–13
Bozo filters, 91
BP Solar, 184, 186, 188, 189
Brady Report, 72
Brahmagupta, 55
Branscomb, Ann Wells, 42
Brazil, 150
Brinkley, Joel, 139
Britain. *See* United Kingdom
British Petroleum, 188, 189
"Brochureware," 92
Brown Boveri, 180
Browne, John, 188
Buchanan, Patrick, 229–30, 231
Buffett, Warren, 76
Burroughs Computer Company, 56
Business reporters, 234
Business Software Alliance, 39
Business Week, 232, 243
Byrnes, Christian, 62

Cadmium-telluride, 184
Cameron, James, 109
Canada: computer software sales in, 48; deindustrialization in, 9; and discount brokerage industry, 81; fast trains in, 195–96; income in, 9, 233; and trade in cultural products, 104
Canon, 120, 123
Capital investment: in computer software industry, 45, 55; in Japan, 123, 130–31, 215; in manufacturing, 18–19, 30–31; in steel industry, 158, 163; in textile industry, 152
Carbon fiber, 154
Care International, 167
Carnegie, Andrew, 168
CASE (computer-aided software engineering), 56
Caterpillar company, 54
Cathode-ray tubes, 140–42
Cavanagh, John, 31
CBS Records, 105
CD industry, 15, 25–26, 105, 133, 244
CD players, 133, 134, 225
CD-ROMs, 133, 135, 144, 205

Cellular phone, 225
Ceramics industry, 143
Challenge, 67
Chartists, 74
Chemical companies, 189
Chihaya, Akira, 161
Chile, 181
China: CDs in, 25, 105; ceramics industry in, 143; computer software industry in, 52–53, 61; energy resources for, 178, 180, 181; industrialization speed in, 169; piracy in, 40–41, 105; silicon industry in, 127; steel industry in, 157, 161; textile industry in, 151; Three Gorges Dam in, 180; train system in, 193, 194; travel by Chinese, 190, 192
Christian Science Monitor, 214
Chrysler, 216
CIS. *See* Copper indium diselenide (CIS)
CISC (complex instruction set computing), 222
Cisco Systems, 51, 57
Citibank, 55, 57
Clinton administration, 195, 200, 225
Cloning, 101
CNN, 102–03
Cobbin, Edgar, 42
Coca-Cola formula, 92
Coherent, 132
Colamosca, Anne, 16, 54
Colgate-Palmolive, 33
Commerce on Internet, 94–97
Commerzbank, 80
"Commodity" products, 205–6
Communications. *See* Information industry; Internet; Telecommunications
Compact disks. *See* CD industry
Compaq, 57, 220
Competitive Intelligence (Kahaner), 21
Computer City superstore chain, 95
Computer games, 47
Computer industry, 95, 205. *See also* Computer software industry; Computers; *and specific companies*
Computer productivity paradox, 63–67
Computer software industry: body-shopping in, 61; capital required for new software business, 45, 55; in China, 52–53, 61; classification of, as manufacturing industry, 4; and computer productivity paradox, 63–67; and creativity, 16, 45; cultural barriers to export prospects of, 13, 41–42; in developing countries, 15–16, 45–46, 48–50, 54–58, 187; export performance of, 13, 40–44; and financial services industry, 59–60, 66–67; forward planning in, 56–57; in Germany, 47–48; and government regulation in U.S., 66; growth factors for, 59–60, 62–67; imports as threat to U.S. software industry, 44–54, 61; in India, 54–59, 61–62; and intellectual property rights protection, 14–15, 42–43; in Ireland, 50; in Israel, 50–51; in Japan, 42, 47; as labor-intensive industry, 45; and localization/adaptation of software, 41–42; management in, 51–52; Microsoft's success, 37–39; and piracy, 15, 40–41; postindustrialists' enthusiasm for, 37; and program upgrades, 65; programmers' short-term memory, 45–46; and reverse-engineering, 42, 43; in Russia, 52, 61; sales in, 39, 43–44, 52; in South Korea, 42; in Third World, 15–16; and voice recognition systems, 174; wages in, 39–40, 61–62; word-processing programs, 41–42; workforce in, 38–40, 44, 45–50, 56, 61–62; and year-2000 problem, 60
Computers: desktop computers, 205; early development of, 170; Japanese household ownership of, 208; laptop computers, 173, 225; notebook computers, 205; programming skills

Computers (*cont.*)
and global spread of personal computers, 48–49; voice recognition systems for, 174; "Wintel" standard in, 222. *See also* Computer software industry
Concorde, 192
Construction industry, 57, 160–61
Construction machinery, 116
Consulting, 87
Continuous casting in steel industry, 159
Copiers, 171
Copper indium diselenide (CIS), 184
Copyright, 14–15, 40–41, 104–5
Corning company, 144
Costner, Kevin, 109
Courtis, Kenneth, 80
Craft workers, 187
Creativity, 16, 45, 224–26
Cringely, Robert X., 45–46
Cronin, Mary, 96
CrossComm, 52
CRP Technic, 126
Cultural barriers to postindustrial exports, 12–14, 41–42
Currency markets, 72–73
Curtis, Charles B., 182, 189
Cusumano, Michael A., 51–52
Cyber Patrol, 97
CyberPromotions, 97
Cyberquackery, 97–98
Cymer, 132, 133, 136
Cyprus, 185
Czech Republic, 110

Daimler-Benz, 51, 60, 196
Damuth, Robert, 39–40
Database information services, 87
Dataquest, 128, 223
Deindustrialization. *See* Postindustrialism
Demag, 161
Deming, W. Edwards, 93–94
Denmark: income and income growth

in, 7, 8, 150; shipbuilding industry in, 149–50; wind power in, 182
DePalma, Anthony, 104
Deregulation in financial services industry, 59, 71–72, 76, 81–82
Derivatives, 82, 84
Dertouzos, Michael L., 90, 91, 100
Desalinadoras AVF, 176
Desalination, 176
Deutsche Bank, 80
Developing countries: computer software industry in, 15–16, 45–46, 48–50, 54–59, 187; and desire for manufactured goods, 24; education in, 168; energy resources in, 177, 180, 181, 184, 185–87; final assembly plants in, 26; and investment goods, 168; and manufacturing, 24–26, 166–69; microbanking in, 186–87; prosperity for, 24–26, 166–69; savings and savings rates in, 26–27, 168; silicon industry in, 127; solar energy for, 184, 185–87; steel industry in, 157; textile industry in, 152; travel in, 190. *See also specific countries*
Dickens, Charles, 105
Digital camera, 225
Digital Equipment, 48
Digital television, 50, 137–42
Digital video disk players, 133, 135
Direct mail, 87
Discount brokerage industry, 80–81
Dollar-yen exchange rate, 72–73, 210–11, 245–46
Dow Jones & Company, 99
Dreman, David, 74
Dresdner Bank, 80
Drip systems for irrigation, 175–76
Driver, John, 184, 186
Driverless cars, 191–92
Du Pont, 152, 153

East Asia: Chinese and Japanese languages in, 110; computer software industry in, 52–59; education in, 168; financial crisis of 1997 in, 214; financial services industry in, 79; Japan's status in, 28; manufacturing economies of, 204–6; movies in, 103, 110; and outsourcing, 220–24; press coverage of, 204–6; savings in, 27, 82, 229; silicon industry in, 127; software piracy in, 41. *See also specific countries*

Eastern Europe: computer software industry in, 52; Germany's status in, 28; industrial disruption in, following collapse of Soviet Union, 157; oil industry in, 179; train system in, 193. *See also specific countries*

Eastman Kodak, 22

Eaton, Mark, 141

E-commerce, 94–97

Economic Policy Institute, 209

Economic Times, 61

Economics profession, 232–34

Economist, 81, 176–77, 202, 215, 246–47

EDS, 50

Education in developing countries, 168

Egypt, 151, 180

EIAJ. *See* Electronic Industries Association of Japan (EIAJ)

Eisenhower administration, 230, 235

Eisenstodt, Gale, 153

Electric-arc process in steel industry, 159–60

Electric cars, 191

Electricity, 178, 180–83, 185–88

Electronic Industries Association of Japan (EIAJ), 248

Electronic junk mail, 97

Electronic mail, 90–91

Electronics industry: and automobiles, 117; capital intensity of components side of, 18; and "commodity" products, 205–6; consumer products in, 137, 208, 225; importance of, 116–17; and intelligent cars and roads, 191–92, 195; in Japan, 5, 18, 119, 225; laser industry, 131–37; and Nikon, 117–23; robots in, 173; sales in, 39; semiconductors industry, 128–31, 134, 140; silicon industry, 123–28; stepper industry, 117–23, 144; voice recognition systems, 173–74

Elvis+Co., 52

E-mail, 90–91

EMI, 103

Emmott, Bill, 215

Employment. *See* Workforce

Energy resources, 174–75, 177–89

Engardio, Pete, 49

England. *See* United Kingdom

ENI, 179

Enterprise resource planning (ERP) programs, 47–48

Entertainment industry: and exports, 103–7, 244; and high-definition television (HDTV), 137–44; Hollywood movie industry, 15, 107–11; overseas sales of CDs and videocassettes, 244; recorded music industry, 15, 103, 105; television, 102–3, 104, 137–44; and Viacom, 105–6; and Walt Disney Company, 106–7

Environmental protection, 174–75, 191

Epstein, Jason, 97

Erickson, Jim, 46

ERP programs, 47–48

ESPN sports channel, 107

Ethernet switches, 50–51

Ethical issues in financial services industry, 82–86

E*trade, 81

Etzioni, Amitai, 8

EU. *See* European Union (EU)

Eubanks, Gordon, 39

Euro, 59–60

European Union (EU), 22, 23, 28, 104, 230

Eurosolar, 189

Exchange rates, 10–12, 72–73, 210–11, 245–46

Executive incentive plans, 85, 228

Exports: adjustments of manufactured goods for sale in foreign markets, 240–41; and computer software industry, 13, 40–44; cultural barriers to postindustrial exports, 12–14, 41–42; and entertainment industry, 103–7, 108, 244; financial services as, 77–82; of Germany, 204; and information industry, 12–13; and Internet, 95–96; of Japan, 209, 215, 247, 248; and movie industry, 108, 110; and piracy, 14–15, 104–5; and postindustrialism, 12–15, 17; and recorded music industry, 15, 103; and regulation in financial services industry, 14; and television programming, 104; of United States, 217, 240; wind turbines as, 182. *See also* Trade

F.I.A.S.C.O. (Partnoy), 84

Fahri, Paul, 108

Fallows, James, 231

Fasol, Gerhard, 135–36

Fast trains, 193–96

Faxing, 90

Fearnleys Review, 146

Feature films. *See* Movie industry

Feder, Barnaby J., 124, 126

Ferren, Bran, 88, 89

Fiber optics, 25, 144

Fiji, 186

Film industry. *See* Movie industry

Financial services industry: and currency markets, 72–73; and deregulation, 59, 71–72, 76, 81–82; and derivatives, 82, 84; ethical issues in, 82–86; and euro, 59–60; export potential of, 77–82; and financialism, 70–77; and "front running," 83; and insider trading, 83; international operations of U.S. firms, 77–82; investment in manufacturing by, 30–31; in Japan, 10, 31, 207, 213–14, 239, 246–47; microbanking in developing countries, 186–87; and mutual funds, 75–77, 84; and Black Monday crash of 1987, 71–72, 76; and portfolio insurance, 72, 76; postindustrialists' enthusiasm for, 68; regulation of, 14, 31, 79–82, 234–35; revenues from, 79; and selective allocation, 83–84; software demand in, 59–60, 66–67; wages in, 68, 228; workforce in, 79; and yen-dollar exchange rate, 72–73, 245–46

Financial Times, 155, 176, 188

Financial World, 62

Financialism, 70–77

Finland, 147–48

First World. *See specific countries*

Flat-panel displays, 141

Flavin, Christopher, 181

Floating airports, 149

Forbes, 76, 153

Ford Motor, 13, 38

Foreign Affairs, 243

Forrester Research, 95

Fortune, 40, 97–98, 105, 190, 202–03, 204

Founder Group, 52–53

FPSOs (floating production, storage, and offloading vessels), 148

France: automobile industry in, 195; fast-train technology in, 194, 195–96; housing in, 208; steel industry in, 158; textile industry in, 154; and trade in cultural products, 104; train system in, 193, 194

Franchising, 87

Free-market ideology, 28, 71–72, 200

Freud, Sigmund, 225–26

"Front running," 83

Fuel cells, 191

Fuji Photo Film, 21–22

Fujitsu, 205

Future in Sight (Minkin), 88–89

Galbraith, John Kenneth, 232
Gambling, 98
Gartner consulting firm, 60
Gas turbines, 182
Gates, Bill, 38, 39, 40, 43, 46, 47, 52, 62, 76, 174
GCA Corporation, 122
Gelbspan, Ross, 174
General Electric, 55, 180
General Motors, 195
Germany: automobile industry in, 60, 115, 195; chemical companies in, 189; computer software industry in, 47–48; computerization in, 63; electrical companies in, 180; exports of, 204; fast-train technology in, 194–95, 196; financial services industry in, 80; hydrology in, 176; income and income growth in, 7, 8; laser technology in, 132; leadership role in European Union (EU) and Eastern Europe, 23, 28; manufacturing in, 5, 8, 19, 28, 204; Motorola plant in, 19; press coverage of manufacturing in, 204; printing equipment industry in, 144; profits in, 29; and "purchasing power parity" exchange rates, 10; reunification of, 22–23; savings in, 82; silicon industry in, 124, 125–28; solar energy industry in, 183; steel industry in, 157, 161; textile industry in, 152; train system in, 193; and transfers of production know-how, 27–28, 31; unemployment in, 22–23; wages in, 10, 19, 22, 32, 48, 128, 204, 240; wind turbine industry in, 182
Gigot, Paul A., 83
Gilbert, W. S., 105
Gingrich, Newt, 99–101
Glass industry, 143–44
Glassman, James K., 77
Globalism: challenges to, 231–32; and financial services industry, 77–82; and national identities, 235; and transfer of manufacturing know-

how to foreign subsidiaries of U.S. companies, 32; and U.S. manufacturing wages, 32–33; and virtual reality medicine, 99–102
Glossbrenner, Alfred, 13
Grameen Bank, 186–87
Graphical user interfaces, 56
Great Betrayal (Buchanan), 229–30
Great Britain. *See* United Kingdom
Greece, 104, 185
Greenberg, Daniel S., 97
Greer, Germaine, 94
Greider, William, 38, 222
Gresham's Law, 90
Grove, Andrew, 39
Guenier, Robin, 60

Haloid, 171
Hamilton, Martha M., 152
Hamrin, Robert, 216
Handycam, 47, 225
Haney, Jim, 98
Hangul & Computer, 42
Hansell, Saul, 95, 96
Hard industries: action plan for, in U.S., 227–35; advantages of, 17–23; definition of, 4–5; future of, 23–28. *See also* Manufacturing; *specific industries and countries*
Harland and Wolff, 148
Harrison, Bennett, 17–18, 231
Harwood, Richard, 201
HCL Corporation, 56–57
HDTV, 137–44
Health care, 97–98, 100–102, 153–54, 175, 186
Heart pacemakers, 101
Heart transplant, 101
Heidelberger Druckmaschinen, 144
Helicopters, 195
Heller, Robert, 224–25
Herzer, Heinz, 127, 128–29
Hewlett-Packard, 48, 123, 220, 221
High-definition television (HDTV), 137–44
High-speed transport, 192–96

Hitachi, 57, 180, 196, 205
Hoagland, William, 188
Hoechst, 152
Hokkaido Takushoku, 207
Holiday Inn, 58
Hollywood movie industry, 15, 107–11
Holstein, William, 49, 213, 214–15
Home shopping, 88, 95
Home Shopping Network, 95
Hong Kong: CD industry in, 105; movie industry in, 110; per capita income in, 110; piracy in, 41, 105; publishing companies in, 52
Hoover administration, 230
Household appliances, 116
Housing, 208
Howell, David, 18
Huntington, Samuel P., 109
Hutton, Will, 231
Hybrid cars, 191, 195
Hydrology, 175–76, 180, 186, 187

Iacocca, Lee, 216
IBM, 13, 38, 42, 46, 47, 48, 50, 53, 57, 73, 93, 170, 176, 202–3, 222
Ichitaro, 42
IdeaMarket, 202
IFPI. *See* International Federation of the Phonographic Industry (IFPI)
Iguchi, Masakazu, 191–92
Iijima, Hidetane, 151–52
Imports: rising imports of postindustrial services, 15–17; and savings rates, 26; software imports as threat to U.S. software industry, 44–54, 61; of United States, 199, 203, 217–18. *See also* Trade
Income and income growth: international statistics on, 7, 8–10, 55, 110, 233; and manufacturing, 7–9, 22; postindustrialism and, 7–12, 199
India: computer software industry in, 51, 54–59, 61–62, 164; education in, 55; image problem of, 54–55; per capita income in, 55; program-

mers from, 49, 61; textile industry in, 151, 187; wind turbines in, 181
Indonesia, 25, 168, 181
Industries. *See* Hard industries; Manufacturing; *specific industries and countries*
Information industry: cultural barriers to exports, 12–14, 41–42; definition of, 4; and e-mail, 90–91; and exports, 12–14; Third World competition in, 15–16. *See also* Computer software industry; Internet; Postindustrialism
Infosys, 55
Ingres Corporation, 42
Innovative products, 170–77
Insider trading, 83
Institute for the Future, 133
Intel Corporation, 39, 48, 93, 117, 125, 130, 171, 222
Intellectual property rights, 14–15, 42–43, 104–5
Intelligent cars and roads, 191–92, 195
Interactive Gambling Council, 98
International Federation of the Phonographic Industry (IFPI), 105
International Herald Tribune, 108, 109, 212–13
International issues. *See* Globalism; Trade; *and specific countries*
International Monetary Fund (IMF), 215
International Planning and Research, 41
Internet: advertising on, 95; bookstores on, 96–97; "brochureware" on, 92; business information on, 92–94; commerce on, 94–97; compared with printing, 90; cynics' view of, 88; databases on, 144; and discount brokerage industry, 80–81; electronic junk mail, 97; and e-mail, 90–91; export potential for Internet-based information businesses, 12–13; gambling on, 98; informational potential of, 91–94, 242–43;

and international commerce, 95–96; journalists' use of, 201; medical quackery on, 97–98; paid-for information on, 93; and piracy, 15; postindustrialists' enthusiasm for, 87–89; as research tool, 91–94, 242–43; sales of businesses operating on, 98–99; scientific information on, 94; search engine companies, 99, 243; sex-related sites on, 97; software know-how disseminated on, 49

Investment. *See* Capital investment

Investment goods, 168

Iona Technologies, 50

Ireland, 8, 50

Irrigation drip systems, 175–76

Israel, 50–51

Italy, 8, 18, 179

Iwasaki, Kowata, 123

Iwasaki, Yataro, 123

Jain, Nirmal, 58

Japan: aerospace industry in, 21; affluence in, 207–8; American movies in, 108; automobile industry in, 115–16, 195, 218–19, 240; banking in, 10, 31, 207, 213–14, 239, 246–47; capital availability and capital investment in, 123, 130–31, 215; chemical companies in, 189; computer industry in, 205; computer software industry in, 42, 47, 48; computerization in, 63; and creativity, 224–25; current account surpluses of, 33–34, 209, 215, 245–46, 248; downplaying of economic strengths by, 211–12; economy during 1990s, 9, 10, 23, 34, 73, 206–16, 248; electrical companies in, 180; electronics industry in, 5, 18, 119, 225; fast trains in, 193, 194–96; GDP and GNP of, 209–10, 246; government budget in, 212, 213; high-definition television (HDTV) in, 137–38, 139; household electronic gadgetry in, 208; housing in, 208; hydrology in, 176; income and income growth in, 7, 8, 9; industrialization speed in, 169; and intellectual property rights protection, 105; labor system in, 122–23, 145; laser industry in, 133–36; life expectancy in, 11, 12, 209; liquid-crystal displays manufactured in, 20; living standards in, 207–9; local service support for products, 96; manufacturing in generally, 5, 8, 20, 204–6; modesty ethic in, 212; net external assets in 1990s, 215; Nikon in, 117–23; and outsourcing, 220, 222, 248; photographic film industry in, 21–22; press coverage of, 204–6, 207, 211–15; printing equipment industry in, 144; profits in, 29; publishing companies in, 53; and "purchasing power parity" exchange rates, 10, 11–12; real estate industry in, 10, 207, 213–14, 239; road construction projects in, 208; savings rate of, 215, 248; semiconductor industry in, 129–31, 134, 223, 248; shipbuilding industry in, 147, 148–49, 150; silicon industry in, 124, 128; solar energy industry in, 189; steel industry in, 93, 158–64, 245; stock market in, 10, 207, 211, 213, 239, 247–48; and supersonic passenger plane, 192; textile equipment industry in, 156; textile industry in, 151–52, 153; and trade, 33–34, 209, 211, 215, 245–46, 247, 248; and transfers of production know-how, 27–28, 31; transportation industry in, 173; travel and tourism by Japanese, 208; unemployment in, 22, 23, 209, 248; wages in, 10, 22, 32, 33, 40, 48, 116, 120, 131, 220, 240; wind turbine industry in, 182; yen-dollar exchange rate, 72–73, 210–11, 245–46

Japan Institute of Social and Economic Affairs, 22
Japan Storage Battery, 195
Jasinowski, Jerry, 216–19, 223
Java Beans, 53
Jensen, Michael C., 75
Jobs. *See* Workforce
Jobs, Steve, 43
Johnson, Chalmers, 231
Johnson, Samuel, 67
Journalists. *See* Media; Newspaper industry; *and specific newspapers*
Judas Economy (Wolman and Colamosca), 16, 54
Judis, John, 231
Just-in-time inventory control system, 51
Justsystem Corporation, 42

Kahaner, Larry, 21
Kawasaki Heavy Industries, 149
Kaye, Steven D., 83
Kelly, Kevin, 12
Kemper Financial Services, 83–84
Kennedy administration, 176, 211, 235
Kenya, 186
Kerosene, 177
Kipwee Display, 141
Kirimoto, Takeshi, 163
Know-how in manufacturing. *See* Proprietary know-how
Knowledge industry. *See* Computer software industry; Information industry; Internet
Kobe Steel, 161
Komatsu, 133
König & Bauer-Albert, 144
Korea. *See* South Korea
Kraar, Louis, 105
Krayushkin, Sergey, 136–37
Kristof, Nicholas D., 71
Kumagai, Osamu, 134
Kuttner, Robert, 72, 158, 231
Kuwait, 176

Kyocera, 143, 189

Labor force. *See* Workforce
Laissez-faire model, 28–29, 30, 34, 211, 231–35
Lambda Physik, 132
Land, Edwin, 22
Landauer, Thomas K., 63–66
Landler, Mark, 94
Laptop computers, 173
Laser diodes, 133–36, 140, 205
Laser industry, 131–37, 140, 171, 205
Latin America. *See specific countries*
Latvia, 53
Layoffs, 145, 228
Leahy, Austin, 100
Lee Kuan Yew, 229
Legal profession, 14
Levy, Steven, 65
Lewis, Michael, 84
Leybold Systems, 126
Life expectancy, 11, 12, 209
Lightbulbs, 135–36
Light-emitting diodes, 135–36
Ling Rui-ji, 53
Liquid-crystal displays, 20, 141, 205, 225
Lithuania, 200
London Stock Exchange, 58
London Underground, 58
Los Angeles Times, 183
Lovins, Amory, 174–75
Lovins, Hunter, 174–75
Lufkin, Eric, 74
Luxembourg, 7, 8, 158

Machine tools, 116
Made in America, 204
Made in Japan (Morita), 166
Madrick, Jeff, 67
Magaziner, Ira, 225
Maglev train, 194–95, 196
Magnets, 136–37
Making It in America (Jasinowski), 216–19

Malaysia: CD sales in, 25; computer software industry in, 52; financial crisis of 1997, 214; silicon industry in, 127; wages in, 51

Malkiel, Burton, 74

Management: of computer software companies, 51–52; "managerial laxity," 65–66; of manufacturing operations, 51, 227, 228

Mandel, Michael, 232

Mann, David W., 122

Mannesmann, 161

Manufacturing: action plan for, in U.S., 227–35; adjustments of manufactured goods for sale in foreign markets, 240–41; advantages of, 17–23, 34; balanced with postindustrialism, 5; capital investment in, 18–19, 30–31; and computer productivity paradox, 62–67; computer software classified as, 4; and creativity myth, 224–26; and developing countries, 24–26, 166–69; and energy resources, 177–89; entry barriers for new entrant to industry, 19–22; and environmental protection, 174–75; and First World consumers, 169–73; foreign nations' industrial policies for promotion of, 29–30; foreign subsidiaries of U.S. companies, 31–32; future of, 23–28, 165–96; higher levels of, 4–5; improvements in efficiency in, 24–25; income growth and, 7–9, 22; of innovative products, 170–77; jobs in generally, 6, 17–18, 204; and laser technology, 132–34; management in, 51, 227, 228; outsourcing trend in, 220–24, 248; political case for, 27–28; press coverage of, 204–6, 220; of production machines, 5, 117–23; proprietary know-how in, 19–22, 31–32; return on manufacturing investment, 228; and savings rates, 30; subsidies for, 29; and tariffs, 229–31; and trade generally, 23; and trade protection, 29–30; training in operation of high-tech production machinery, 17–18; transfers of production know-how, 27–28, 31–32; type 1 and type 2 computer applications in, 64; and unemployment, 22–23; U.S. comeback myth for, 216–19; U.S. decline in, 28–34, 204; U.S. high-tech manufacturing, 219–24; and wages generally, 12, 32, 33; water resources for, 175–76; yield in, 20, 133–34. *See also* Trade; Wages; Workforce; *specific industries and countries*

Marketing on the Internet, 95, 96

Marlin Partners, 55

Marsh, Peter, 155

Masie, Elio, 98

Massachusetts Institute of Technology (MIT), 90, 91, 100, 204

Matsushita Electric, 195

MCA, 105

McGuire, Jeff, 153

Media, 87, 93–94, 144, 200–206, 220, 232–35. *See also* Entertainment industry; Television; *and specific newspapers*

Medical quackery on the Internet, 97–98

Medicine. *See* Health care

Megatrends (Naisbitt), 9, 150

Mehdorn, Hartmut, 144

Mehta, Dewang, 55

Membranes for medical field, 153–54

MEMC Electronic Materials, 124, 126, 128

Merrill Lynch, 57, 60, 78–79

Meta consulting firm, 62

Mexico: income in, 9; profits in, 29; solar energy in, 186; and trade in cultural products, 104

Microbanking, 186–87

Microchips, 121, 125, 129–31

Microprocessors, 171, 222
Microsoft, 37–44, 46–52, 59, 76, 80, 93, 117
Microsoft Secrets (Cusumano and Selby), 51–52
Mighty Whale, 148
Millennium problem, 60, 65–66
Miller, Glenn, 193
Milliken & Company, 152, 153
Millipore, 96
Minkin, Barry Howard, 88–89
Mishel, Lawrence, 209–10
Mishra, Raman, 49
MIT, 90, 91, 100, 204
MIT Commission on Industrial Productivity, 85, 225
Mitsubishi Electric, 139
Mitsubishi group, 122, 123, 196
Mitsubishi Heavy Industries, 144, 148
Mitsubishi Motors, 195
Mobius, J. Mark, 168, 169
Mohanagopal, Sreenivasan, 57
Mongolia, 181
Monsanto Corporation, 153
Morgan Stanley, 84
Morita, Akio, 166
Morton, Nathan, 94–95
Motion Picture Association of America, 107
Motorola, 19, 48, 50
Movie industry, 15, 107–11
MTV, 106
Multimedia Super Corridor, 52
Murdoch, Rupert, 95
Murthi, N. R. Narayana, 55
Music industry, 15, 103, 105
Mutual funds, 75–77, 84

Nadar, Shiv, 56–57
Nader, Ralph, 38
Nagatsuka, Seiji, 147
Naisbitt, John, 9, 12, 115, 150
Nakamura, Shuji, 135
Nanotechnology, 176–77
National Renewable Energy Laboratory, 181–82

National Software Testing Laboratories, 51
NCR, 33
NEC, 57, 130–31, 205
Netherlands, 153–54
Netscape, 98
New Economics (Deming), 93–94
New Economy. *See* Postindustrialism
New School, 17–18
New York Times, 33, 71, 75, 80, 94, 95, 96, 104, 139, 171, 207, 212, 234
New Yorker, 201
New Zealand, 8, 81
Newcomb, Peter, 25
Newspaper industry, 144, 200–206, 220, 232–35. *See also specific newspapers*
NexGen, 49
NHK, 137–38
Nichia Chemical Industries, 135, 136
Nickelodeon, 106
Nielsen, 102
Nikon, 117–23
Nippon Steel, 161
Nishi, Kazuhiko, 47
NKK, 161, 245
Nobel Prize, 16, 67, 232, 233
Nordstrom, 55
Norris, Floyd, 207
Northern Light search engine, 243
Norway, 7, 8, 11
Notebook computers, 205
Novell, 39, 50, 57
NTT, 57
Nuclear power, 179
Nucor Corporation, 159
Nylon, 153

OECD. *See* Organization for Economic Cooperation and Development (OECD)
Oil industry, 148, 179
Oil rigs, 148
Oil tankers, 148

One World, Ready or Not (Greider), 165, 222

OPEC oil cartel, 179

Optimetrix, 120

Oracle Corporation, 42, 48, 50, 51

Organization for Economic Cooperation and Development (OECD), 7–10, 23, 212, 240

Ormerod, Paul, 231

Oswald, Gernot J., 186–87

Outsourcing, 220–24, 248

Ovonic, 195

Paramount Pictures, 106

Paravia, Joseph, 98

Partnership for a New Generation of Vehicles, 195

Partnoy, Frank, 84

Patents, 19, 42

PB Solar, 184

Perceptron, 132

Personal computers. *See* Computers

Peter Wolters, 126

Peters, Tom, 216

Peterson, Wallace C., 193

Peugeot, 195

Pharmaceuticals industry, 39, 116

Philip Morris, 13

Philippines, 29, 51

Photographic film industry, 21–22

Photovoltaic silicon, 183–84, 189

Piracy, 14–15, 40–41, 104–5

Planes. *See* Airplanes

Plasma display, 141

Poland, 52, 110

Polaroid, 21, 22

Political case for manufacturing, 27–28

Pollack, Andrew, 107

Pollution control, 174–75

Polyester, 152–53

PolyGram, 103

Pool, Robert, 89–90, 172

Pope, Alexander, 28

Portfolio insurance, 72, 76

Portugal, income growth in, 8

Postel, Sandra, 175–76

Postindustrialism: action plan for reversing, in U.S., 227–35; and balance of payments, 17, 23; balanced with manufacturing, 5; characteristics of postindustrial services generally, 4, 34, 87; and childlike faith in efficacy of free markets, 28–34; and exports, 12–15, 17; and imports, 15–17; and income, 7–12, 199; job mix for, 6, 9; as labor-intensive services, 15; press coverage of, 200–206; and "purchasing power parity" exchange rates, 10–12; and trade, 12–17, 199–200; and wages, 9, 29, 32–33. *See also* Computer software industry; Financial services industry; Internet

Poverty, 24, 55, 166–67, 169, 186–88, 199

Power-generation equipment, 116, 180

Preece, Sir William, 170

Prestowitz, Clyde, 129, 231

Princeton University, 184

Printing compared with the Internet, 90

Printing equipment industry, 144

Procter & Gamble, 13

Production machines: and developing countries, 168; manufacture of, 5, 117–23; steelmaking equipment, 161; textile equipment industry, 154–56; training in operation of high-tech production machinery, 17–18

Productivity: and capital intensity, 18; computer productivity paradox, 63–67; improvements in, 228; in mature manufacturing industries, 145, 158; in steel industry, 158–59; and wages, 18

Profits, bias toward, 29

Program upgrades, 65

Proprietary know-how: in computer software industry, 49; in manufac-

Proprietary know-how (*cont.*)
  turing, 19–22, 31–32; in semiconductor industry, 131; in silicon industry, 126–27; transfers of
  production know-how, 27–28,
  31–32
"Purchasing power parity" exchange
  rates, 10–12

Quinkert, Norbert, 19

R/3 software, 48
Railroads, 193–95
Raza, S. Atiq, 49
Reagan administration, 129, 231
Real estate industry, 10, 207, 213–14,
  239
Recorded music industry, 103, 105
Recruit Company, 53
Regulation: and computer software in-
  dustry growth, 66; environmental
  regulation and automobile industry,
  191; of financial services industry,
  14, 31, 79–82, 234–35; press bias
  against, 234–35. *See also* Deregula-
  tion
Reingold, Edwin M., 166
Relevant Knowledge, 97
Renewable energy. *See* Energy re-
  sources
Reverse-engineering, 42, 43
Rhône-Poulenc, 154
Ricardo, David, 30
Rieter, 155, 156
RISC (reduced instruction set comput-
  ing), 222
Roach, Stephen, 63
Road freight transportation, 195
Robots, 47, 134, 173, 175, 177
Roland company, 144
Romer, Paul, 172–73
Romm, Joseph J., 182, 189
Rosenfeld, Megan, 108
Rothschild, Michael, 6
Ruling engines, 121
Russia: computer software industry in,

52, 61; laser industry in, 136–37;
  software piracy in, 41

Saffo, Paul, 133
Sales: in automobile industry, 39; in
  computer hardware, 95; in computer software industry, 39, 43–44,
  52; in developing countries, 167; in
  electronics industry, 39; in HDTV
  industry, 142; of microchips, 129;
  by Nikon, 123; in online commerce,
  98–99; in solar energy industry,
  189; in steel industry, 159, 163
Salomon Brothers, 84
Samuelson, Robert, 95
SAP, 47–48
Saudi Arabia, 176
Saurer Gruppe, 155–56
Savings and savings rates: in advanced
  manufacturing nations, 30, 82; in
  developing countries, 26–27, 168;
  in East Asia, 27, 82, 229; of Japan,
  215, 248; in United States, 30, 82,
  215, 228–29; use of savings in own
  country, 82
Schafer, Andreas, 190, 192, 196
Scheer, Hermann, 189
Schlafhorst, 156
Schmidt, Eric, 39
Schmitt, John, 209–10
Schneider, Sue, 98
Schwarz, John E., 199
Science and Government Report, 97
Scientific American, 188, 190
Scotland, 101
Scrubbers, 174
Search engine companies, 99, 243
Securities and Exchange Commission
  (SEC), 83, 84, 221
Securities industry, 58, 71–77, 82–85,
  207, 212–14, 228, 234. *See also*
  Stock market
Selby, Richard W., 51–52
Selective allocation, 83–84
Semiconductor industry: and high-
  definition television (HDTV), 140;

Intel as leading manufacturer, 222; and intelligent roads, 195; in Japan, 129–31, 134, 223, 248; and outsourcing in, 221–24, 248; and silicon chip production, 123–28; state-of-the-art semiconductor factory, 128–31; and stepper industry, 127–23, 132, 133, 144; U.S. comeback myth on, 223–24; and voice recognition systems, 174; workforce in, 129, 130–31, 222; yield problems in, 134

Senegal, 186, 187

Service industries. *See* Postindustrialism

Seuss, David, 243

Sex-related Internet sites, 97

Sharp Corporation, 20, 205

Shell/Royal Dutch oil group, 21

Shiller, Robert J., 71

Shimizu, Hisayuki, 119, 120–21

Shimomura, Mitsuko, 166

Shin-Etsu Chemical, 124, 128

Shingosen fabrics, 153

Shipbuilding industry, 117, 145–50, 173

Shopping on Internet, 94–97

Showa Shell Sekiyu, 189

Shukla, Ravi, 75

Siemens corporation, 101, 180, 183

Siemens Solar, 183–84, 186, 188, 189

Silicon industry, 121, 123–28, 183–84

Silicon Snake Oil (Stoll), 65

Singapore: hard industries in, 5; income in, 150; savings in, 27, 82, 229; shipbuilding industry in, 150; unemployment in, 22; wages in, and "purchasing power parity" exchange rates, 10–11

Smith, Adam, 76

Software industry. *See* Computer software industry

Solar energy industry, 183–89

Solarex, 189

Solow, Robert, 67

Solutia Corporation, 153

Sony Corporation, 26, 47, 103, 133–35, 140, 166, 195, 205

Sony Handycam, 47, 225

Soros, George, 76, 231

South Africa, 101, 181

South Korea: automobile industry in, 116; CDs in, 25; computer software industry in, 42; economic problems during 1997–1998, 9–10, 214; income growth in, 8, 9–10; manufacturing in generally, 8, 167; photographic film industry in, 1; piracy in, 104; shipbuilding industry in, 146–47; train system in, 193; wages in, 116

Soviet Union collapse, 157. *See also* Russia

Spain, 8, 176

Spectraphysics, 132

Spinning. *See* Textile industry

Spinning mill, 18

Squandered Computer (Strassmann), 65

Stanford University, 132, 172

Staudigl, Rudolf, 128

Steel industry, 17, 93, 156–64, 168–69, 173, 178, 219, 245

"Step and repeat" process, 121

Stepper industry, 118–23, 132, 133, 144

Stich, John, 138, 140

Stipp, David, 98

Stock market: Black Monday crash of 1987, 71–72, 76; and "chartists," 74; explosion in financial trading, 70–77; and financialism, 70–77; and "front running," 83; and insider trading, 83; in Japan, 10, 207, 211, 213, 239, 247–48; London Stock Exchange, 58; and Microsoft, 38; and portfolio insurance, 72, 76; proposed transaction tax on stock trades, 228; and securities analysts, 74, 234–35; trading software, 58, 66. *See also* Securities industry

Stoll, Clifford, 65, 89

Strassmann, Paul, 63, 65–66
Stringer, Howard, 103
Subsidies, 29
Sullivan, Arthur, 105
Sulzer Ruti, 155, 156
Sumitomo Metal Industries, 162–64
Sun Microsystems, 52, 57, 222
Superconductivity, 175
Supersonic passenger plane, 192
Sveriges Riksbank, 232
SVG, 120
Sweden: economic policy of, 233; life
    expectancy in, 11; per capita income
    in, 7, 233; steel industry in, 157;
    and trade in cultural products,
    104
Swissair, 58
Switzerland: electrical companies in,
    180; income and income growth in,
    7, 8, 158; manufacturing in, 5, 7;
    profits in, 29; savings in, 82; securi-
    ties industry in, 58; steel industry in,
    157; textile equipment industry in,
    155–56; unemployment in, 22;
    wages in, and "purchasing power
    parity" exchange rates, 10
Syal, Ashok, 56
Symantec, 39, 50
Synthetics industry, 152–53
Syria, 200

Tagliabue, John, 80
Taiwan: income in, 152; manufactur-
    ing in generally, 167; piracy in, 41,
    104; publishing companies in, 52;
    textile industry in, 152; train system
    in, 193; wages in, 152
Tariffs, 229–31
Tata Consultancy Services (TCS), 56,
    58
Tata Infotech, 56, 57
Tata Sons, 56
Taurus trading program, 58
Tax incentives, 227
Taylor, Alex, III, 190
Taylor, Roger, 181–82

TCS. *See* Tata Consultancy Services
    (TCS)
Technology Review, 175
Telecommunications industry: and
    computer software industry, 45, 55;
    computerized production tech-
    niques in, 117; and developing coun-
    tries, 167; drop in international tele-
    communication costs, 45, 55; fiber
    optics in, 25, 144; and invention of
    telephone, 170; and labor relations,
    89; and lasers, 171, 205; materials
    used by, 25; solar energy for, 185,
    186, 187; video telephones, 88, 89;
    and virtual reality, 99–102. *See also*
    Internet
Telegraph industry, 170
Telephone, 88, 89, 170, 186, 225
Television: in developing countries,
    187; digital television, 50, 137–42;
    and entertainment industry, 102–3,
    104, 106, 107; ESPN sports chan-
    nel, 107; exporting of television pro-
    grams, 104; high-definition televi-
    sion (HDTV), 137–44; MTV, 106;
    Nickelodeon, 106; in United King-
    dom, 104. *See also* Entertainment in-
    dustry
Texas Instruments, 48, 138, 140
Textile equipment industry, 154–56
Textile industry, 18, 151–56, 187
TGV, 193
Thailand, 25, 41, 200, 214
Thatcher, Margaret, 231
Think tanks, 87
Third World. *See* Developing coun-
    tries; and specific countries
3-Com, 49, 50, 51
Three Gorges Dam, 180
Thurow, Lester, 231
Thyssen steel group, 182
Titanic, 109, 110
To Renew America (Gingrich), 99–100
Tomen, 182
Toray, 152, 153
Toshiba, 57, 140, 180, 205

Tourism. *See* Travel and tourism
Toyoda, 156
Toyota Motor, 13, 51, 136, 195
Trade: cultural barriers to postindustrial exports, 12–14, 41–42; and entertainment industry, 103–7, 108, 244; and import increases, 15–17; Internet and exports, 95–96; Japan's current account surpluses, 33–34, 209, 215, 245–46, 248; and manufacturing, 23; and movie industry, 15, 108, 110; and nontariff barriers for protection of manufacturing, 29–30; and piracy, 14–15, 40–41, 104–5; and postindustrialism, 12–17; and regulation in financial services industry, 14; software imports as threat to U.S. software industry, 44–54, 61; software industry's export performance, 13, 40–44; and tariffs, 229–31; U.S. current account deficits, 23, 33–34, 44, 199–200, 203–4, 215, 218. *See also* Exports; Imports
Trade secrets, 31–32
Traded stock options, 76
Trading Places (Prestowitz), 129
Traffic lights, 136
Training of workers, 17–18, 122
Trains, 193–96
Transfers of production know-how, 27–28, 31–32
Transistors, 171
Transportation industry, 57–58, 173, 189–96
Travel and tourism, 190, 192, 208. *See also* Transportation industry
Trczinka, Charles, 75
Trouble with Computers (Landauer), 63–66
Trumpf, 132

ULSAB (ultra light steel auto body) research programs, 157
Unemployment, 22–23, 209, 240, 248. *See also* Workforce

United Arab Emirates, 176
United Kingdom: advertising agencies in, 13–14; challenges to laissez-faire in, 231; computer software industry in, 47; and discount brokerage industry, 81; economy of generally, 202, 210; financial services industry in, 68–69; government budget deficit in, 212; housing in, 208; income growth in, 8–9; industrialization speed in, 169; movie industry in, 109; postindustrialism in, 8–9, 202; shipbuilding industry in, 150; solar energy industry in, 184; steel industry in, 157, 158, 219; telegraph industry in, 170; television in, 104; trade deficits of, 23; wages in, 47, 240; and year-2000 problem, 60
United States: action plan for manufacturing in, 227–35; automobile industry in, 39, 115, 195, 218–19; computerization in, 62–63; and dollar's depreciation, 217, 218; energy consumption in, 177; exports of, 217, 240; financial regulation in, 31; foreign subsidiaries of U.S. companies, 31–32; GDP and GNP of, 210, 217, 246; government budget deficit in, 212; Great Depression in, 207, 229–30; high-definition television (HDTV) in, 138–39; high-tech manufacturing in, 219–24; imports of, 199, 203, 217–18; income in, 7, 8, 199, 210, 233; industrialization speed in, 169; manufacturing comeback myth in, 216–19; manufacturing's decline in, 28–34, 204; net external liabilities in 1990s, 215; outsourcing by, 220–24, 248; poverty in, 199; productivity rates in, 67; return on manufacturing investment in, 228; savings rates in, 30, 82, 215, 228–29; and tariffs, 229–31; trade deficits of, 23, 33–34, 44, 199–200, 203–4, 215, 218; train system in, 193–94; and transfers of

United States (*cont.*)
  production know-how, 27, 31–32;
  travel in, 190; unemployment in,
  22, 209; wages in, 18, 22, 32–33,
  203–4; wind power in, 181; yen-dollar exchange rate, 72–73, 210–11,
  245–46. *See also* Manufacturing;
  Postindustrialism; *and specific industries and companies*
U.S. Department of Labor, 23
U.S. News & World Report, 83, 97,
  213, 214–15
USX-U.S. Steel, 159

Valentine, Donald, 51
Vanguard mutual fund group, 75, 242
Veba, 126
Viacom, 105–06
Victor, David, 190, 192, 196
Video compression, 50
Video telephones, 88, 89
Videotape recorder, 225
Vietnam War, 27
Virtual Gaming Technologies, 98
Virtual reality, 99–102
Voest-Alpine, 161
Voice recognition systems, 173–74
Volkswagen, 195

Wave power electricity-generating
  plants, 148
Wachs, Martin, 189
Wacker, Alexander, 125
Wacker-Chemie, 124, 125–28
Wages: in advanced foreign nations
  and "purchasing power parity" exchange rates, 10–12; in automobile
  industry, 116, 120; and body-shopping, 61; in capital-intensive businesses, 18–19; in computer software
  industry, 39–40, 61–62, 164; in
  financial services industry, 68, 228;
  in Germany, 10, 19, 22, 32, 48, 128,
  204, 240; globalism and U.S. manufacturing wages, 32–33; in Japan,
  10, 22, 32, 34, 40, 48, 120, 131,
220, 240; and manufacturing generally, 12, 32–33, 33, 235; in movie industry, 107; and postindustrialism,
  9, 29, 32–33; and productivity, 18;
  in semiconductor industry, 131; in
  silicon industry, 126; in steel indus-
  try, 164; in United States, 18, 22,
  32–33, 203–4
Walkman, 225
Wall Street Journal, 83, 202, 212, 214
Wallace, James, 46
Walt Disney Company, 106–7
Ward, Steve, 91
Washington Post, 1, 144, 212, 234
Water resources, 175–76, 180, 186,
  187
Waterworld, 109
Waxman, Sharon, 109
Weaving. *See* Textile industry
Web gambling, 98
Weber, Jonathan, 183
Western Union, 170
Westernization, 231
Westinghouse, 180
What Will Be (Dertouzos), 91, 100
White, David, 176
Williams, Robert, 184
Williamson, Gilbert, 33
Wind power, 180, 181–82
Wind turbines, 181–82
Wintel chips, 222
Wireless LAN, 50
Wolman, William, 16, 54, 231
Word-processing programs, 41–42, 59.
  See also Computer software industry
Workforce: and body-shopping, 61; in
  computer software industry, 38–40,
  44, 45–50, 56, 61–62; in financial
  services industry, 79; Japan labor
  system, 122–23; job cuts in mature
  manufacturing, 145, 158, 228; and
  job security, 228; in laser industry,
  133; for manufacturing generally, 6,
  17–18, 204, 220; in movie industry,
  107; for postindustrialism, 6, 9; in
  printing equipment industry, 144;

for product development, 223; in
semiconductor industry, 129, 130–
31, 222; in silicon industry, 125–26;
in solar energy industry, 189; in
steel industry, 158, 163–64; in stepper industry, 119–20; in textile
equipment industry, 156; training
for, 17–18, 122; unemployment, 22–
23, 209, 240, 248; U.S. executives'
disregard for, 33; wages and postindustrialism, 9, 10–11, 18, 32–33.
See also Wages
World Bank, 175
World Health Organization, 186
World Wide Web. *See* Internet
Wyatt, Edward, 75

Xerox Corporation, 42–43, 63, 65,
171

Y2K problem. *See* Year-2000 problem
Yahoo!, 99
Yamaichi Securities, 214
Year-2000 problem, 60, 65–66
Yen-dollar exchange rate, 72–73, 210–
11, 245–46
Yield in manufacturing, 20, 133–34
Yoshida, Shoichiro, 120

Zeiss, 122
Zurich Kemper Investments, 84